Wildlife Country

How To Enjoy It

Blue Ridge dawn: breakfast comes early before a bird walk.

Library of Congress CIP Data: page 207

Wildlife Country

How To Enjoy It

NATIONAL
WILDLIFE
FEDERATION

Contents

Return to the wild

Beneath the campsite's towering oak trees, my mother balanced a big griddle on top of the Coleman gasoline stove. Flapjacks bubbled in brilliant early sunlight. As she sat on her folding canvas chair under the tent's awning, nothing was far from reach: the black, cast-iron Dutch ovens in the campfire, the spatula and pot holder, the engine crank for crowning the rattlesnakes that never dared appear.

The rich smells of our breakfast arose to the surrounding ridges. My sister and five brothers and I, called from pup tent to camp table, soon were scraping the bottoms of our tin plates. Now the whole broad sweep of Arizona's Yarnell Mountain region beckoned. For the youngest, there were cool, high swings on the car's spare tire suspended from an overhanging limb. For my older brothers and me, the day might bring long sweaty stalkings of bobcat shadows or mountain-lion paw prints. Or perhaps the excitement of tracking thirsty bees from our swimming hole to their hollow oak-tree homes—then smoking the bees out and winning as much as 40 pounds of honey. Or catching and bringing back blue gills and bass hung from our belt loops on hooks whittled from willow sticks. There would be chores, too, from the gathering of firewood to the burying of garbage far enough from camp, and deep enough, to foil skunks and raccoons. And always there was the unexpected, the breath-taking moment when a deer caught our eye, a Gambel's quail called. For us it was a time of great happiness, a time of innocence.

Elsewhere, autos much like ours, carrying American families much like ours, clogged rutted roads to national parks, Pike's Peak, and other scenic wonders. Their broad running boards were piled with wicker baskets, leather trunks, semi-retired camping gear from World War I. This was the first wave of campers-for-pleasure in U.S. history. By 1920, membership in the American Automobile Association was soaring into the tens of thousands. These tin-lizzie campers were not like the grand rich of the previous generation, wealthy Easterners and European royalty who had paraded into Yellowstone and the other newly opened national parks, staying in elegant hotels and marveling at Old Faithful. The people of the new wave were working families, benefiting from rising incomes and the first paid vacations, eager to claim their heritage of the wilds.

While setting out to write this introduction, I found myself smiling with fond recognition at pictures of that first American camping generation, of which I happened to be a young part—at the primitiveness of their equipment, their joyful embrace of the new meaning of summer, their zeal for such ambitious causes as the Appalachian Trail (America's first North-to-South footpath), their casual unawareness of the harm their litter might cause. How different from us today! And what an even greater difference between their glad rediscovery of a tranquil outdoors and the stern necessity that drove their frontier forebears to subdue it! But despite those generational differences, I am most impressed in retrospect by the *continuity* of the American wilderness and wildlife experience.

For all American outdoor adventurers, the way from past to future was opened by a titanic breed of men. Not far behind Lewis and Clark and Daniel Boone came Ralph Waldo Emerson, Henry David Thoreau, and John Muir, pioneers of a different sort, leaving trail blazes in the mind for all who would follow. They expressed a consistent philosophy of nature strong enough to bind together the pioneer era, the naive decades, and the conservation mind-set of today.

Emerson urged that the wilderness homes of bear and panther not be "civilized off the face of the earth"; he proposed in 1844 that "the forests should become graceful parks, for use and delight." At about the same time, Thoreau theorized that the aesthetic and spiritual healing powers of our woodlands were as important to U.S. citizens as were the West's mineral resources. A generation later, Muir

A city family explores the new back-to-nature lifestyle of the tin lizzie era.

professed the Indians' creed that the wilderness exists as a place to go in search of fresh vision, exhorting us "to climb the mountains and get their glad tidings." They sought far more than the creation of national parks; they pleaded with us to regard the preserved wilderness areas as shrines.

An unusual concept, perhaps. But for my family—my great grandfather, my grandparents and parents, and for my wife, children, and me—it has always made a kind of internal sense, whether or not we fully understood and articulated it. My great grandfather, David Kimball, was sent by the Mormon leader, Brigham Young, to colonize southern Arizona in the middle years of the 19th century, before the war with Mexico. He and other settlers found good farmland around what's now St. David, Arizona. My grandfather helped to settle eastern Arizona along the Gila River. Theirs were the hard years of exploring, breaking ground, coping with the elements and the animals they found there. It was Grandfather, wise in the ways of nature, who years later showed us how to smoke the honeybees out of the hollow trees. He loaned us his beekeeper's hat and taught us to respect the bees' business by leaving some honey in the tree. Thus there would be bees and honey again next year.

Father left old ways behind when he abandoned farmer's work—almost as if in response to historian Frederick Jackson Turner's decree that America's frontier days were past—and became a professional pharmacist, opening the first drugstore in Phoenix. But he did not, probably could not, completely abandon that vital relationship with the hills and the birds and the air. In summer, Phoenix's 100-plus degrees were too much for anyone; returning to the wilds was also a means of survival. Up in the mountains, away from prescriptions and apothecary jars, he taught my brothers and me to live as woodsmen, able to read wildlife signs in the browsed shrubs; alert to the tracks, droppings, sounds of the non-human creatures who were, with us, inheritors of the land. For me, the outdoors was an ever-unfolding story, learning the ways of wildlife more than a holiday spree. It became my life's work.

My first job was with the Arizona Fish and Game Department and my assignment to conduct the first complete inventory of Arizona's wildlife. Because I had to keep moving around the state, I was issued a pickup truck to live and travel in. "The first modern camper in Arizona," I called it. From the back I could pull a drop-down bed rigged with a tarp in case of rain. On one side, a 55-gallon tank freed me to drive for days between gasoline pumps; on the other, a 50-gallon water drum enabled me to make "dry camp" wherever animal migrations or calving times might lead me. Tent, canvas chairs, and a satchel-type folding table completed my rig.

About the same time, magazine advertisements tried to persuade their readers that camping and easy living could go hand-in-hand. In newspapers and magazines, bold type presented "A Summer Home on Wheels," "At last—A Real Toilet Tent," and "Wear-Ever Camp Cooking Outfits," products that guaranteed perpetual service. But, compared to my own sturdy inventions, many appeared to be flimsy or faddish, balky to operate, or heavy as lead to carry around.

By contrast it is a delight to see the ease with which today's vacationing Americans can seek solitude or find adventure in the outdoor world. In summer and winter (as shown in the chapters that follow) adults and children alike are observing natural wonders and logging thousands of trail miles in comfort unknown even to the last generation. Now the outdoor market has become a $400 million-a-year business; now such organizations as the North American Family Campers Association foster fellowship among the vast numbers of outdoor Americans. And yet, I wonder if they all find what they are seeking, whether they are making the most of their rich opportunities to see and enjoy the wildlife that is out there.

Gorgeous advertisements of people equipped with gear splendid enough for moon assaults somehow mock my memories of our simple, early camping days. I wonder if these modish campers have heard Emerson's and Muir's message: I'm

The delights of flipping flapjacks in the pine woods and collecting decals from the national parks swelled the tide of car campers who overran the parks' meager facilities in the 'twenties. In the 'thirties, F.D.R.'s Civilian Conservation Corps built trails, roads, and campgrounds to relieve crowded tent cities. For many, the pursuit of wildlife became a matter of proper leisure attire and the latest camping gadgets, such as the adjustable grubstake stove at left.

True outdoorsmen left cars at trailheads and plunged into wilderness. Boy Scouts fashioned their own packboards Trapper Nelson style, though few would carry one 500 miles on Sierra trails as did William Johnson (left) in 1928. Honeymooners found idyllic hideaways to beach their canoes along the Hudson, and dusty riders found no trail too steep to reach the best trout streams in Idaho. Capturing each proud moment was the ubiquitous camera, keeper of the memories of a people who had never traveled so far so fast nor so exuberantly.

afraid they may not find in our camping wonderlands the re-creation, the recovery from urban alienation that they seek, because of their preoccupation with outdoor trappings. I also fear that those who invade the wilderness without a strong outdoor ethic may further scar those fragile areas.

The tendency to overindulge in expensive outdoor gear probably cannot be blamed on women. I think of my mother, roughing it with us in the mountains, her face reflecting the campfire's flicker. And my wife, Arvella, cheerfully sharing my nomadic existence as I roamed all over Arizona in the 'thirties. Mother rejoiced when we replaced our Coleman stove with one "you don't have to pump up," and much later Arvella was glad to see the air mattress and sleeping bag replace the canvas Army cot; but each knew a dozen ways to keep camp life comfortable yet simple, the food plain but soul-satisfying.

Not many of us could or would follow the austerities of Thoreau or the saint-like economy of Muir. When Muir was climbing in the California mountains, he generally carried bread broken into small pieces or some kind of meal, plus sugar and tea. The food bag tied to his belt sometimes also contained dried meat and fruits. So long as he could find water, he could hike for a week and more, fasting and stretching his body and his senses. On return, civilization would give him more food and rest than he needed—as it does us.

In the Southwest of the 1930's, a mainstay of camping was sourdough bread. I learned about it when I managed Arizona's buffalo herd for the Fish and Game Department. Our cook would start the batter by pouring the sourdough starter right into the top of a 100-pound bag of flour. Then, after working it with his hands until it had the right feel, and letting it rise there, he'd form balls of dough, dip them in grease, and pop them into the Dutch oven. Hungry hunters, squatting with me around the fire, knew what to do when the big biscuits were done: punch a hole in the top, pour in butter and honey while the bread was still hot, and you'd have the best chow of your life. ("Punch-hole biscuits" they're called in the South, friends have since told me.) The cook knew the essential trick of the process—he always kept some of the batter for next time.

For next time: that's what I regard as the secret of the outdoor experience. As soon as my son Tom was old enough to ride well, he accompanied me on a horsepacking trip into the high country of the Teton Wilderness. Officially, the purpose was to survey the big game populations up there; personally, my objective was to be with Tom. And to enjoy the countryside all the more because, in a certain way, I was passing it on to him. Although that pack trip took place in the early sixties, we both have vivid memories of it. When I asked Tom about it the other day, he recalled the immense herds of elk we'd seen on their summer range, and how we'd had "trout for breakfast, trout for lunch, and trout for dinner—served with that great sourdough bread." Because he'd caught some of the rainbows and the cutthroats himself, throwing back the small ones and stopping fishing when we had enough for the next meal, he'd seen for himself how we help nature save some for the next time.

The words and pictures of this book, showing American families enjoying wildlife adventures today in highly individualistic ways, give me hope that other people's children as well as my own are getting the feel for Wildlife Country—and learning how to enjoy it. The book is dedicated to all those philosophically and physically bold Americans who would reach out like the young woman in the Rockies on the cover and make contact with a Clark's nutcracker. Perhaps for others their perch would be serenely by a stream rather than daringly on a mountaintop, but their purpose and joy would be the same. Their pursuit of the modern wildlife experience takes stamina, discipline, and a deep objective respect for nature in all its ways.

In the bicentennial book presented to our readers by the National Wildlife Federation, *The History of Wildlife in America*, we demonstrated how our society from its earliest beginnings has advanced in company with wildlife. Now that association has a new dimension: Americans are looking to wildlife as a resource not just of food but of wonder. Today's campers have unprecedented opportunities, if they will take them, to learn about animals even before the family car rolls out of the carport. Thanks to books, magazines, television, and nature centers, they can go into wildlife's world prepared to meet them first hand, and then to grow in understanding the vital, subtle connection between all animals and the human kind.

When our editors started work on this book, their first concern was to spread the word of the recently rediscovered and updated outdoor ethic. They sought to communicate to everyone who hoists a pack or skis a trail in the 'seventies or 'eighties the breakthroughs of those who learned in the last decade how to live and hike in the spirit of latterday Emersons and Muirs. The 'sixties were a difficult, revolutionary, but profoundly revealing time in our national experience; they helped us turn away from the chrome and tail-fin era that preceded.

To impart the spirit of this new trail-honed philosophy along with practical tips on finding and enjoying wildlife (and for eating and sleeping well in the wilderness at the same time), the editors turned to some of America's most experienced nature writers. Their generous and enthusiastic response has given us an album of real-life family adventure stories interlaced with "how to" chapters of instruction on key aspects of outdoor living.

Our authors have been chosen not only for their wisdom but also for the joy they find in getting out into the wildlife world: in backpacking with a knowledge of the animals whose habitats they are traveling through; in riding with a respectful eye for the proper maintenance of the animals' trails and waterholes; in canoeing with an awareness of and sensitivity to migration and behavior patterns. These are writers and photographers who know and admire their subject.

While reading their stories and delighting in their pictures, it has been fascinating for me to note the similarities in their approach to the outdoors. Consider, for example, the manner of their going: quietly in canoes and rubber rafts rather than wastefully and noisily in motorboats. Quietly on skis or snowshoes rather than in snowmobiles, on foot rather than on motorbike. Consider, too, their eating and cooking: their willingness to master a new cuisine of lightweight, dried foods in order to minimize weight and cooking time (saving room in their packs for cameras and time in the field for wildlife), yet providing excellent, energy-rich meals, as the trail recipes on pages 64-69 attest; featherweight, portable stoves instead of open fires wherever possible; and proper dousing of fires and removal of the fire ring whenever open fires are used.

I'm particularly impressed by the authors' knowledge of wildlife seasons and their willingness to go to extra effort to win a genuine wilderness experience: members of the Kemsley party hiking an extra 27 miles to cache food in the desert floor of the Grand Canyon so the family could avoid crowded campgrounds, and planning the trip for March when their young children would not be in danger of scorpions or snakes; the Clyde Smiths seeing a deer swim across the bow of their lead canoe as a reward for their paddling and portaging 15 miles one Indian summer weekend; Kent and Donna Dannen skiing more than 100 miles on the Continental Divide in search of the ptarmigan in its snow-white winter plumage. And of course I'm struck by the strong technical bond that unites all of these outdoor families, the common emphasis on planning and organization—the discipline that excludes the temptation to take ecologically costly shortcuts.

This is, then, a most practical book, filled with solid instruction. It tells how to use a map and compass, how to make trail gear, where to find the great flocks and herds of wildlife, and how to photograph them. It is at the same time an idealistic book that reflects the heritage of my own family and the cherished traditions of all who share a love for wildlife.

Thomas L. Kimball
Executive Vice President
National Wildlife Federation

Some sought ice caves in summer, playing follow-the-leader into Mount Rainier's Paradise Glacier. Others chose winter adventure, donning snowshoes in hopes of crossing paths with rabbit or fox. Today, families find no season too cold or too hot to explore wildlife country—and to learn more about the creatures who live there.

Make it a family adventure

William Kemsley, Jr.

New Yorkers Molly and Will Kemsley, ages 11 and 5, pause on a muddy switchback of the Kaibab Trail to survey the awesome dimensions of the family adventure unfolding before them—a 40-mile hike in the Grand Canyon. Their first level walking will be on the Tonto Plateau some 3,000 feet below. From there the thin ribbon of the Kaibab drops into the Inner Gorge for a zigzag plunge of another thousand feet to their first campsite at Phantom Ranch. The children's father, William Kemsley, Jr., editor and publisher of Backpacker *magazine, started planning the trip nine months earlier so that their party of ten might eat well, sleep safely, and explore the Canyon most enjoyably.*

It was snowing again on the morning that we were to begin our hike down into the Grand Canyon. We had already waited three days at the South Rim. If we were to keep the schedule called for on our camping permit, we had to get moving. As we adjusted our heavy packs and started down the Kaibab Trail at Yaki Point, the snow stopped briefly, just long enough to give us a clear view of the wonderland below.

Do you know that thrill you get when you realize that you are finally on your way? For me, there is hardly anything else like it. It's a soaring feeling. My family and I began to sing as we headed down the first switchback. The trail is wide as it winds back and forth down the side of the Canyon, but we were carefully watching our footing. We were the first people to go down the steep, slippery trail since the last snow fell and we had no ice creepers on our boots.

Soon the snow-covered piñon and juniper anchored in the trailside rock gave way to an occasional bare blackbrush as the snowy trail became a muddy path. Still, it was a relief. With the mud came warmer temperatures. At our first rest stop in a clearing on top of O'Neill Butte, I pulled out a sack of pistachio nuts which no one knew I had packed. We had been building up to this trip for nine long months and here we were enjoying our first rest stop on the trail with a special treat to boot. As we gazed out across the mile-deep Canyon and down onto the tops of the mountains within it, my wife, Marcella, and I had a sense of triumph that our commitment to family backpacking had survived all the preparations for this, our most ambitious trek.

Because Marcella and I had backpacked most of our lives, we had to find ways to continue when our first child arrived. And as the children kept coming, we had to devise ever more ingenious ways of coping with youngsters on the trails. We were living in White Plains, a suburb of New York City, when we decided the time had come for the whole family to explore the Grand Canyon. To allow time for the children's slower pace, we set aside a two-week vacation for it. At that time Molly was 11; Katie, 6; Will, 5; Andrew, 3; and Maggie, 9 months.

Andrew Kemsley (right) precedes his father (opposite) down snow-crusted Kaibab Trail, followed by his mother with Maggie on her back, Jana Bergins with Katie, and Molly with Will. Gary Page shoulders a heavy pack to compensate for light loads carried by the children along the U-shaped route (see map). Each small child is securely roped and his leash held by an older person at all times on the steep, slippery trail—for the children's safety and their parents' peace of mind.

With children of these ages, we knew we would have to have some other experienced backpackers along in case of an emergency. It made good sense to invite our nephew, Kenn Petsch, 21, a camera salesman in Arizona and one of the most experienced desert hikers we know. Next, we asked Gary Page, my charge from the Big Brother program in Queens. At 16, Gary was a veteran backpacker, having been my most frequent hiking companion in the past eight years.

With Kenn and Gary, we felt we could cope with any problem on the trail. Since Kenn and I had backpacked in Grand Canyon before, we felt we had had enough experience to get the park rangers' permission for our party to spend several days in a wilderness part of the Canyon. Later we added one more competent and enthusiastic trekker, a 15-year-old neighborhood girl, Jana Bergins, who offered an enticing bonus: she would baby-sit for us on the trip.

We had planned our great adventure for mid-March at the time of the children's spring vacation. We also chose this time of year partly because the temperatures in the Canyon would be perfect for hiking. But more important, mid-March is still too early in the season for snakes and scorpions. With young children, one of the most serious considerations is the possibility of their reaching behind rocks or into bushes and surprising a rattler or scorpion. This danger is considerably reduced by avoiding the hot summer season.

Because we wanted everything about the trip to go right, we began our planning the preceding July. First we ordered topographical maps of the Canyon. By Labor Day we had decided upon a route, requested camping reservations from the Park Service, and started to list the gear we would take.

Right after Christmas I began shopping for the special items we would need to add to our backpacking equipment. Soon we were all involved in the excitement of searching catalogs and discussing choices. Two items looked particularly useful for the trip. One was a varmint-proof container for storing our food supplies in the wilderness. (The plan was for our strongest backpackers to precede the family on our proposed route and set up food caches.) We ordered six of the five-gallon metal cans from an outfitter in San Francisco who sells them for use on packhorse trips in the Sierras.

We also needed a water container that was collapsible enough to be carried conveniently in our packs when not in use. At one of our wilderness campsites we would be waterless for three days, so we would need enough of these containers to carry 10 gallons at a time. We chose large, Army surplus, leak-proof polyvinyl bottles from a supply house in Buena Vista, Colorado.

With our equipment problems solved, we turned to that part of the trip preparations that always gets our whole family involved: the food. Early in January I made out a week's menus. Then the fun began. First, the shopping. For large trips we usually find about a third of the goods we need in a supermarket, about a third in a backpacking supply store, and about a third in a gourmet food shop.

By mid-February we were cooking for a trip that was still one month away. I made three kinds of the trail snack known to all backpackers as gorp, while Marcella made a date-nut-molasses loaf, and granola from our own recipe. The granola requires long, slow baking and sends an aroma through the house that

Refreshed by the glories of spring at Phantom Ranch, the Kemsleys cross the Colorado River (below) to picnic and rest before moving on (opposite) to their preferred wilderness campsite at Horn Creek. The food and fuel awaiting them there had been cached by Kenn Petsch (right) and Gary Page who hiked 27 extra miles to make the family adventure possible.

gets everyone's taste buds clamoring for a sample. Of course we had some, warm right out of the oven, in bowls with fresh milk. I portioned out the rest into plastic bags, one for each day it appeared on the breakfast menu. To save weight, we repackaged all the store-bought goods into plastic bags, in single-meal quantities. The gorp was divided into 63 individual bags, so each person (except Maggie) could carry his daily supply in a pocket. Altogether, the bottles and cans we emptied for this Canyon trip weighed 8½ pounds.

The shopping, cooking, and packing made us feel as if the countdown had started. We pitched the tents in the backyard to make sure that everything was still there—poles, stakes, tie downs—and that no repairs were needed. Will, Katie, and Andrew played inside them and got underfoot, but I really enjoyed their excitement. Everyone tried on his pack and boots to be sure they still fit. Katie and Molly had outgrown their boots, so Marcella took them shopping for new ones, and the girls broke them in by wearing them to school day after day. One of the last jobs was to pack our sleeping bags in small nylon stuff sacks so the down would not get too compacted.

The children told everyone at school about their coming trip to Grand Canyon. Katie's first grade teacher got her to write a story about the trip. Molly's teacher asked her to read a book about Navajo and Havasupai Indians because the Canyon country is their homeland. Jana called several times to ask about cacti, an essay subject she had chosen for her science course. Gary wanted to know about the controversy over deer and burros in Grand Canyon because he had made a bet with his study hall adviser. I began to read about John Hance, Seth Tanner, Ben Beamer, and other 19th century prospectors who explored the Canyon.

Suddenly departure day was here—March 12. Jana's father drove us to the airport. There was barely breathing room with all of us and our gear in his station wagon. When we landed at Grand Canyon Village, we found six inches of snow on the ground and more falling. We stayed at Moqui Lodge while completing our plans and spent our first day sightseeing and meeting with the back-country rangers. They wanted to know how much Canyon backpacking experience we had had, what gear we were taking, names and addresses of all members of our party, and a list of places we would be staying each night. Satisfied that we met all requirements, they confirmed our permit.

Then a freak accident threatened to undo our months of planning. I broke my thumb and had to go to a hospital in Flagstaff to have it set. Suddenly, I was something of a liability to our party instead of a strength, and I felt it would not be wise for us to travel so deeply into the more remote wilderness parts of the Canyon as we had planned. The rangers adjusted our permit and we resigned ourselves to spending part of our time in what is known as the "heavy use corridor" in the Canyon. It is the route of daily mule trains to Phantom Ranch, the tourist hotel at the bottom of the Canyon next to highly developed, ranger-attended campgrounds.

We had to wait yet another day while Kenn and Gary set up our food cache. We kept hoping that it would stop snowing long enough for us to hike safely down through the snow zone. We knew that each 1,000 feet we descended would be like traveling 300 miles south and that we would pass through several biotic life zones, ending up in the Lower Sonoran Zone which is pretty much like a tropical desert. Though it was still snowing at the Rim, we expected it to end about 1,500-

Katie explores the shore of Bright Angel Creek in her own way, perhaps looking for a lizard like the harmless whiptail (below) found by Jana and Molly. On the way to Horn Creek the family held a staring match with a pair of burros. The children found these feral beasts fascinating and were sorry to learn that their growing numbers threaten the grazing for desert bighorn (opposite) and mule deer in the Canyon. Gary learned it is unlawful to take from the Park the deer antler topping his pack (below). Discarded antlers yield calcium to gnawing desert rodents.

2,000 feet down and evaporate altogether before it hit the bottom. As I kept telling everyone, "It never rains on the bottom of Grand Canyon." So I thought.

By the time we stopped for lunch that first morning, the snow had stopped. We were enjoying our Gouda cheese and pilot biscuits when it suddenly began to hail and then to rain. We pushed on anyway, and the children had already begun to ask, "When will we be there, Dad?" when we dropped down over the edge of the Tonto Plateau into the Inner Gorge. There the clouds opened up—thunder, lightning, and a torrential downpour. Soon everyone was soaked to the skin. The thunderstorm set first Katie, then Will and Andrew off in a constant wail. We had already hiked about seven miles. For the first time in my life I wondered if I could be something of a sadist to inflict this kind of abusive treatment upon our children.

What to do? Hike on. We simply kept right on hiking. What was the point in stopping? There was no place to get out of the pelting rain.

Well, the children survived. When we arrived at the bottom of the Canyon, it stopped raining. I left the family by the side of the trail while I went to inquire about our campsite. When I returned, I jokingly said, "It's only another mile."

Little Will stamped his foot. "Damn it, Daddy, I don't want to hike any more." He so well expressed the feelings of everyone that we all broke up laughing. I didn't have the heart to reprimand him for his language.

My family was amazed to discover how dry the air is at the bottom of the Canyon. Our clothes dried completely right on our backs by the time we had finished cooking dinner and unrolled our sleeping bags.

The next morning was sunny and clear. It was as if we had hiked down through a faery maelstrom, weathered the storm, and were now in the garden of paradise. Springtime was in full bloom at the bottom of the Canyon. The cottonwoods and arrow weed were clothed in their light green leaves. Beavertail cactus, turpentine broom, and globe-mallow were in full blossom.

We dawdled about camp until mid-morning, then took a day hike down to the sandy north bank of the Colorado where it is joined by Bright Angel Creek, so named by John Wesley Powell in 1869 when his party stopped there for a few days' rest. One of the vital secrets we have learned about successful family backpacking trips is to allow for frequent rest days, and this was the first one for this trip. Gary, Kenn, and Jana tried to throw stones across the Colorado. In the midst of a hearty game of Capture the Flag, we were all amazed to find a brown pelican among the cottonwoods. We learned later that the bottom of the Canyon is a minor flyway for such varied species as juncos, Canada geese, and other migrating birds that sometimes follow the Colorado River into the Canyon and winter there.

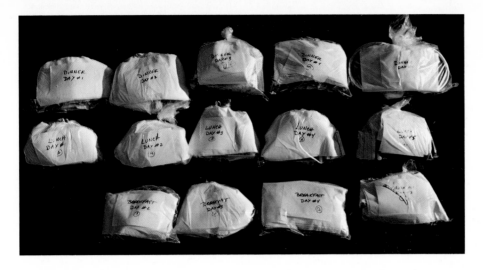

After lunch the little children occupied themselves by building a fort in the sand while Maggie napped. The roar of the river rapids washed away all sound of voices around us as Marcella and I basked, reveling in the remoteness wrought by the Canyon's vertical walls. Recalling our seven-hour journey of yesterday, down through the layers of gray-white limestone and pale brown sandstone at the distant Rim, past the blues, greens, and purples of the Tonto Platform and the red rock of the Inner Gorge, we tried to fathom the Colorado River's journey down through five million years of rock formation.

Time itself acquires a different meaning in this place of vast heights, depths, and distances. The children felt it in the shortness of the day. The sun never came over the rim until mid-morning and passed the other rim by mid-afternoon. As soon as the shadows fell, the temperature cooled rapidly from around 75 degrees to the low 40's, summoning us back to camp. Along the way Molly was the first to notice several bats swooping about in the twilight.

Our third day required our longest hike, 10¼ miles and an ascent of 1,700 feet. It would take us up to Horn Creek, the most primitive campsite of our trek and the place where our food was cached. Food accounted for more of the weight in our packs than it normally does because Maggie is allergic to milk and her special soybean formula had to be carried in cans.

The next day Gary and Kenn went on ahead of us to set up camp. Then they hiked back three miles from the new camp and met us for lunch at Indian Gardens, excited over some mule deer they had seen. Since the new camp had no water supply, we filled our Army surplus bottles at Indian Gardens with enough water to last us through the first night and morning there. Then, because we planned to stay at our new wilderness campsite for three nights, some of us would hike back the six miles' round trip for more water.

On our way to Horn Creek, it was very revealing to us to be hiking the "heavy-use corridor," where we met other hikers and long mule trains carrying either passengers or supplies. We had never intentionally hiked such a crowded trail before. It took us through Indian Gardens which, like our Phantom Ranch campground of the two previous nights, was one of the most heavily used back-country campsites in Grand Canyon National Park. Here were some 75 people jammed side by side into campsites with picnic tables, plumbing, electric lights, and pumped water. Yet, only a very easy three-mile hike away was Horn Creek—completely undeveloped, no sad scars of man, quiet, and almost completely unoccupied except for us. We saw one camper there the first night, a Flagstaff minister, William H. Denlinger, and only two other hikers the rest of the time we were there. I have a hunch that most backpackers do not really want solitude, but rather want to do their social thing in a nature setting.

Mr. Denlinger told us he had seen a desert bighorn sheep the day before, so we spent our first day at Horn Creek exploring the side canyons to the west of our

Visiting an Anasazi ruin (right), the Kemsleys learn how families lived here a thousand years ago. Besides irrigating what is now Indian Gardens Campground to grow corn, squash, and beans, they harvested the wild agave (below). After maturing for 12 to 20 years, this plant shoots up a 12-foot flower stalk, then dies. Occasionally Havasupai Indians still prepare agaves in the ancestral way. They roast the stalk 48 hours, then eat it or grind it into meal. To nourish the giant stalk, the agave's thick leaves hoard the same rain and snowmelt that seeps into Deer Creek (opposite). It refreshes today's visitors, as it did the Anasazi, with the boon of a waterfall in the desert.

camp in the vicinity of Mr. Denlinger's bighorn sighting. We did not find the bighorn, but we did find deer tracks and a pair of burros. Skunks visited our campsite at night, forcing us to rig our hiking staffs into a derrick to suspend some foods out of their reach. Fortunately they didn't vent their frustration on us.

When our time at Horn Creek was up, there was a sadness among us. While the trip was not yet over, we knew we were now on the last leg. We had only 7½ miles to hike back out. Still, we had allowed two whole days to do it, because it included 4,000 feet of vertical ascent. By mid-morning we were back at Indian Gardens, in good time to set up camp and take off on a day hike to some Anasazi ruins. Surprisingly, these Indian ruins, located within sight of the most heavily used trail in the park, the Bright Angel Trail, are remarkably unscathed.

That night we reorganized our gear and prepared for an early morning departure back up to the Rim. Of the 308 pounds of supplies we had carried into the Canyon, we had 45 pounds of trash to carry out in our now-empty metal cans. The 45 pounds included an excessive amount of trash from the baby—empty food jars and cans, and disposable diapers—but our theory is that if you change very little in the way the baby is accustomed to being treated at home, you'll have a more contented baby and, ergo, a more enjoyable trip.

We began the long climb out of the Canyon about eight o'clock that last morning. We let three-year-old Andrew lead the procession because it would be particularly difficult for him. Kenn and Gary were far ahead of us on the premise that they could get to the Rim, leave their packs, and come back to help us, if need be. Since the rangers do not allow any camping along this stretch of trail, we had to go all the way to the top. We were confident the children could do it, after their week of trail-hardening.

What we could not have imagined, though, was how easily it would go. We made it all the way out—four miles—in 4½ hours, not counting stops. I doubt Andrew could have, or would have been willing to try to make this record during the first days of the trip. But because the whole adventure had been so much fun, he was willing to put forth the effort. We've found that youngsters have far more hiking stamina than we think they do. The trick is to make it interesting enough for them. The ever-changing rocks, plants, and animals beside Bright Angel Trail were a big help, as was the trail itself, twisting its way upwards through one ecosystem after another.

Back on the South Rim we turned for a last look into the immensity of the Canyon. Already it was hard to believe we had really been part of it. We found we had no way to express the sense of vastness and the mystery of time that it had given us. So, just as Andrew and Will and Katie had mastered it one little step at a time, it was the little things we talked about—the lizards and the burros, the bats, the prickly pear cactus, and the Indian ruins—and how much we all wanted to come back to see them again sometime.

From a campsite facing the Grand Tetons, Peggy Bauer prepares to join her husband for a day of photographing Wyoming wildflowers and wildlife.

EQUIPMENT— YOUR KEY TO COMFORT ON THE TRAIL

Erwin A. Bauer

Late on a silent, gray afternoon toward the tag end of September, my wife, Peggy, and I hurried down a steep mountain path toward a trailhead, our trek's end, still seven miles and about 2,000 feet below. Pausing briefly, Peggy tightened a shoelace while I studied the lowering clouds which threatened to bring a miserable end to a delightful week. At that moment, a light rain began to fall.

Normally, September is a golden rather than a rainy period to be on top of Wyoming. Quaking aspen leaves have turned from summertime's gray-green to yellow, and most days are cool and dazzlingly bright. No month offers more to us less gregarious woodsmen who prefer to have the trails and the wildlife watching to ourselves. Still, September rarely passes without at least one brief storm, perhaps a heavy snow squall that subtly begins on such a somber afternoon as this one in the high country. Now I had a premonition about an even more drastic change in weather. As if to confirm it, the light drizzle increased to a steady rain.

"It's still about two hours, maybe three, to the car," I said. "Should we push on or find a camp near here?"

"I'll vote for here," Peggy answered. My wife is never one to end a pleasant trip before it is absolutely necessary.

We soon found a level and firm campsite nearby, well out of sight of the trail and where no clearing whatever would be necessary. In less than ten minutes we were ensconced comfortably inside our nylon mountain tent, which I had pitched with special care in case the rain developed into a severe storm. Using a mini-stove, we cooked what was not quite the last of the freeze-dried rations in our packs. When the wet night finally fell, we were fast asleep.

At daybreak we found six inches of fresh, soft snow covering everything, including our tent. We must have slept through a wild storm because everywhere small, dead evergreen limbs littered the lovely landscape. The snow now softened the outlines of rocks and muted the sound of our footsteps as we moved around preparing breakfast. The low clouds were breaking up, giving us sunlit glimpses of white mountain peaks above. By the time we were ready to strike the tent, the sky was clear and blue again. The last part of the trip to our trailhead was so idyllic —completely dry below the snowline —that we used up four hours instead of two for the downhill saunter. Part of that time was spent shooting pictures of a fine bull moose which had only recently shed the velvet from his huge palmate antlers. We also made color photos of a ruffed grouse that strutted nearby rather than flush as most of that species usually does.

I relate this incident for one reason only: proper backpacking equipment made the happy ending possible. We experienced no discomfort, despite the sudden whim of the weather. It could too easily have turned out another way.

Today more than ever before, backpacking and camping in the American wilderness can be a rich and rewarding activity. For many it has become the ultimate experience.

Yet for some, backpacking amounts to little more than hard toil on a tough trail and may even become a never-to-be-repeated ordeal. Backpacking enjoyment depends on three factors: mental preparation, physical conditioning, and equipment. Equipment is as important as the other two; even the most muscular person with a wholesome attitude can soon be turned away from the outdoors if he is ill-equipped.

However, there is such a bewildering amount and variety of camping and backpacking gear on the market today that a beginner is likely to be confused. Even a good many veteran outdoorsmen disagree about which equipment is best. So I'll attempt to simplify the

Put your feet first

In boots with **cemented** construction (right), the leather upper (1) is folded under the inner sole (2) and cemented to the midsole (3), which is cemented to the lug sole (4). No stitching is used, and cheap boots may not have midsoles. Cemented boots without out midsoles cannot be resoled.

Littleway construction appears mostly in lightweight boots. The upper (1) is inserted between inner sole (2) and midsole (3) and the three pieces are sewn together (5). Filler (6) cushions the foot and stiffens the sole. The stitching is inside the boot, protected from water and dirt. A reputed disadvantage is excessive stiffness caused by the inside seams. Littleway-constructed boots can be resoled.

Most medium- and heavy-weight hiking boots, including the high tops worn by the author (above), have either Goodyear or Norwegian welt. In **Goodyear**, upper (1) is placed next to inner sole (2); a thin strip of leather—the welt (7)—is placed against bottom edge of upper, and all three are sewn together (5). Welt is then bent back and down and sewn (5) to midsole (3).

In **Norwegian** welt, the upper (1) is stitched (5) to inner sole (2) and then bent out to edge of midsole (3) and stitched (5). A welt (7) may be present. Goodyear and Norwegian boots contain deeper layers of filler (6). Both are more flexible than littleway boots and can be resoled.

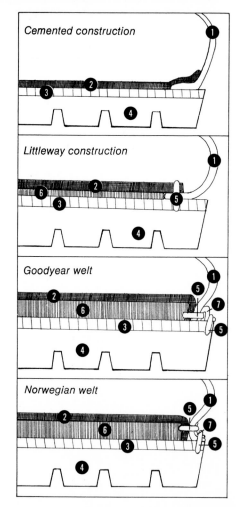

Cemented construction

Littleway construction

Goodyear welt

Norwegian welt

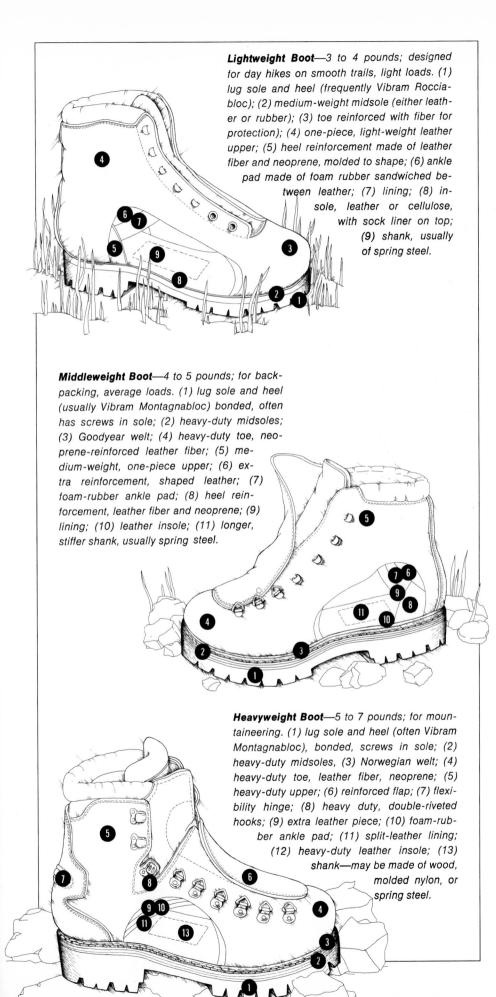

Lightweight Boot—3 to 4 pounds; designed for day hikes on smooth trails, light loads. (1) lug sole and heel (frequently Vibram Rocciabloc); (2) medium-weight midsole (either leather or rubber); (3) toe reinforced with fiber for protection); (4) one-piece, light-weight leather upper; (5) heel reinforcement made of leather fiber and neoprene, molded to shape; (6) ankle pad made of foam rubber sandwiched between leather; (7) lining; (8) insole, leather or cellulose, with sock liner on top; (9) shank, usually of spring steel.

Middleweight Boot—4 to 5 pounds; for backpacking, average loads. (1) lug sole and heel (usually Vibram Montagnabloc) bonded, often has screws in sole; (2) heavy-duty midsoles; (3) Goodyear welt; (4) heavy-duty toe, neoprene-reinforced leather fiber; (5) medium-weight, one-piece upper; (6) extra reinforcement, shaped leather; (7) foam-rubber ankle pad; (8) heel reinforcement, leather fiber and neoprene; (9) lining; (10) leather insole; (11) longer, stiffer shank, usually spring steel.

Heavyweight Boot—5 to 7 pounds; for mountaineering. (1) lug sole and heel (often Vibram Montagnabloc), bonded, screws in sole; (2) heavy-duty midsoles, (3) Norwegian welt; (4) heavy-duty toe, leather fiber, neoprene; (5) heavy-duty upper; (6) reinforced flap; (7) flexibility hinge; (8) heavy duty, double-riveted hooks; (9) extra leather piece; (10) foam-rubber ankle pad; (11) split-leather lining; (12) heavy-duty leather insole; (13) shank—may be made of wood, molded nylon, or spring steel.

subject as much as possible. But first, another, even more important matter must be considered.

In the past, before so many Americans escaped each year to the wilderness, before trails were as heavily tramped as they are now, a camper or backpacker could plan to live off the land, at least to some extent. He could cut and burn all the firewood he needed for fuel. Evergreen boughs could be cut to make a comfortable bed each night. He could even hope for the thrill of cooking his own fresh-caught fish or game. But suddenly the number of campers began to multiply and trails became crowded, with alarming consequences for the wilderness they had come to enjoy. Too few gave any thought to the fact that they were littering and polluting streams, and even scarring the land by the way they pitched a tent. Out of the genuine concern of dedicated wilderness travelers there has emerged a new wilderness ethic for all backpackers. It affects every aspect of wilderness living, but it can be stated in one short sentence: leave no trace of your visit except your footprints. Campers who take this ethic seriously must begin with the selection of their equipment.

Let us begin with footwear because every hiking activity depends upon it; without good, serviceable boots you will not need any of the other camping equipment very long.

Any boots are satisfactory if you happen to be used to them and find them comfortable day after day. I have hiked in every conceivable kind of boot, from the high-heeled lumberman's boots and military-issue combat boots to rubber-bottomed pacs and the old, reliable, twelve-inch high moccasin-style "bird shooters" preferred by upland hunters. But for several years I have settled on the now standard hiking boot. Developed originally in Europe for alpine hiking and climbing, it is designed to give maximum support to the arch and the ankle. It laces from low on the toe up to the ankle, is about six inches high, and has fairly stiff, lugged "waffle stomper" soles. The leather (sometimes padded

Dress in layers for comfort

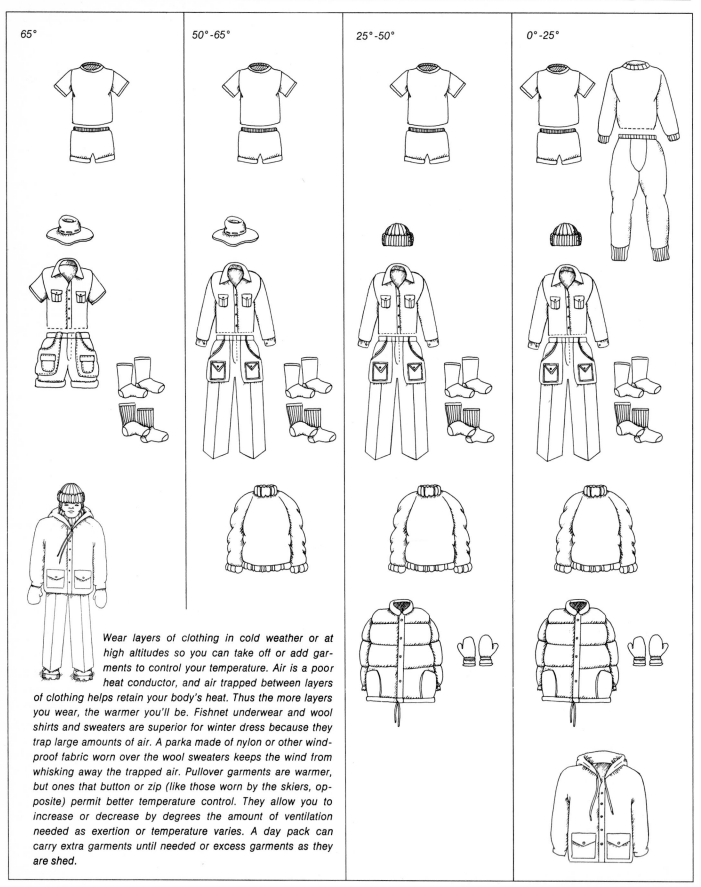

65° 50°-65° 25°-50° 0°-25°

Wear layers of clothing in cold weather or at high altitudes so you can take off or add garments to control your temperature. Air is a poor heat conductor, and air trapped between layers of clothing helps retain your body's heat. Thus the more layers you wear, the warmer you'll be. Fishnet underwear and wool shirts and sweaters are superior for winter dress because they trap large amounts of air. A parka made of nylon or other windproof fabric worn over the wool sweaters keeps the wind from whisking away the trapped air. Pullover garments are warmer, but ones that button or zip (like those worn by the skiers, opposite) permit better temperature control. They allow you to increase or decrease by degrees the amount of ventilation needed as exertion or temperature varies. A day pack can carry extra garments until needed or excess garments as they are shed.

around the ankles) is shaped to hold the foot snugly and is heavy enough to protect the entire foot when traveling over rough or rocky ground. A standard hiking boot superficially resembles a mountain climbing boot, but a climbing boot is even stiffer and heavier, too stiff and heavy for typical trail travel.

The most important single point in selecting a boot is fit; it has to feel comfortable right from the beginning. Don't walk out of any shop with boots about which you have any doubts. If you buy by mail order, order several pairs so you can choose the best-fitting one. The money you paid for the boots you return will be refunded. Believe me, it's worth the extra effort to find well-fitting boots.

To make sure a boot fits, try it on over the hiking socks you normally wear. My strong recommendation is for two pairs of medium-to-heavy woolens, the year around, mainly for cushion and comfort. Try on both boots and, without lacing, push each foot forward as far as possible. Now stand up and use an index finger to feel whether there is a little space (as there should be) between your heel and the heel of the boot. Next, move your foot all the way back into the boot and lace it tightly. While walking about, twist and flex each foot and try a few deep knee bends. Your heel should not move or rub against the boot, and your toe should not touch the boot's toe. In other words, the boot should feel snug, but not restrictive.

If possible, try on several pairs for comparison, perhaps a different boot on each foot at the same time. If two boots feel equally comfortable, select the lighter of the two, since a pound carried on the foot is equivalent to five pounds carried on the back. Many of the best-made, medium-weight hiking boots weigh three to four pounds a pair. Beyond this is too heavy, unless you definitely plan to get into mountaineering, for which stiff, heavy boots are needed.

Welt refers to the manner in which leather tops and insoles are attached together and to the sole of the boot. The type of welt is likely to determine

the cost of the boot, and what is generally known as the Norwegian welt (reputedly the most waterproof and flexible) is the most expensive.

As I stated earlier, of all backpacking equipment, boots are the most crucial; skimping on quality is false economy. At this writing, a few good ones are still available at less than $45 per pair. But most adult-sized boots that will last for years and hundreds of tough but comfortable trail miles are in the $50 to $70 range.

Most hikers have normal feet and will be able to find boots that fit in an outdoor or mountain shop. But you may have to do some searching if you need unusual sizes. Once you've located exactly the right "off-size" boot that really fits, it's sound advice to buy a second pair for the future.

No footwear—absolutely without exception—should be worn on a trip without first being completely broken in. To do otherwise is to risk destroying a good pair of feet.

For constant hiking in wet situations, wear shoe pacs (shown on page 35), slip-on rubbers over boots, or canvas "jungle-type" boots developed by the military services for use in Viet Nam (available in some Army surplus stores).

Campers and backpackers need no uniforms and need not be slaves to changing fashions. It's only chic to dress comfortably, and that usually

means inexpensively. Cotton clothing is hard to beat for typical hiking from May through September. It's cooler and more absorbent than pure synthetics, although some part-cotton, part-synthetic fabrics are ideal for summertime outdoors because they are both absorbent and quick-drying. Well-worn (therefore soft) blue jeans are also excellent for warm weather backpackers, but denim weighs more than khaki or cotton-synthetics. Denim also dries more slowly, a serious consideration in cold weather.

Far more important than the type of fabric is the way the clothing fits. Fit is particularly important in trousers. Tight pants restrict movement and result in unnecessary fatigue. But very loose, baggy slacks are a nuisance—even a potential hazard—because they catch on trailside shrubs and sharp rocks. The best pants and shirts are loose (maybe a size too large) and have plenty of pockets to carry film, compass, or other small items.

Many enthusiastic backpackers prefer knickers and even more wear shorts for the most complete freedom of movement. But, even in warm weather, it's hardly wise to take only shorts because of the possibility of insect bites, scratches from brush or rocks, sunburn (especially at high altitudes), or unexpected drops in temperature.

The same kinds of clothing are not suitable at all elevations, even in the same area. During the midsummer of 1976, Peggy and I spent a month trekking in the Himalayas of Kashmir, India's northernmost region, and into Ladakh, or Little Tibet. We hiked for more than 150 miles at altitudes ranging from 6,500 feet to almost 14,000 feet. Although we could wear cottons comfortably at the highest elevations on sunny days, it was necessary to switch to woolens on cloudy days. Woolen sweaters or jackets were welcome on mornings and evenings when we were not underway on the steep trails. Any backpacker should keep in mind his entire route when selecting clothing for a trip. Old, well-worn garments often prove to be the best.

No hiker should venture far from his base without carrying foul-weather outer garments. Especially in the mountains, an afternoon thunderstorm can change the brightest day into a dismal experience. The best choices for protection are ponchos that fit over the backpacker and his pack alike, or one- or two-piece (parka and pants) nylon rainsuits that protect the walker, but not his pack. Special covers just for packs are available. A disadvantage of ponchos is that they have a lot of loose material that snags on bushes and flaps in wind; but they are more versatile than parkas since they can serve as groundcloths or emergency shelters. My own preference has always been to take a parka and to find some natural, temporary shelter until the worst of the rain passes. Why seek shelter? Because, when walking in the rain, your body's moisture will condense on the inside of any waterproof garment. In fact, perspiration may make it as wet underneath a parka or poncho as it is on the outside. So I wait out short squalls.

When choosing foul-weather clothing, try to avoid the very cheap items that obviously will rip easily and probably will not survive the first wet trip. Test by pulling the material with your hands before buying. Look for the nylon or "rubberized" nylon things that will withstand rough use and may cost as much as $25 for a large parka.

In selecting other garments for wet weather, remember that both wet wool and wet polyester-filled clothes are warmer than wet down clothes. Wet down becomes very heavy and loses its insulating effect. Other advantages of polyester-filled clothes are that they cost less than down and dry in a fraction of the time down takes.

Long experience and common sense have taught me to trim my checklists of clothing to a minimum. In warm weather that is good advice to anyone. But there are a few exceptions. Depending on the length of a trip, I carry several pairs of socks, trying to wash and keep dry as many of them as possible as I go along. I do not wear worn or darned socks, common causes of blisters. A camper who plans to wander at high altitudes or in uncertain weather may want to take long underwear that

is at least part wool. Some kind of broad-brimmed hat or billed cap is useful for protection against intense sun. My own preference is for inexpensive straw cowboy hats that provide a sunshade and are well ventilated at the top. For winter hiking, a balaclava helmet, which when completely unrolled protects the face and neck as well as the head, is useful.

All clothing for campers is available in a surprising range of prices. The most expensive is not necessarily the best, so time devoted to comparing items is usually well spent. Neatness of the exposed stitching and reinforcement around stress points are good indicators of quality. Also check to see if the zippers work smoothly and the buttons are securely sewn. If you still feel unsure about judging workmanship, ask a knowledgeable clerk to help you. Otherwise, stick to familiar brand names with solid reputations in the outdoor equipment field.

Before obtaining a pack, realistically assess your needs. Are you going to stay out on the trail overnight? For several nights? Will you move on each day or establish a convenient base from which to take short hikes each day? Do you have a small child to carry? Will you and your trailmates share loads? All these factors affect your choice of carrier.

For day hiking only, a nylon or waterproofed cotton-synthetic bag known as a daypack (see illustration on page 34) is carrier enough. Daypacks provide just enough space to tote a rain parka, lunch, knife, matches, suntan lotion, insect repellent, camera, and so on. They usually have one or two compartments and are worn over the shoulders. Daypacks can be multipurpose, being used for carrying schoolbooks or groceries or when biking, fishing, hunting, or cross-country skiing. They range in price from about $8 for the simplest to about $25 for those with zippered side pockets and large capacity. Beltpacks—light carriers that fit around the waist—are also adequate for day hikes. Some have compartments and adjustable waistbands and can carry lots of gear.

Backpacks differ from daypacks in that their capacity allows a person to carry enough supplies to be self-sufficient for one or more nights. That means that backpacks can hold all essential gear—food, stove, mess kit, tent, sleeping bag, first aid kit, survival kit, toilet items, knife, map and compass, extra clothing, flashlight—and a fair amount of non-essential gear like a camera and field guides.

Today's backpack has become somewhat standardized, with a choice of two styles: the more popular external aluminum tube frame with the carrier bag that fits onto it, and the internal frame pack in which the frame, usually flat, fits inside the bag. The latter packs are called body packs or rucksacks and are more popular with mountaineers and cross-country skiers than with backpackers.

The pack itself—the nylon, water-repellent bag that attaches to the aluminum pack frame—often comes in two styles: packs that have a single, large compartment and packs that are divided into two or more internal compartments. The more compartments, the better you can organize the contents. But compartments may prohibit distributing the load exactly the way you want it. You can eliminate having to make an either/or choice by buying a bag with zippers inside the compartments. When they are zippered, there are compartments; unzipped, there is one large compartment.

In the last decade or so backpackers have started carrying more weight on the hips where, for many (perhaps most) of us, it is much easier to tolerate. A wraparound hip belt transfers weight from the back and shoulders to the legs, which usually are three to four times as strong as the back and shoulders. Many of the better pack frames are now built with these padded waist bands. A good pack frame will also be adjustable to better fit an individual, to slightly shift the load up or down, to permit the weight to be carried on the hips or shoulders or both. Some frames have extensions at the top that permit you to tie on additional lightweight, bulky gear. Sometimes a minor adjustment makes carrying a

Don't let body heat escape

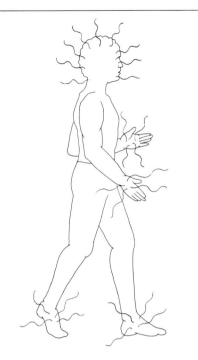

The body's extremities are major areas of heat loss. Feet cold? Don a hat. Head and neck lose the most heat; prevent that loss and more heat circulates to your feet.

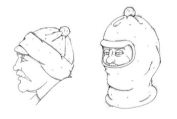

The versatile wool or orlon balaclava helmet is probably the best hat for really cold weather. Unrolled, it prevents heat loss from head and neck, and protects the face against frostbite.

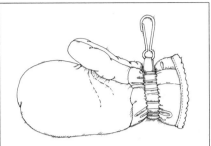

Mittens are warmer than gloves because they allow the fingers to snuggle together and warm each other. Two popular kinds are the down-, polyester-, or foam-filled ones (top) and those that combine an outer shell of nylon and leather with a wool liner (below). Either style should have gauntlets that cover the parka sleeve and fasten securely in place to keep snow out, warm air in. Gloves (bottom) are useful in mild weather and for doing chores.

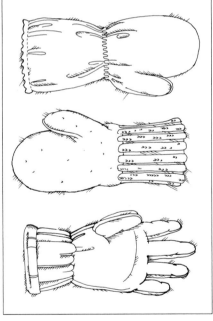

A shoe pac (near right) has a rubber bottom to keep foot dry. A felt liner can be inserted for extra warmth. A nylon gaiter (far right), snugly zipped, keeps snow out of the boot top. A cord runs under the boot to prevent the gaiter from riding up.

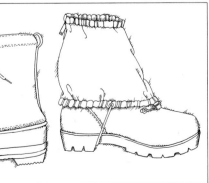

loaded pack much more pleasant. So experiment before buying.

Let's assume you are buying your first pack. If you plan only normal summertime camping trips of a week or less—and will be carrying less than 35 pounds—a frame that puts most of the load on the hips is almost certainly preferable. Carrying heavier loads than that on the hips will probably cause undue fatigue.

Before actually buying a pack, test to find the one that fits you best. Borrow different models from friends, or rent them. Many shops offer rentals and deduct the rental rates from the price if you decide to buy. Go into a shop and try as many as are available. Adjust the pack carefully to your body. Next load the pack with heavy items handy in the store, say 20 to 25 pounds' worth, because any sack can feel good empty. Wear it full for awhile; walk around. If possible, climb some stairs. Granted, that does not duplicate how a pack feels after a few hours on an uphill trail, but it does provide a basis for comparison with other packs similarly loaded.

As when buying any camping equipment, the purchaser should look for quality in design and construction. Nearly all of the frames now on the market (all those made by well-known manufacturers) are strong enough to stand long, hard use, well beyond what is normal. Not so with all shoulder straps, however. They should be padded and wide enough (two and a half to three inches) not to cut. Webbed nylon straps are likely to slip in the buckles, so check the buckle system carefully to make sure that it holds the straps securely in place under stress. Check to see if the hip belt is well padded, as it should be, particularly for thin people.

The storm flap that covers the open top of the pack should be large enough (and then some) to cover the opening when the bag is fully loaded. The rows of stitches on a backpack, inside and out, should be straight and even—evidence of good workmanship. The thread should be nylon, and the more stitches per inch the better. Look for reinforcing at all stress points in

A good pack lightens your load

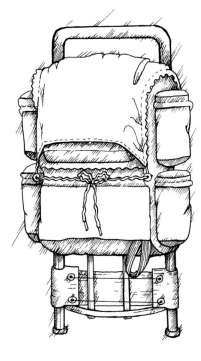

The external frame pack, used by most backpackers, supports heavy loads— 40 to 75 pounds.

The day pack, sometimes carried in larger packs to use on side trips, can be a book bag at home.

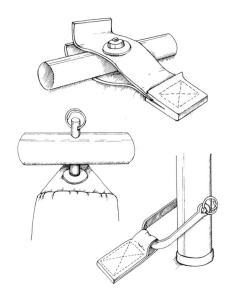

In attaching straps to pack frames, strength is all-important. One good way bolts the strap to the frame (top). Another inserts a clevis pin through the frame and a grommet in the strap (middle). A split ring keeps the frame from slipping off the pin. A third design combines a U-ring and clevis pin fastening (bottom).

Each of these styles of packs is designed for a different use. The **rucksack** (left), is favored by cross-country skiers and mountain climbers because its narrow, back-hugging design provides the stability those sports require. Some rucksacks have frames (aluminum or fiberglass stays or tubes) that fit inside the bag and next to the back to steady the load. For extended hiking trips, most backpackers prefer an **external frame pack** (above left). Its aluminum frame (U-shaped, H-shaped, or rectangular with welded-on horizontal bars for reinforcement) makes walking with a load easier. The frame may be straight or slightly curved to match body contours. The water-repellent, nylon bag has one or two internal compartments and pockets sewn on outside. The nylon **day pack** (above) has no frame and is intended for light loads on short trips.

The rucksack, or soft pack, holds a load of up to 35 pounds, most of it borne by the shoulders.

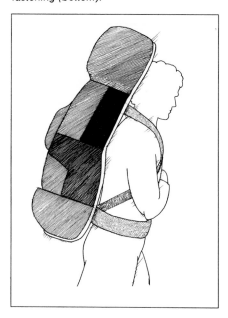

A properly loaded pack is an easier riding pack. The idea is to distribute the weight of the various items so that the heaviest things are next to the pack frame and near your shoulders. The next heaviest items go just below them, and the lightweight items fill the rest of the space. That makes it easier to keep your balance when walking and reduces the strain on back muscles.

the bag, such as the corners and where the bag fastens onto the frame. Check also for reinforcing around zipper ends and where pockets attach to the main bag. Test zippers to be sure they work smoothly; you may prefer heavy-duty ones. For winter camping, nylon zippers are preferable to metal ones, which are more likely to freeze up. Finally, check to see that there are at least three grommets (four are better) on each side of the pack. Grommets secure the bag to the frame and should be reinforced sufficiently to support a full load.

Remember that there are many cheaply made and poorly designed backpacks on the market. Any backpack selling for less than $35 or so probably should be avoided. On the other hand, there are very expensive backpacks with price tags beyond $100 which are equally bad bargains. The best values for the money today are found in those backpacks that are manufactured by reliable companies and that sell in the $50 to $75 category. They will serve for many years and many miles.

A warm, comfortable sleeping bag is essential for a restful night, so choose wisely. You can avoid overspending by learning about sleeping-bag fillers, weights, and shapes.

The two principal filler ingredients are down and polyester. Down is millions of light, fluffy filaments, the underplumage and insulating layer of waterfowl. When plucked from ducks and geese, down retains its insulating properties. It is light and compressible without losing its great resilience, known as loft. Down is the warmest insulation for its weight, so it is no wonder that goose and duck down are widely used in outdoor garments, perhaps most of all in sleeping bags.

In recent years, synthetic fibers have been developed that seriously compete with down. For some uses, such as warm summertime and wet weather camping, synthetic fibers are better. Polyester fibers are water-resistant and retain their insulating capabilities even when wet. Once soaked, they dry much faster than down. Synthetic sleeping

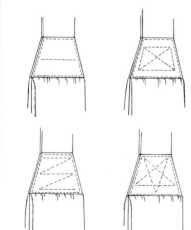

The author's pack (above)—loaded for four days' fishing in Montana's Beartooth Mountains—weighs 30 pounds. His fishing pole carrier doubles as a map case.

Straps must be securely sewn to shoulder pads. The more stitches per inch, the more angles in the pattern, the stronger the bond. Of the four patterns of stitching at left, three will do the job. The single row (top left) is inadequate. The star pattern (bottom right) is the strongest, though the other two are probably secure enough.

35

bags are less expensive and more durable than down ones and are easier to repair and keep clean. But a synthetic bag that keeps you as warm as a down bag under the same conditions weighs 1½ to 2 times more than the down bag. So you make your choice.

Some down bag manufacturers occasionally are careless in filling their bags. They use the advertised quantity of down, but they overfill some sections and underfill others. Thus, when selecting a down bag, check to see that all areas are equally filled. Look at the surface of the bag, too. You can expect some tiny feathers to poke through here and there, but be suspicious of a poor-quality product if many do.

Beyond those tests, selecting your first bag may be reduced to picking the right size, the best shape, and the correct weight. If the bag that passes these tests happens to be made by a known, reliable manufacturer, the odds are then good that you will be able to sleep comfortably and stay warm in your bed wherever you unroll it.

No one bag will serve every camping need, from warm summer nights in the Carolinas to bitterly cold hunting camps high in the Rockies. But for most summer holidays, consider a bag of two pounds of down, or 3½ or 4 pounds of synthetic. (*Three-pound bag* means only that it contains three pounds of insulation. Total weight may be 4½ pounds.) There are adult-sized, four-pound polyester bags, for instance, that are great for June-through-August trekking and which sell for $35 to $45. A down bag of the same weight will be warmer and cost more.

Bags come in rectangular, barrel, mummy, and semi-mummy shapes. Child-sized bags are available and are cheaper than adult sizes. Compatible couples can buy "doubles" that zip together. A mummy bag of the same length as another style of bag has less material and weighs less in a backpack. But not all campers can sleep comfortably in a mummy bag. Learn whether you can before making a large investment.

When examining bags, keep in mind that the "warmth rating" often given may be misleading. Buy a bag by weight, size, shape (as described just above) and the maker's reputation. Avoid the really inexpensive (often very colorful) bags stocked in such abundance in discount stores. These may be filled with cotton batting or hair or kapok and are not worth carrying home. But do remember that if you become cold while sleeping, whatever style of bag you are using, you can remedy the situation by wearing more clothes inside the bag and by keeping your head (but not your face) tucked snugly inside the bag's hood.

Take care of any bag and it will last longer. Mostly that means keeping it as clean and as dry as possible. Put a mattress (inflatable air or foam) or at least a ground cloth (the floor of the tent, a sheet of plastic, a poncho) between bare ground and the bag. If you use your bag frequently, launder it periodically, especially around the open end where it gets dirtiest. Repair any rips or tears before storing so it will be ready to use on short notice. (See pp. 112-113—Ed.)

For some people, the combination of great fatigue after a hard hike and unwillingness to carry any extra weight may make a mattress superfluous. But for the majority of backpackers a ground pad is nearly as important as the sleeping bag, both for the cushion comfort and for added insulation against the cold ground. Experienced backpackers greatly prefer a simple polyurethane foam pad from ½ to 2 inches thick and just long enough to extend from shoulders to hips, the main pressure points. This pad can be rolled up and lashed onto the backpack. However, some short and very light inflatables are now available, and a growing number of trail campers seem to prefer them.

Consider an interesting fact: you may not need a tent at all. At least not in the beginning.

Assume that you will only be trekking in summer, in a generally dry area, where weather is fairly predictable. Maybe you will travel where there are refuges from rain at intervals along your route. If so, why not sleep under the stars and save the tent money for something else? Carry along a poncho to cover your sleeping bag until a brief rain squall passes. Or take a waterproof ground cloth and a couple of collapsible aluminum poles to improvise a tent (see illustrations on page 39). Peggy and I have done it many times and thereby have saved lugging four pounds or more.

The inside story on sleeping bags

Down bags need an inner construction called **baffling** to keep the down from shifting. When inner and outer shells are **quilted**, the stitching lets in cold air. Baffles separate the shells, creating uniform areas of dead air. In **box tubes**, down may fall away from baffles, creating cold spots. **Slant tubes** are warmer because the tubes overlap. **Overlapping V** construction requires more baffling, costs more. **Laminated** construction is less popular because extra fabric adds weight.

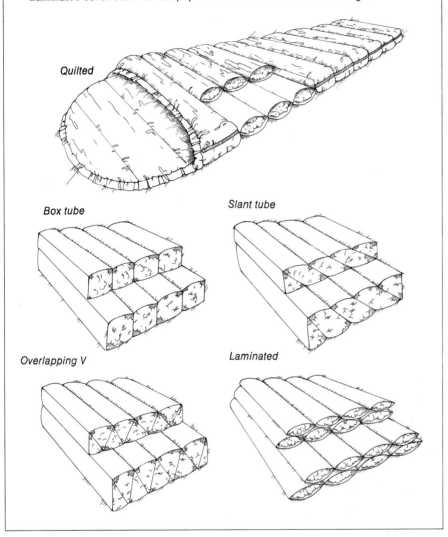

Quilted

Box tube

Slant tube

Overlapping V

Laminated

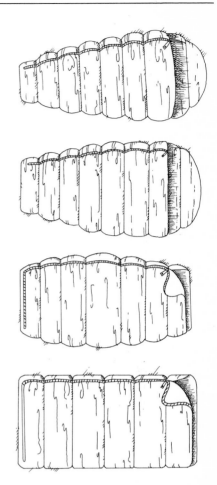

Sleeping bags come in four basic shapes (above): mummy; semi-mummy (more foot space); barrel (more elbow and leg room); and rectangular. The mummy bag is warmest because there is less dead air to warm and lightest because there is less fabric. But if you toss in your sleep, it may be the least comfortable. The rectangular bag is roomiest but heaviest and least warm. Whatever shape you choose, air out the bag (photo, opposite) after each use.

Baffling is unnecessary in polyester sleeping bags (left) because the fibers don't shift. But the fiber needs to be secured so the edges don't curl and leave uninsulated areas. A common method (1) is to stitch through both shells and batting to form tubes of fiber, but the seams let in cold air. Another way (2) is to sew the shells to the batting only where the zipper attaches. The zipper baffle keeps out the cold from the seam. A better method (3) is to overlap two quilted layers of batting to trap insulating air between the inner and outer shells. In a few bags a third layer of fiber is sandwiched between the quilted layers.

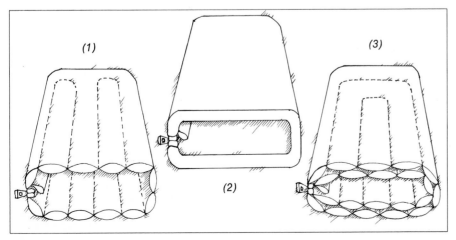

(1)

(2)

(3)

When you do contemplate buying a tent, consider your actual needs carefully. The main reason for using a tent is to have shelter from cold, rain, wind, and insects. In lowland areas where mosquitoes can be troublesome, you need something that is insectproof. Where the weather is generally warm and dry, there's no use choosing something large and elaborate. But where damp weather is likely to keep the camper and his gear trapped inside for days at a time, a roomy tent can be worth its extra weight. A backpacker who ventures above timberline or takes his tent ski touring in winter will want something that can withstand high winds and snow.

Backpacking tents come in many models, some very strange. But most are A-shaped or inverted U-shaped to resemble miniature quonset huts. Quality tent designs give as much room, shelter, and ease of erection as possible while keeping the weight to a minimum. Because the manufacturers are very competitive, some extremely good designs have resulted. A backpacker can surely get his money's worth from many different brands and styles of tents.

Some campers will disagree, but I submit that ventilation is the most important factor to consider when acquiring a tent. One reason is that provision for ventilation is the least standardized aspect of tents. Nearly all tents are made of durable material such as ripstop nylon and nylon taffeta. Most tents can be pitched by anyone in just a few minutes, after a trial or two. And the limits in light weight (for the materials now available) have surely been reached. But not all tents are well, or even adequately, ventilated.

A properly designed tent permits any vagrant summer breeze to blow through its vents, making it livable rather than like a bake oven when the occupants are zipped up inside. Proper ventilation also prevents moisture from condensing on the inside of the tent (see illustration on page 39).

Either in the store or on trial at home or on a short trip (some stores rent tents), erect the tent yourself and check it carefully before buying. Ex-

Modern backpacking tents are marvels of lightweight yet sturdy designs. The traditional A-frame tent has many competitors, such as the quonset-shaped tent (top) with vestibule for protecting gear. Some tents have external aluminum tubular frames (center right) that don't require guylines or stakes. The four-man, center-pole tent (center left) has been adapted from the Indian tepee design. A variation of the quonset design is shown at right. All of these tents (though not all tents on the market) are made of breathable ripstop or taffeta nylon, except for the waterproof floors. The tents can be fitted with waterproof rain flies for stormy weather.

Buy a tent or make one

A tarp tent is often adequate for summer trips, especially in dry, mosquito-free country. A plastic ground sheet or coated nylon tarp can be shaped into several types of shelters. All you need is a tarp (8 by 9 feet for one person, 9 by 12 for two) with grommets, some rope or cord, two or more short aluminium extension poles, and your imagination. (You can add grommets yourself by purchasing a kit consisting of grommets, washers, and a metal punch.) The first three methods illustrated below offer protection from wind and some rain; the last method is good for protection from the sun. Whatever you do, don't leave your plastic in the woods. Carry it out!

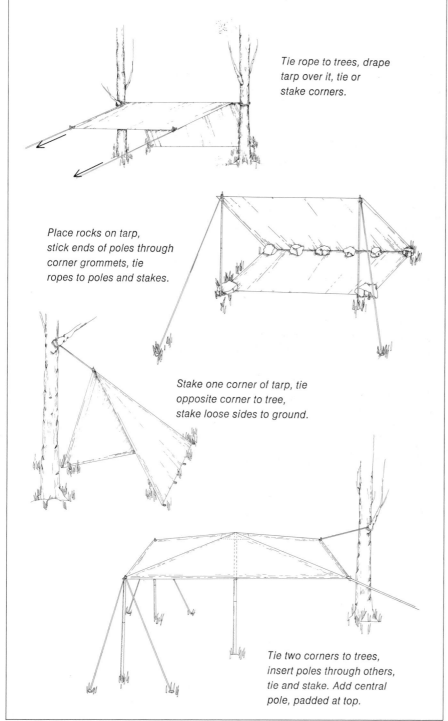

Tie rope to trees, drape tarp over it, tie or stake corners.

Place rocks on tarp, stick ends of poles through corner grommets, tie ropes to poles and stakes.

Stake one corner of tarp, tie opposite corner to tree, stake loose sides to ground.

Tie two corners to trees, insert poles through others, tie and stake. Add central pole, padded at top.

Ventilation is critical in tents. A sleeper can exhale and perspire a pint of moisture during the night. A tent made of fabric that breathes—lets that moisture pass through it—also lets in rain (top). A waterproof tent (center) keeps rain out, but body moisture condenses on the inside and the tent becomes clammy in cold weather or a steam bath in summer. The solution? Use a tent that breathes and that has air vents high along the ridgeline to let breezes carry away the rising warm air, and cover the entire tent with a waterproof fly (bottom). The fly keeps out rain, and the air space between it and the tent permits drafts to carry away the moist air that escapes through tent roof.

Mini-stoves leave no trace

You need a windscreen because WIND

Blows away layer of warm air and steam, thereby cooling the food near the top of the pot.

Increases heat loss by cooling the sides of the pot.

Deflects the flame and its heat away from the pot.

Cools the stove, reducing the fuel pressure needed for gas stoves to operate.

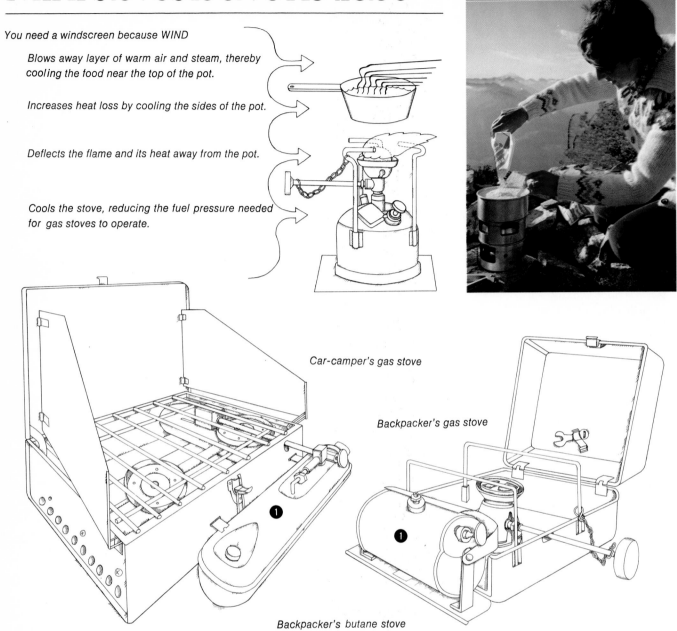

Car-camper's gas stove

Backpacker's gas stove

Backpacker's butane stove

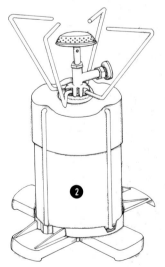

The famous Coleman two-burner stove (above), which burns white gas, has a just reputation for reliability. But this model of stove is intended for car or, possibly, canoe camping; it is far too heavy and bulky for backpacking. Small, lightweight (1 to 2-pound) stoves that burn white gas, kerosene, or alcohol, like the gas stove above, right, are the long-time standbys of backpackers and mountaineers. Another model, shown in the photograph at top, is enclosed in a windscreen designed especially for it. Efficient and reliable, though sometimes finicky to start, they work well in hot and cold weather, at low and high altitudes. All gas stoves have pressurized fuel tanks (1) fitted with safety pressure-release valves.

LP (liquefied petroleum) gas stoves that burn propane or butane (left) are popular because they are clean and easy to operate. These stoves are safe when treated with respect. In operation, the cartridge (2) should never get too warm to hold in your hand. With all mini-stoves, take these precautions against overheating fuel tank or cartridge: avoid using oversize pots that reflect too much heat downward; provide a well ventilated windscreen (e.g., don't surround the stove with rocks—they reflect heat); never refuel a hot gas stove (fill it **before** you begin to cook); don't throw supposedly empty cartridges into a fire—they might explode. Don't bury them, either. Carry them out with you.

amine the ventilation system first. Next see if the walls stretch tightly and smoothly. (Loose or sagging tents are especially annoying in a wind.) Also check the sewing to see if it is neatly done. There should be substantial double, even triple, rows of stitches around corners, stake tabs, and other stress points. There will be eight to ten stitches to the inch in a tent made to last.

Notice whether or not the flies and flaps adequately cover tent openings. The waterproof, sewn-on floor should extend about six inches up the tent walls all around, and that includes forming a sill at the door (to keep out rain, snow, and small animals). Poles and stakes should be included in the whole tent package. Be sure to carry the pegs with you: it's against the backpacker's code, and in some places against the law, to cut fresh wooden stakes.

Three- and even four-person backpack tents are available, but those for two are far more common, because larger ones are so much heavier.

The wise beginning backpacker pitches his tent in his backyard for a night or two of trial camping before charging out on an ambitious expedition. This rehearsal becomes crucial, rather than just advisable, if the initial trip is scheduled for cold weather. Obviously, children are best introduced to camping gently by allowing them to sleep outdoors near home.

A backpacker will pay from $80 to $150 or more for a tent that can be used in spring, summer, and fall and weighs from three to six pounds at the most. However, for pleasant-weather trekking, it is possible to get by with a very inexpensive shelter. I have recently seen some excellent bargains in lightweight, summertime tents for as little as $35 at nationwide department stores.

I always try to keep cooking to a minimum in warm weather. There is a great variety of nutritious foods available that need no cooking—and I feel that cooking only subtracts from time that can be better spent in a wilderness. On short trips I may carry homemade mixtures of gorp, homemade beef or venison jerky, or freeze-dried foods to which only water need be added. It is not actually necessary to heat all freeze-dried foods, so, unlike most hikers, I usually don't. Besides, some heat (in fact a surprising amount during summer middays) can be obtained by setting the prepared food in a metal container on a rock exposed to the sun. By not heating my food or by letting the sun heat it, I don't have to unpack, set up, and attend my stove. That way I can take a quick nap or use the extra time to read my map or enjoy looking at the scenery and taking photographs.

When I do cook, I don't use campfires unless I happen to be in one of the established campgrounds in which wood and cooking hearths are supplied for campers.

For long trips to cooler altitudes, I carry a small alcohol-burning stove-and-cooking set. The unit consists of an alcohol burner into which the following items nest perfectly: a two-cup teapot, a cover that also serves as a flat fry pan, two sauce pans, and a removable handle. The whole set (it often isn't necessary to carry all of it), including a half pint of fuel, weighs two pounds. The unit heats quickly and will not blow out even in a very strong wind.

The field of small gas stoves for mountain use has long been dominated by European imports, although some American brands are fast gaining a solid reputation. They all burn alcohol, kerosene, or white gas and weigh one to three pounds. Some are not always easy to light and operate, depending mostly on the type of fuel they burn. Kerosene, for example, is more difficult to start than white gas. But, once lit, kerosene burns hotter than white gas. Alcohol gives off less heat than either white gas or kerosene. These factors should be understood and, if possible, tested for in the shop before buying. Be sure any stove is operable before hitting the trail. You may have to cook inside your tent during severe weather conditions, but do so only as a last resort. If you do cook inside, open the tent's vents to let the carbon monoxide escape. Even in the worst kind of weather, *all* stoves should be fueled and lit *outside* the tent—*without exception.*

Recently a number of tiny one-burners that use standard ten-ounce cans of compressed LP (liquified petroleum) gas (propane and butane) have become popular. They are reliable and trouble-free, and some can provide up to four hours of cooking time, which is often enough for four days on the trail. One disadvantage of propane is that it must be stored under greater pressure than butane, so propane canisters are heavier than butane ones. With the LP gas stoves' conveniences of easy starting and cleanliness come their inconveniences—not knowing how much fuel is left in a cartridge, putting up with their reduced heating efficiency as the pressure in the cartridge drops, and having to carry out used fuel cartridges. Also, cold weather sharply lowers the efficiency of LP gas stoves, particularly butane ones. You have to calculate your needs and make your choice. My personal view is that LP gas stoves are the safest source of fuel to use and carry during a wilderness adventure, especially when children are along.

As for cooking utensils, families often are able to assemble enough from whatever odds and ends are available at home, perhaps adding an item from the supermarket. We have managed, for example, with just one saucepan for heating and empty yogurt or cottage cheese containers for bowls or plates. One each of the feather-light plastic forks, spoons, and knives (which are normally wasted as throwaways) are fine as utensils for Peggy and me.

Boots, clothing, packs, sleeping bags, tents, and cooking stoves of high quality are essential for successful trips to the wilderness. But don't leave this chapter with the impression that equipment is all-important—it isn't. Good equipment is important only insofar as it permits you to enjoy your outdoor experience to the fullest, without worry or discomfort. So, select your backpacking gear with care, then relax on the trail!

Paddle through wilderness waters

Clyde H. Smith

The cry of a loon at dusk, haunting symbol of wilderness mystery, may signal mating, greeting, annoyance, or alarm. When the cries increase in frequency and intensity, Indian lore says, they herald the approach of a storm. To Tracey Smith (opposite), the loon's wail evokes memories of family canoe trips like this one led by her wildlife photographer father, Clyde Smith. With family and friends they have come to say farewell to Indian summer and to the wild creatures of Adirondack waters before the coming ice drives both man and bird to winter havens. For its imminent flight, perhaps all the way to Texas, the loon has already changed to winter-brown plumage from its natty summer pattern of black and white.

Flames swirled upward in the chill dusk as Ed Hixson added a log to our campfire on a tiny pine-tufted island in Adirondack State Park. A cheer went up across the darkening water as the children acknowledged his signal by racing their canoes back to camp. Minutes later nine youngsters stumbled up the hill in growing darkness with breathless reports of who beat whom and who almost fell into the water. My wife, Elizabeth, poured hot chocolate for everyone. Grasping warm cups in chilled hands, our young voyageurs snuggled down with Ed, Elizabeth, and me around the fire. Eventually the talk about our day of paddling and portaging died down, tired muscles relaxed, and a hush fell as the timeless sorcery of glowing embers had its way with us.

Suddenly a long, mournful ha-oo-oo-oo echoed from out over the pond. Again, the eerie call pierced the darkness, this time answered by another ha-oo-oo-oo from the opposite direction. Nothing in all of creation is quite like the call of a loon. It is a sound that sends shivers running up your spine, tingles your imagination, and lingers hauntingly in your memory long after its plaintive echo has faded away.

From the deep timber on the far shore came the chilling hoot of a great horned owl. The loon seemed to reply. Spellbound, we listened as two creatures of the wild engaged in a duel of primeval cries. The echoes of their tattoo crossed and recrossed the water. What a thrilling way to end our first day's adventure afloat.

Our wilderness home that crisp autumn night was only one of thousands of miniature islands dotting the blue-green kingdom of the Adirondack Mountains in upper New York State. This intriguing patchwork of lakes and streams is a six-million-acre legacy of the glaciers that gouged out its deep ravines and valleys thousands of years ago. Most of these ancient mountains are forested, and seasonal rains seep down their gentle watersheds, forming innumerable lakes, ponds, streams, marshes, and bogs. It is an Eden for waterfowl, fish, deer, and other wildlife—and for canoeists who want to enjoy them, especially in autumn when all of nature is in a quiet mood.

Dressed for a final fling in bug-free October's midday sun, the Hixson youngsters (top, center) scramble to see who can be the first afloat while their elders greet another party. Cold nights follow warm autumn days, so the author (opposite, center) decreed that everyone bring down-filled parkas and sleeping bags. Beth Paxson and Tracey Smith (opposite, far right) stuff theirs into plastic bags, then into waterproof duffel packs, and stow them beneath the canoe's thwarts, spreading the packs evenly to balance and trim the craft. To keep gear from shifting in rough water, all items except life jackets are lashed in place. Even in flat water, veterans as well as novices keep them handy. Below, Robin Smith and Sue Reit lead the flotilla into a narrows.

Spring canoeing in the Adirondacks is something else. Then torrents of snow-melt whip every stream to an icy froth and put every comer to the test. It was on just such a wild river that I first met Dr. Edward Hixson of Saranac Lake, New York, one of the most competent white-water canoeists I know. Our friendship has grown through the sharing of high adventure on New England's most challenging rivers, and has led to a number of family trips such as this one on the Adirondacks' flat waters.

A lingering Indian summer had extended the canoeing season, and we were all hoping the golden days would last until our children's next school holiday. Ed planned to bring his five children, Heidi, Eric, Peter, David, and Sam, ages 5 through 16. Elizabeth and I would bring my teenage girls, Robin and Tracey, and their friends, Beth Paxson and Sue Reit.

Like all successful canoe trips, this one started at home with careful planning of every detail. First we pored over topographical maps to select a circular route through the maze of lakes in the Saranac area—one that would be challenging enough for adults yet not too difficult for young paddlers and that would require us to pitch camp only once. Next we decided on our canoes. We chose five, ranging from my 20-footer, which easily carries my family and all our gear, down to 16-footers which the teenagers, working in pairs, could handle well. Ordinarily a 20-foot canoe is considered too large and heavy for small lake trips, especially when portages are involved. But mine is unusually light, having cedar ribs and planking covered with one layer of plastic cloth—called polypropylene—and epoxy adhesive. This material is similar to fiberglass, but is even stronger and more resilient. Once when my canoe crashed hard on a rock in some rapids, seven of its ribs were cracked yet the polypropylene skin remained intact and did not leak, allowing me to complete a trip of many miles before repairing the broken braces.

With the choice of canoes for this family trip settled, Ed and I went over each craft very carefully to make sure it was in good condition. There's nothing so discouraging as coping with a leaky boat loaded with camping gear. Still, accidents do happen on trips. The one repair item I always take is a two-inch roll of silver duct tape which I buy at a hardware store. This miracle adhesive is strong and waterproof, and it will take care of minor cracks or punctures in fiberglass, wood, canvas, or aluminum canoes.

Next, we had everyone select a paddle. Blades, shafts, and handles vary; each individual must experiment in the water to discover the kind and length of paddle that suits him best. As a safety measure, we always carry at least one spare per boat. On white-water trips we take an extra paddle per person. A broken or lost paddle at a crucial moment in the rapids can mean big trouble.

Astute map-reading of the Adirondacks'
100,000 miles of navigable waterways enables the author's party to select a 15-
mile circular route interrupted by only
1½ miles of portaging. Little Eric
Hixson (far right) grips a gunwale to help
his father and brothers in a four-man
portage of their 85-pound canoe. Sam Hixson
(opposite) hefts a 65-pounder, letting
his shoulders bear the brunt, while Beth
Paxson carries two packs and two paddles.
Sam makes it look deceptively easy to balance the unwieldy 16-foot canoe, but he
knows a two-man overhead carry can be
harder than toting it solo. With two
people, neither portager can see far
ahead, and it's difficult to pick up and
set down the canoe. The centuries-old
portage trails, started by warring Algon-
quin and Iroquois tribes, are maintained
by the New York State Department of Environmental Conservation. To avoid a portage, Sue Reit (opposite, top) guides
her fully loaded craft through a culvert
under an abandoned railroad line.

Even on calm water, losing a paddle makes more work for the other canoeist. We also checked the sizes and condition of the life jackets which we always carry, and which even veteran canoeists wear in white water.

That left the food, clothing, and tents to prepare. All that menu-planning, list-making, shopping, and packing might seem like work, were it not our own fun and comfort that we plan for so solicitously.

When departure day finally came, the weather reports were still favorable. Less than two hours' driving brought both families to our launching site at the edge of Hoel Pond. People and equipment poured out of the cars, greetings were exchanged with other launching parties, and eager hands passed the gear to Ed and me to stow in the canoes. By ten o'clock we were on the water. Everyone was a bit rusty at first, but so glad to have a paddle in his hands again that we all beamed as we worked to smooth our strokes and develop a rhythm with our partners. Each pull on the paddle thrust everyday problems farther behind us and stirred the reflections of red-gold maples, dark green firs, and white birches on the quiet water.

Ed's two older boys, Sam and David, were first to reach the opposite shore. There they discovered a large culvert running through the embankment of an old abandoned railroad line. It offered a tempting shortcut to Turtle Pond. David charged over the bank, suddenly peering back at us from the far end of the culvert, looking quite small.

"I think you can ride the canoe through," he shouted to Sam, "there's about four inches of water running all the way through." "I'm going to try it," Sam announced with a grin as he paddled into the dark interior. Whoops and hollers— and scraping noises—echoed from inside, cut short by a loud splash as Sam and his canoe dropped two feet into the next pond. "Everything all right?" I shouted through the concrete tunnel. "Sure," David shouted back, "Sam almost fell in, but I saved him."

The rest of us decided we'd walk our boats through the culvert—we really were not up to a spill so early in the trip. Everyone had to crouch awkwardly and, with all the bumped heads, it was a howling contingent that emerged at the far end. The drop to the next pond wasn't bad, but when we saw the clutter of slippery logs and stones surrounding the outlet, we realized how lucky Sam had been to have made a safe splashdown there.

Turtle Pond was long and slim, and we were immediately conscious of entering wilder country. At our approach, scattered groups of mallards burst out of little inlets. A flash of white on the far shore told us a white-tailed deer had seen us before we saw it. The pond narrowed into a zigzag channel which took us into Slang Pond. As we poked our bows into a tranquil cove, more ducks— mergansers—lifted off with a panicky flutter of dripping wings. We all got a cold shower as they passed directly over our heads.

At the far end of Slang Pond we faced our first portage. The canoes were pulled out onto a small log landing and unloaded; Liz, Dave, Tracey, and Beth grabbed gear and loose paddles and began walking along the well-marked trail. The rest of us carried our canoes by the gunwales or hefted them in an overhead carry. No matter how many times we've done it, our portaging nearly always turns into an awkward, hilarious affair. This time, as usual, it ended in a chuckling, staggering effort to stay on the trail and to endure. At each rest stop on the half-mile trek the hungry ones dug into their pockets for the little bags of dried fruit, nuts, cheese, and cookies which we all snack on as needed rather than make a formal lunch stop.

The portage took us to Long Pond where all canoes were repacked and put back into the water. This was a larger lake, full of rocky outcrops and tiny islands, but they were too small to be the camping spot we were now seeking. The map showed some that looked about the right size farther down the lake, so we charted

a course in their direction. We had left the brilliant autumn maples behind and were now surrounded by tall, dark evergreens—pine, spruce, balsam, and hemlock. All at once a piercing cry riveted our attention to an enormous nest in the top of a dead pine tree. An osprey had just lifted off with a loud flapping of wings. The great bird circled above us, enabling everyone to observe clearly its white head and belly. Sometimes called a fish hawk, the osprey has a characteristic notch in its wings that helps identify it in flight.

"Look!" whispered Tracey, "there are more in the nest!" Sure enough, three young osprey, probably this year's brood, were standing on top of the jumbled pile of sticks. I reached for my camera, but before I could get to my telephoto lens, the mother—with a threatening dive and another shrill cry—let us know she didn't like our intrusion, so we quietly glided away.

Farther down the lake we came to a narrow stretch where the water funneled between dark walls of pine. "Something in the water ahead," Ed called softly to me, pulling his canoe alongside mine. We signaled the others to approach quietly. A wake was streaming behind what we now recognized to be the head of a deer swimming the narrows. Everyone dipped his paddle as quietly as possible and our crafts slid closer and closer to the deer. To escape us, the deer put on a burst of energy. In moments it was on shore. Shaking off the water, the young buck gave us one backward glance before crashing headlong into the underbrush. No one said a word; we just looked at each other and smiled.

Where the lake broadened again at the end of the narrows we found a nameless but picturesque little island. It immediately became the unanimous choice for our weekend campsite. It didn't take long to land, unload, and move our supplies to a high vantage point above the water where there was plenty of dead wood for a fire. Famished after a long first day of paddling, it was hard to wait for our small cooking fire to die down so the foil-wrapped potatoes could bake in the coals. Everything was soon unpacked, the youngsters all taking care of their gear and putting up their own tents. Finally the sizzle of Elizabeth's special camper-style hamburgers called us to supper. After our evening campfire, sleep came easily. The last sounds we heard were the cries of the loons and the great horned owl.

Very early the next morning—a foggy, cold one—my dreams were cut short by the loud honking of a big flock of geese, obviously flying low. Poking my head out of the tent for a look, I couldn't even see the other tents only 50 feet away because of the thick fog. Tiny frost crystals etched the tent ropes, and frost whitened the mat of pine needles on the ground. The geese seemed to be circling our island, but as I looked upward, I could see nothing but a ghostly canopy of tree branches. It was tantalizing not to be able to see them. The honking gradually faded as the geese headed south. The whole camp was awake

"My family feels it is a great privilege to see wildlife in the wild," says the author, "and our canoes often serve as front-row seats." The swimming deer (opposite) is one of 50 mammal species that inhabit Adirondack forests and waters. Many are furbearers that barely survived the heavy trapping of 70 winters ago, but now thrive under the park's wildlife management plan. Canada geese (above and opposite, bottom), which the Smiths and Hixsons heard but could not see through a ground fog, are one of many Atlantic flyway transients that pause here to feed and rest—or to molt if the Canadian winter came too soon—en route to East Coast wintering grounds. The ospreys at left, like those that challenged the canoeists' apppproach, are summer visitors. They, too, must soon depart, taking their young to fish in tropical waters somewhere between Florida and Brazil. Spring will bring them back, perhaps to this same nest.

Fishing close to shore in a morning fog allows Ed Hixson (right) to concentrate on luring trout into his canoe, but trying to travel across a fog-shrouded lake without a visible shoreline is a different matter. "It can be spooky gliding along unable to see either land or all the canoes in the party," Clyde Smith admits. "On a river there's usually a current to follow, but on a lake, sky and water blend into one gray sea." Navigating by compass, the author led his party straight to the trailhead they were seeking. Elizabeth (below), following the children on a lake-to-summit dash, enjoys a more leisurely climb through the fog into brilliant morning sunlight.

now, and bundled shapes groped their way out of the other tents to start a crackling breakfast fire. The aroma of coffee, frying bacon, and hot biscuits, mingled with the scent of pines and hemlock, lured the last sleepyhead out of his warm sleeping bag. Fog hung oppressively over breakfast, but shouts went up when we saw a shaft of sunlight pierce the mist.

I passed a map around so everyone could see where we were and discuss plans for the day. At first some wanted to stay in camp and loaf or just paddle around, maybe do some fishing. Others voted to climb Long Pond Mountain, not too far from our campsite. The mountain group won, so we packed a lunch and, as if expecting some sort of warming miracle after the frosty dawn, towels and swimsuits. As veterans of Adirondack Indian summers, we knew that the temperature could rise dramatically by afternoon. We put out our campfire for the day, the children lugging pots of water up from the lake and stirring it in the ashes with sticks to make sure the last coals were dead out.

It looked as if the fog were about to lift, so the canoes, which had been turned upside down during the night, were launched once again. We set out for the trailhead at the base of the mountain, but once we were under way, the fog socked us in again. As lead canoeist, I had the map and used my compass to set our course. On the mist-shrouded water, there was no other way to tell if we were heading in the right direction. It was a relief when Liz spotted land. We beached the canoes, slipped on our day packs, and started the steep climb.

In less than half a mile we suddenly broke through the clammy fog into glorious sunshine. Another half hour of climbing through a notch in steep cliffs brought us panting to the summit. The view was worth it. The fog had nearly disappeared in the valley, revealing miles of undulating forest of reds, yellows, and golds accented by dark evergreens and shining water. The softly rounded peaks of surrounding mountains were framed by the blue sky. It was a perfect Indian summer day.

We lolled around the peak for a couple of hours, shedding our sweaters in the warm sunshine, enjoying the view and our lunch. A lazy, relaxed feeling prevailed as the temperature steadily mounted to what felt like 70 degrees. Although reluctant to leave, we got out the map again and plotted a different route down a wild, trailless side of the mountain. If we followed a stream indicated on the map, we figured we should end up quite close to where we had left the canoes.

A rapid descent of several ledges brought us to a ravine where a stream splashed over smooth, sun-warmed rocks. A mile or so farther the water dropped invitingly over a series of steps gouged with big potholes connected by little chutes. This terraced chain of mini-swimming pools was too much to resist. Out of the packs came those swimsuits. Robin and Sue were first in the bracing water and the rest of us soon followed. The girls tossed white pebbles into one of the deeper pools, then we all took turns trying to retrieve the largest number on one

Elizabeth Smith (above) enjoys a natural whirlpool bath in a pothole flooded by the same mountain stream in which Sue Reit (opposite, right) dives for white stones. Sue and Robin Smith (right) lead the swimming party back to their island campsite. That evening, Elizabeth (standing, opposite, left) supervises the last-night feast of corn-on-the-cob and freeze-dried beef stroganoff. (Room to bring along such fresh, bulky foods as roasting ears is one of the luxuries of canoe camping.) The pot-watching appetites and the weariness exhibited by Sam Hixson, Tracey Smith, and Ed and Eric Hixson reflect their long day of canoeing, climbing, and swimming.

dive. Reluctantly we pulled ourselves out of the slides and potholes in order to get back in time to fix supper before dark. As we paddled back to our island, a large bank of clouds appeared in the northwest. Could it be that this beautiful day was a prelude to bad weather?

The morning of our third day was steel gray. A raw, cold, gusty wind was blowing. It was hard to believe our first two days could have been so mild. At breakfast we looked like Eskimos—everyone huddled around the fire wearing both parka and hat. We lost no time getting tents down and equipment packed. A few stray snowflakes galvanized our efforts. At the last minute before departure, Ed and I rechecked the campsite to make sure that we hadn't left anything and, especially, that our campfire had been thoroughly doused. The way the wind was blowing, it wouldn't take much to reignite it. All tin cans and other non-burnable trash were crushed and repacked in our plastic bags and stowed in the canoes to be disposed of at home. The children had already gathered firewood for the next visitors to this Park-maintained campsite—another little wilderness courtesy that Ed and I have tried to instill in them.

Whitecaps swept across the surface as we headed our boats into our first rough water of the trip. We all leaned low and feathered our paddles, turning them parallel to the water at the end of each stroke to reduce wind resistance. I shouted for everyone to hug the shore as soon as we got across the broad open stretch. Just keeping the canoes headed into the wind was a battle.

On the pond's opposite shore we were relieved to find the portage trail that would take us a little over a mile to Floodwood Pond. Sam and David, pointing to a small stream nearby, suggested that maybe it would be easier to take the canoes down it. "I don't know," I said as I scanned the map, "that thing looks pretty tiny on here—I'm more inclined to take the portage." Everybody but me voted to try the stream. Only Liz stuck with me for this last portage. Even though it was a mile hike and we stopped to rest several times, leaning the canoe on one of the crossarms which are nailed up between two trees for the purpose, Liz and I still beat the rest of the gang to the next pond. They had run into all kinds of blowdowns and ended up half-carrying their canoes down the little stream.

With our flotilla united at last on Floodwood Pond, I was conscious of a rapidly darkening sky. A sudden shower of snowflakes chased us into the next waterway. We could see our breath as we paddled several more miles of easy streams that wound and twisted through Little Square Pond and Follensby Clear Pond. A final sprint across Green Pond brought us to our take-out spot. Ed and I jogged the mile back to our cars and returned to collect canoes, gear, and tired paddlers. We bade farewell to each other, to Indian summer, to this year's canoe season, and started home just as winter's first real snow began to fall.

EAT WELL – IT'S HALF THE FUN

Charlotte Bull

There is something very special about eating camp-cooked foods. For every camper who assures you that he goes camping to enjoy nature, there is at least one who will admit that the highlight of each day is the evening meal. This casts the camp cook in the role of hero and makes the assignment a very satisfying responsibility. It can also be creative, fun, and easy if careful plans are made and certain simple routines are followed.

But the exact way to plan meals varies a great deal from trip to trip. It depends upon the number of campers, their ages and nutritional needs, the location, the expected weather, the availability of fuel and water, time allotted for meal preparation, and cost. Still other vital factors to be fed into the camp cook's mental computer are the length and the type of camping being planned.

Public campground cooks, for example, may have easy access to a store where they can buy refrigerated milk, eggs, and charcoal briquets and enjoy the luxury of corn on the cob. Even in the wilderness, a canoe party or trail riders with pack horses may use canned foods. But backpackers carrying their homes on their backs become acutely aware of the need to give lightweight foods and cooking equipment a high priority in meal planning. After a day of hiking 12 miles of mountain trails, they also want foods that are high in nutritional value. So, to balance all the requirements of the group, a good camp cook becomes first of all a "lister."

List menus. List cooking equipment. List foods on hand. List foods to be bought. List prices. List weights. List foods to be stored until the last minute.

The memory of a good camp cook lingers like the fragrance of wildflowers.

The secret ingredient is planning

For years my family checked and rechecked our lists both before and after each trip until we had developed an effective master list and eventually a refined permanent list for each type of trip we take. By now, planning and packing are second nature to us. Each trip begins with planning the menus.

An overnight outing does not require much attention to food value, but the longer the trip, the more nutritional needs must be kept in mind. Fortunately, many of the proteins, calcium, iron, vitamin C, and carbohydrates we all need happen to be concentrated in such convenient and favorite trail foods as raisins, nuts, chocolate, jerky, dried milk, peanut butter, fruit drinks, and hard candies. If your family has special dietary needs, they, too, can almost certainly be met with careful planning.

To get things off to a pleasant start, the first supper on a backpacking trip may be fairly luxurious. You may have fresh fruit or frozen meat—perhaps in a pocket stew, one of our family favorites which I have included in the recipes at the end of this chapter. However, even the dried soups and noodle dinners for subsequent nights can be lifted out of the ordinary with the right combinations and seasonings. In fact, effortless gourmet meals in the wilderness are quite possible today for those who are willing to pay for freeze-dried shrimp creole or turkey tetrazinni.

At least a dozen companies make more than 175 delicious, lightweight foods for campers, to which you need add only water. Despite all the processing involved, these companies turn out surprisingly appealing dishes, usually easy to prepare under camp conditions, and in enough variety that you can enjoy a long trip without repeating main courses. However, the quality, flavor, and prices do vary. To help you choose among them, there are excellent consumer evaluation reports listed in the Bibliography.

Still, nothing beats making your own taste tests before hitting the trail. Experienced camp cooks sample all new foods and try all recipes on the backyard grill before taking them on a long trip where a mistake is more costly. Families who are just beginning to sense the lure of the wilderness are also wise to deliberately break away from their traditional hamburger-and-baked-bean habits. Car camping and overnight hikes offer good opportunities to fieldtest equipment as well as foods for later use in the wilds.

For one thing, you will find that the actual amount of prepared food in each package of the freeze-dried foods varies greatly, and campers learn not to be fooled by the "Four-Man Serving" labels on some products. Two hungry hikers may find these insufficient. Four may be satisfied only if the cook adds soup, stewed fruit, skillet bread, and instant pudding to the menu. We look for the brands that tell you the actual cups of food in the completed product.

Freeze-dried products are relatively expensive, however, and most must be ordered from mail-order catalogs (firms and addresses are included in the consumer reports) or purchased at a camping or mountaineering specialty store. So, if you are concerned with costs, stick with your local grocery store. If you are willing to carry a little more weight, you can eat well and economically up to a week on food purchased there. If you dry fresh fruits and vegetables in season, you can save even more.

Getting down to specifics, let's assume you are ready to start planning a trail menu for your family. What kinds of meals are possible?

For breakfast you might have a powdered fruit drink; an instant hot cereal with raisins, sugar, and dry milk added; toaster pastries heated in a pan, on a stick over the fire, or eaten cold; and hot chocolate. For larger appetites, or when you want to take time to do more than boil water, you could plan on scrambling reconstituted dried eggs and bacon bits to serve with biscuits and trail jam. Or you could fry reconstituted hash-browned potatoes and onions with a can of corned beef. You may also enjoy the many excellent granola products available in cereal or bar form as well as a variety of dried fruits. Fig-bar cookies make a good concentrated quick breakfast treat, too.

Trail lunches are usually a series of snacks and munchies, not an actual noontime meal. My family seldom carries sandwiches and fresh fruit except on the first day. Both to keep energy at its peak and for the needed break in routine, we find that several snack breaks are more desirable than a lunch stop with a heavy meal. Popular with most backpackers are peanut butter on cocktail rye bread, cheese and crackers (the big seeded ones that do not crumble easily), jerky, meat sticks, nuts, sunflower seeds, dried fruits, fruit leathers, hard candy, chocolate, and firm cookies.

Fruit drink powders provide a great deal of energy; they also mask the blandness of melted snow and the mineral flavors of some springs. Instant lemon teas are excellent, too. Calorie-conscious packers need not worry about the sugar in these drinks—you need it for energy. No one in our family has ever gained weight on a trip.

The most popular and versatile main dish for camp suppers is the one-pot stew in which spaghetti, noodles, rice, or potatoes are the main ingredients. Combined with dried vegetables and canned or dried meats and blended with a sauce, they are hearty and easy to prepare in a variety of ways.

Supper menus also include hot breads, often in the form of a skillet bread or dumplings cooked in the stew. For dessert most campers rely on the quick and easy instant puddings, or on dried fruits eaten as is or stewed. Other cooks are more inventive, making one-pot fruit cobblers or dried-fruit fritters. A hot beverage—coffee, tea, bouillon, or instant soup—completes the meal.

When your trip menu is complete, and the family has given its stamp of approval, the next step is to list the

More than half the work involved in every memorable outdoor meal is done at home, including menu planning, shopping, assembling the utensils and ingredients, and packing them to travel well. A countdown check list makes it impossible to forget the onions.

Dried parsley (at right) and the other dry ingredients for a savory stew are being measured and packed together in one plastic bag ready to be opened in camp, dumped into a pot of water, and cooked by hungry hikers. Bouillon cubes and dried mushrooms will be added to onion flakes, carrots, potatoes, and beef jerky already in the bag to complete the one-pot meal for four. The other meals in this photograph have been packed in double thicknesses of plastic bags, with a label indicating the meal and the day on which it is to be enjoyed inserted between the bags. Cooking instructions are also enclosed. Then breakfast, lunch, and dinner for each day may be placed in a larger bag, which is slipped into a waterproof stuff sack. It, in turn, goes into someone's backpack. All the staples needed for each meal, such as dried milk, sugar, picnic shakers of salt and pepper, tea bags, and coffee (and perhaps a favorite herb mix in a 35 mm filmstrip can) are put into still another bag and kept handy.

Pictured below is a deluxe 3-pound mess kit for a family of four. The three aluminum pots have tops that double as frying pans (with handles that tuck around the top for packing). With a folding pocket knife and a plastic spatula and serving spoon, the kit provides for just about every trail cooking need. It also sets the camp table with stainless steel forks and spoons, plastic plates and cups. Everything nests inside the largest pot and the plates go into a stuff sack, easily retrievable when hunger strikes. Liquid ingredients such as honey or ketchup travel neatly in airtight waterproof, plastic jars with screw-type caps (lower right). This is also a good way to carry margarine (which keeps better than butter in summer) and shortening. Fresh eggs can travel as a liquid, too, but only in winter and for a couple of days. All this homework lightens the backpacker's load and saves the cook's time in camp. It also encourages meticulous menu planning, assuring better eating on the trail.

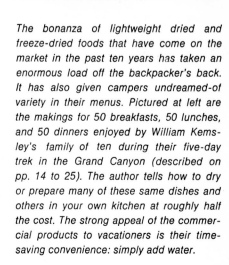

The bonanza of lightweight dried and freeze-dried foods that have come on the market in the past ten years has taken an enormous load off the backpacker's back. It has also given campers undreamed-of variety in their menus. Pictured at left are the makings for 50 breakfasts, 50 lunches, and 50 dinners enjoyed by William Kemsley's family of ten during their five-day trek in the Grand Canyon (described on pp. 14 to 25). The author tells how to dry or prepare many of these same dishes and others in your own kitchen at roughly half the cost. The strong appeal of the commercial products to vacationers is their time-saving convenience: simply add water.

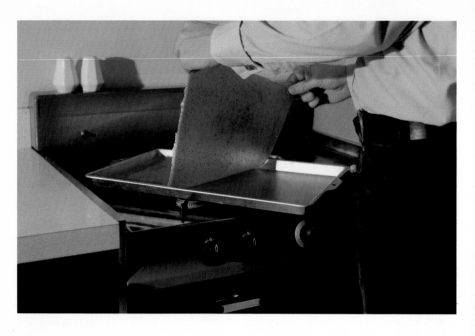

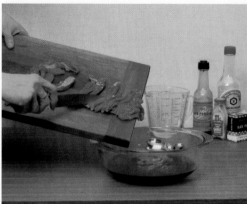

"There's nothing mysterious about drying food," the author declares, "it's a valuable skill for the serious camper who uses a great deal of lightweight foods." To dry food, but not cook it, the oven is set at 150 degrees F. and the door left open a crack for 6 to 8 hours.

The sheet of strawberry fruit leather being peeled from the drying pan above went into the oven as a ¼-inch-thick puree. The leather comes out pliable enough to peel, roll, and slice into bite-size pieces. Recipes for making a variety of fruit leathers (vegetable and meat leathers, too) are found on page 64.

Peaches and other fruits may also be dried in 2 days in the sun or in 10 to 12 hours on a wire-screen tray in the oven or in an electric dehydrator (below). An interior fan ensures more even drying and a softer, chewier product. Dehydrators also dry simultaneously such varied foods as onions, meat, and bananas without blending the odors. Some vegetables must be steamed or blanched before drying, but not the camper's most useful stew vegetables—peppers, onions, zucchini, mushrooms, and parsley.

At right are shown the steps in making jerky. The partially frozen, lean meat is sliced thinly, marinated 2 to 3 hours in soy sauce, garlic salt, and pepper; blotted dry on paper towels; placed apart on oven rack; and dried until meat is brittle. Homemade jerky is a delicious, additive-free food that goes well with such other highenergy trail snacks (photo opposite) as granola and fruit leathers.

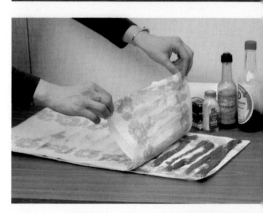

Dry your own trail snacks

basic cooking equipment you will need for *every* meal—the stove, fuel, and matches; a bowl, cup, and spoon for each person to eat with; the towels, soap, scouring pad, and one large pot for dishwashing. Then, starting with breakfasts, list the amount of each food needed and the specific additional equipment required to prepare and serve it, each time it is needed—such as a pot to boil water in or a skillet and spoon for scrambling eggs.

After listing lunches and dinners in similar fashion, total up all the food and equipment needed and make any changes that will simplify matters. Why take a box of 100 tea bags when you find you need only ten? If the can opener will be used only once to open a can of tuna, it makes sense to leave both at home and switch to a can of Vienna sausages that has a pull-tab opener. To keep utensils at a minimum, you will probably decide, as most backpack cooks do, that you prefer occasionally to wash out a cooking pot or skillet to reuse for the second or third course rather than carry an extra one. This need not be a problem, however. The one-cup instant soups will stall hunger pains while you wait for the main course to cook. Actually, our children have always loved the long supper hours, playing around the campsite between courses.

With your menus adjusted and lists refined, you are at last ready to go shopping. You have anticipated your every need, listed all foods and utensils, and cut out nonessentials. The menu is appealing and well balanced. Everyone is satisfied that he has been consulted about his food preferences and is looking forward to a great trip. If you have chosen all your dishes from the meals described above, you can purchase all the ingredients at the grocery store. However, by shopping at a mountaineering store for a few special items such as freeze-dried shrimp or cottage cheese, you could add some interesting highlights to your meals and have more free time in camp.

When it is time to pack the food, clear off the kitchen table and spread out all of the food you plan to take. We find an important aid to packing is to keep all camp equipment stored in one area and all camp foods on a separate shelf. You can pack much faster if you do not need to rummage around looking for the plastic bowls or the home-dried vegetables.

Packing involves much more than just finding a place to put things in the car or your pack. Actually, it is mostly *repacking* things. To save space and reduce weight, you first discard boxes and repackage the food in heavy-duty plastic bags of the kind designed for freezing foods. I use double bags for some items such as sugar, and use rubber bands, twist'ems, or pipe cleaners to close each bag securely. As you pack each item, check it off the list.

This is also the time to combine many items for ease of use in camp. For instance, it helps to empty a 3-ounce box of powdered instant pudding mix into a quart bag with 2/3 cup of dried milk. At dessert time all you will need to do is add a scant two cups of water to the mix.

The next step is to pack all of the separate parts of each meal together in a larger, plastic "meal bag." Not only is it convenient to pull out of your pack on the trail, but the large bags make it easier to load and balance a pack.

One of the most important decisions a camp cook makes is what to leave at home. If your list shows that an item was not used on several trips, it might

be omitted in the future—unless, of course it is the first aid kit! Your kitchen scale is a big help in clarifying final choices. When you discover that your five-pound binoculars weigh the same as a two-day supply of food, the two-day extension of the trip will undoubtedly win out, and the binoculars stay at home.

Bathroom scales are handy for loading individual packs or for balancing saddle packs or laying out a canoe load. It is almost always dismaying to learn that your planned menu weighs as much as it does. Beginning backpackers find that bulk, too, has to be anticipated with great care.

When the food has all been repackaged and labeled, my husband spreads out absolutely everything we want to take on a trip, lines up the empty backpacks, and then packs in stages, weighing and rearranging each pack at each stage. First he packs the essentials such as the tent and sleeping bags. Then the pots, utensils, and meal bags. Finally he adds the extra socks and down jackets. It is only at this point that we consider the luxuries—extra food treats and personal items such as cameras, nature guides, and sketch books. The packs are all kept equally loaded at each stage until each child's and each adult's weight limit is reached.

After a few trips you'll probably find yourself looking for ways to adapt the basic recipes to accommodate personal tastes. This makes camp cooking still more fun, and may be a necessity to cope with food allergies.

Some of the supper combinations you might whip up are Spanish rice, chicken stew, or beef stroganoff. You can tailor these dishes to your family's tastes by combining the various starchy bases with your own dried vegetables, prepared sauces, herbs, and dried and canned meats. Two of our favorites which I have included in the recipe section are hearty green pea soup and deluxe macaroni and cheese.

"Many campers are surprised to learn that breads and desserts can be baked on a tiny camp stove," says the author, "and that they can be one of the most creative aspects of camp cooking just as they are at home."

Elizabeth Jones (right), art editor for this book, steps from her office at the National Wildlife Federation's Laurel Ridge Conservation Education Center in Vienna, Virginia to the nature trail there to fieldtest Charlotte Bull's recipe for bannock biscuits, the Bulls' all time favorite skillet bread. Adding a cup of water to the dry ingredients which she combined in a plastic bag at home, she mixes them and drops the dough by spoonfuls into a frying pan which has been coated with oil. Next she fries the biscuits slowly, about 4 minutes on each side, until they are lightly browned and cooked all the way through.

When the author makes bannock for her family over a campfire, she uses all the dough to make one large, skillet-sized biscuit. To finish cooking the interior, she improvises a reflector oven by tilting the skillet on its edge, on the ground close to the fire, and lets the glowing coals complete the baking while she slowly rotates the bannock in the skillet.

The author also uses her versatile bannock recipe as dumplings in a camp stew, to make pancakes by adding dried eggs, or make a shortcake for wild berries with a pack of reconstituted whipped cream mix. She also adds wild berries to the bannock biscuit or dried fruit to make a fruit cobbler —all on a camp stove.

Canoe campers and car campers can carry a reflector oven like the one below in which breakfast rolls are baking while ham sizzles in a skillet. A good reflector oven is made of heavy aluminum, folds flat for easy carrying, and weighs about 2 pounds.

60

Hot breads—a moveable feast

A culinary challenge of a different sort arises when you come across a patch of ripe blueberries or when the anglers in your party proudly present you with an unplanned catch. Although you cannot count on nature's bounty, it's good to carry a little extra sugar for making a cup of trail jam, and flour or cornmeal for the fish. Just remember that fish should be cleaned thoroughly, at once, kept dry and cool, and cooked as soon and as simply as possible. Nothing can beat crispy fried trout right out of the pan with a sprinkle of salt and pepper and a squeeze from a handy plastic lemon. To achieve a golden brown, fried but almost fat-free fish, use very hot, but not smoking, fat which just covers the bottom of the skillet. A heavy, cast-iron skillet is ideal for car campers, but weight-conscious backpacking cooks must settle for an aluminum one.

To satisfy a hiker's need for bread, try bannock biscuits, the versatile skillet bread illustrated at left, or the dumpling technique. A spicy dessert of applesauce made from diced dried apples and topped with a gingerbread batter is very good.

Because hikers burn up lots of calories, I add a big spoonful of margarine to every stew or boxed dinner to ensure the energy required on steep trails. The Indians knew what they were doing when they added rendered fat to powdered dry berries and jerky to create that perfect trail food, pemmican. However, we are careful to limit the amount of fried foods in our menus. Men alone on a hunting or fishing trip often tend to fry everything instead of taking the time to bake or boil, and this greasy diet can result in stomach problems. This can also happen on trips on which supplies are carried by pack animals and the riders or hikers are not working off the calories. But hardworking backpackers may enjoy tiny fried pies made from a stick of pastry dough and applesauce or jam and browned slowly in a skillet; or doughnuts made from the bannock mix and rolled in cinnamon sugar when done. (Incidentally, a small can of cinnamon is worth its weight on long trips for applesauce, oatmeal, cookies, and other foods.)

There is really no end to the ways you can work within the limits of your pack and still come up with good meals topped with applause-winning desserts. For our youngest daughter's July fourth birthday in the high country of the Colorado Rockies, I once made a cheesecake from a boxed mix and chilled it in a snowbank. Snow is handy for setting gelatins, too, and in the summer our children make snowcones with highly concentrated fruit drink powders. Clever cooks can even improvise trail ice cream from dry milk and eggs plus hot chocolate mix and clean snow.

Although we use both campfires and stoves on our trips, like many campers practicing the new wilderness ethic, we feel no need to sit by the traditional fire every night. We much prefer to get a good night's sleep and an early start in the morning. We find a camp stove is the ideal solution for most camp cooking, one that avoids nearly all of the campfire problems that concern environmentalists as the number of campers increases. Even public campgrounds discourage campfires nowadays—in such effective ways as requiring campers to bring their own firewood or charcoal. Where fires are allowed in the wilderness we use only "squaw wood," the small dry branches easily broken over the knee. We do not even carry an ax or hatchet. We also strongly advise learning to operate your camp stove first in the backyard, winter as well as summer. You'll learn how to keep the stove clean and operable and how much fuel you need to carry for a trip. Good care of your stove is especially important in winter camping when hot food is a necessity.

Winter campers enjoy a very special type of wilderness experience. An area that would not get a second look in summer can become a scenic wonder in the winter, and both skiing and snow-shoeing make wonderful family outings. When our three girls were all under six we spent an exciting three days at an Adirondack shelter only 500 yards from a road. Later, we bought snowshoes for everyone and spent weekends in the Catskills, pulling our equipment on the toboggan. These were some of our very best camp trips—lots of winter fun and no bugs and no noise.

However, winter camping requires much more advance planning and several important alterations in your usual camping routines. For example, you will need many more hot liquids. Even at lunch stops, a cup of instant soup or hot chocolate made from snow melted on the camp stove can make the difference between just being chilly and being chilled to the bone. A hot drink at the crucial moment can be a bona fide life saver, as my husband can attest after a grueling winter summit climb on Colorado's highest mountain.

You also need to take even more high-energy foods, such as chocolate bars, maple-sugar candy, and dried-fruit candy bars. There are many recipes for such concentrated food treats, but some should be carried only in a winter pack. In a summer pack they may melt all over your extra socks. Winter is also the time to splurge on the more expensive instant stews that need just boiling water. They are especially valuable at high altitudes where it takes so long just to boil water, let alone cook rice or macaroni. Because snow melts more slowly than most campers realize, however, even those marvelous instant suppers take more than an instant to prepare. It helps to save a few spoonfuls of boiling water to add just at the last minute to reheat the rapidly cooling stew on a frigid day.

Winter camping also dictates a few changes in your choice and handling of equipment. Food stays hotter in plastic bowls than on metal plates. You may find yourself sleeping with your canteen in order to have water to use for brushing your teeth in the morning or just to keep it from freezing and bursting the seams. For this reason we buy plastic water bottles rather than metal canteens for year 'round use. On a winter morning you may also find that you need to tuck the camp stove inside your parka or warm it between your hands before it will start.

Winter or summer, we always carry one full day's extra food allotment as an emergency precaution on each trip. This bag contains only foods that can be eaten without cooking or adding water—jerky, leathers, chocolate, cookies, nuts, cheese, or gorp. Once we hiked into an Adirondack shelter and found the spring had dried up, leaving us with insufficient water to prepare the macaroni dinner on our menu. That extra supply of high-energy snacks was a lifesaver.

Such experiences also prove the wisdom of always carrying a full canteen for each member of the party. All of our children began carrying a small daypack with their canteen, jacket, and teddy bear as soon as they began walking the trail. A bedroll was added as soon as they could manage it, around the age of five.

It is also wise to keep food divided among several packs in case someone gets separated from the group. Just having your own supply of chocolate and fruit makes you feel more secure.

Wildlife sightings are a prime reason we enjoy our trips, but we have learned to protect ourselves from freeloading visitors. We once lost an entire pack to a bear in an isolated area of upstate New York. But no animal has ever threatened us personally, not even the bear who shared our campsite on a Canadian island for two days. We have, however, learned how inconvenient it can be to have a mouse eat your boot laces or a porcupine chew up your paddle. Chipmunks can also chew a hole in a pack.

One of the best ways to save yourself from kitchen visitors is not to tempt them in the first place. Keep strong-smelling foods like bacon tightly tinned. Don't leave dishes unwashed or food in your tent at night. The worst offend-

Keep it beautiful

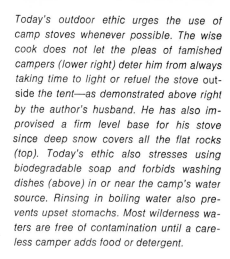

Today's outdoor ethic urges the use of camp stoves whenever possible. The wise cook does not let the pleas of famished campers (lower right) deter him from always taking time to light or refuel the stove outside the tent—as demonstrated above right by the author's husband. He has also improvised a firm level base for his stove since deep snow covers all the flat rocks (top). Today's ethic also stresses using biodegradable soap and forbids washing dishes (above) in or near the camp's water source. Rinsing in boiling water also prevents upset stomachs. Most wilderness waters are free of contamination until a careless camper adds food or detergent.

ers are probably the camp cooks who do not burn their garbage and fishermen who carelessly dispose of fish entrails and heads.

We once spent a long night banging pots together to scare off the bears from a garbage dump where previous campers had discarded loaves of bread and a bag of sugar. The children thought it was exciting though we were in no danger at any time. Most camping books suggest ways to store food or to hang packs in trees, but chipmunks and mice can be very clever at circumventing your complicated inventions. It is better to carry packs unless someone can stay in camp to watch them, but most important is being scrupulously clean at all times.

Of course the use of a camp stove prevents the burning of garbage and papers so the modern camper *must* be especially careful to pack out everything—cans, foil, plastic, and paper. Use your empty plastic bags to pack all non-burnable items such as soap pads, tin cans (cleaned and flattened), and plastic containers. Carry leftover food home or take it far from camp and water supply and bury it under a rock.

Do *not* scatter food for the animals. Carelessly discarded food attracts wildlife in the middle of the night or offends campers who follow you. Feeding wildlife should be limited to offering peanuts or cookie crumbs to the birds or small mammals you meet.

O f course everyone should share the responsibilities of cooking, housekeeping, washing dishes, and keeping the campsite neat. When these tasks are fairly divided and expeditiously completed, there will be all the more time to hike, fish, or just sleep in the sun—together.

Whatever the mode of transportation that gets you into the wilderness, camping is characterized by an exhilaration and freedom of spirit. Even the chores of camping, undertaken with imagination and in the spirit of fun, can be part of the total joy of being self-sufficient, of being changed, of being content. Give it a try. Start planning a trip now. All you need is a pencil and a pad of paper to start your very first list!

The responsible campers above have built their cooking fires on old fire sites or have established a fire ring in places where fire danger is low, and where nature provides a surplus of dead branches. They have also kept their fires small, and are using rock-supported grates to cook several dishes at one time. When the meal is over, they douse *the fire (left), and then rake through the ashes for unburned materials which they will pack out. When cool enough to handle with bare hands, the ashes are scattered. Then the campers use branches to brush fire area smooth. Last of all, they replace any disturbed ground cover and return the stones to their original locations.*

Trail Snacks

Basic Gorp

1 cup peanuts
1 cup raisins
1 cup M & M candies

Mix together equal amounts of peanuts, raisins, and M & M's. Package the mixture in individual plastic bags to be carried by each camper.

Note: You can substitute or add cashews, walnuts, sunflower seeds (shelled), chopped dates, chopped apricots, or shredded coconut to the basic gorp recipe. In winter you might add mini-marshmallows.

Deluxe Gorp

6-ounce package chocolate chips
6-ounce package butterscotch chips
¼ cup honey
2½ to 3 cups dry ingredients

Melt chocolate chips and butterscotch chips in a double boiler. Add honey. Pour over a mixture of dry ingredients selected from the following: raisins, chopped apricots, chopped dates, cashews, walnuts, peanuts, shredded coconut, instant oatmeal, granola, swiss cereal, wheat germ. Stir well. Press into a greased pan. Cool and break into chunks. This treat packs best in cool weather.

Note: Sticky fruits can be rolled in cereal to make them easier to handle.

Basic Fruit Leather (also called Fruit Taffies or Fruit Rolls)

30-ounce can (or 4 cups) of applesauce

Coat an 11-inch by 16-inch cookie sheet with non-grease spray or stick. Spread applesauce evenly on the sheet so that it is no more than ¼-inch thick. Dry the fruit puree in a slow oven (about 150 degrees F.) with the door open a crack for 6 to 8 hours. When dry, the leather will be translucent, pliable, and barely sticky. Peel the fruit leather from the pan, and roll and slice it into 8 small, individual rolls. Each roll of this pure fruit candy is the equivalent of ½ cup fruit. It makes a good school lunch treat as well as trail snack.

Note: Nuts and spices may be added to the puree for more flavor. The sliced rolls store well in large, air-tight jars.

Cranberry-Applesauce Leather

16-ounce can of cranberry sauce
30-ounce can of applesauce

Blend together cranberry sauce and applesauce. Then dry as for Basic Fruit Leather, but in 2 pans. The two thin leathers will be quite moist and sticky because of high sugar content of the cranberry sauce.

Fresh Fruit Leather

6 pears, 6 peaches, or 18 apricots
3 tablespoons honey

Wash, core (or pit), peel, and slice the fruit. Puree the fruit adding honey to make the leather more pliable when dried. Then heat the puree just to boiling point in a saucepan before drying. Dry as usual.

Note: To give the leather extra body, add ½ cup applesauce to fresh berry purees. Lemon juice may be used to treat the fruit when first cut up, to prevent discoloration.

Tomato Leather

4 cans tomato puree (canned or fresh)
salt, pepper, other seasoning to taste

Dry as for Basic Fruit Leather (heating puree to boiling point first if fresh tomatoes are used). The product will be more brittle than the suede-like fruit leathers. Can be used in vegetable soup or in place of canned tomato sauce in spaghetti dinner or pizza.

Meat Leather

Puree a fully cooked roast in the blender with just enough water or meat juices to form a puree. Pour the puree on a non-grease-sprayed cookie sheet and dry as for fruit leather. Result looks somewhat like insulation board, but makes flavorful addition to a boxed noodle dinner or a vegetable stew.

Beef Jerky

3 pounds lean steak, 1 to 1½ inches thick
¼ cup soy sauce
¾ cup water
2 teaspoons garlic salt
½ teaspoon black pepper

Partially thaw meat. Trim off all fat and slice in thin strips (⅛-inch). Put soy sauce, water, garlic salt, and black pepper together in a bowl. Marinate meat in this mixture for 2 to 3 hours. Drain the meat on paper towels and blot dry. Lay the individual strips on the oven rack so that they are not overlapping. Dry in a slow oven with the door ajar for 6 to 8 hours until the meat is brittle.

Note: Jerky may be made in same way of poultry, wild game, and cured pork, but not of fresh pork. Venison is especially good. Fried hamburger bits and bacon may also be blotted on paper towels and oven-dried on a paper towel-lined cookie sheet, but only for immediate use. (Enough fat remains for them to become rancid.) Make up your own marinade recipe by adding such other ingredients as Worcestershire sauce, chopped onion, red pepper, seasoned salt, ginger root, garlic, cloves, dry wines, or liquid smoke.

Pemmican—Indian Style

jerky
powdered, dried, tart berries
rendered lard

Combine equal parts of jerky, berries, and lard. Roll pemmican into 1-inch by 3-inch rolls or pat into muffin tins or paper cups and wrap in foil to carry on the trail.

Dried Seeds

3 to 4 cups sunflower or pumpkin seeds
½ cup salt

Cover sunflower heads with cheesecloth and hang upside down to dry for a month. (A quicker method is to wash, pat dry, and spread sunflower or pumpkin seeds on a screen covered with cheesecloth. Then place the screen on sawhorses in a warm place. The seeds will dry in about a week.) When dry, add the seeds to 2 quarts of salted water. Bring the water to a boil and cook for 15 minutes. Drain and spread the seeds in a shallow pan and bake at 325 degrees F. for 30 minutes or in a home dryer at 150 degrees F. for 90 minutes. Stir occasionally. Cool. Store in a dry place.

Crunchy Stuff

2 to 3 cups mixed seeds and nuts
2 tablespoons salad oil
½ teaspoon garlic salt

Combine equal amounts of a variety of seeds and chopped nuts (sunflower, pumpkin, sesame, peanuts, cashews, almonds, soybeans) and place in a shallow pan. Mix salad oil and garlic salt (you can also use seasoned salt) and pour over the seeds. Toast in oven for 20 minutes at 350 degrees F. stirring often. Drain on paper towels. When cool, store in a jar.

Granola

3 cups oats or other flaked grains
1 cup each wheat germ, sesame seeds,
  and coconut shreds
1 cup assorted dried fruit, chopped
¼ cup oil
¾ cup honey
1 teaspoon vanilla
1 cup chopped nuts (optional)

Warm oil, honey, and vanilla. Add oats, wheat germ, sesame seeds, and coconut and mix well. Spread mixture on cookie sheets up to ½ inch deep. Bake at 250-degrees F. about 45 minutes or until golden brown. Stir mixture periodically to ensure even baking. Add dried fruits *after* baking. Cool and store in air-tight jars.

Granola Bars

7 cups granola
1 cup dried milk
1 cup whole-wheat flour
1 cup honey
1 cup peanut butter
½ cup fruit-juice concentrate

Combine all ingredients and mix well. If too dry, add liquid fruit juice by spoonfuls until it sticks together. Spread mixture on cookie sheets and pat firm. Dry in a slow oven with the door ajar for 8 hours. Turn over. Dry 4 hours more. Slice into bars. Dry additional 3 to 6 hours.

Apple Granola Crisp

1 cup chopped dried apples
3 cups water
½ cup brown sugar
1 teaspoon lemon juice
½ teaspoon cinnamon
2 cups granola

Prepare dried apples as directed on the package for making applesauce. Add brown sugar, lemon juice, and cinnamon. Sprinkle hot applesauce with granola. Cover and steam until flavors blend, about 20 minutes. Serves 6 to 8.

Peanut Butter Rolls

1 cup peanut butter
¼ cup honey
2 cups dry milk
½ cup peanuts, chopped
½ cup raisins

Mix peanut butter and honey. Add dry milk (not reconstituted) until a stiff taffy is formed. Add chopped peanuts and raisins and knead in with hands. Form into rolls 1 inch wide and 3 inches long, or into hunks like taffies. Chill. This treat is best for winter camping. Makes about 12 rolls.

Note: Chunky peanut butter can be substituted for peanut butter and nuts.

Freakies

¾ cup oil
⅔ cup honey
4 large apples (unpeeled, cored and
  chopped)
2 teaspoons vanilla
3 cups rolled oatmeal
1 cup shelled sunflower seeds
1 cup raisins
1 cup chopped dates

Mix oil, honey, apples, and vanilla together. Add oatmeal, sunflower seeds, raisins, and dates and set aside for an hour. Drop batter by spoonfuls onto a cookie sheet lined with brown paper. Dry in a 150-degree F. oven with the door ajar for 12 to 24 hours until firm. Makes 48 cookies.

Note: Soft ones can be refrigerated. Dried ones pack better for trips.

Fruit Balls or Bars

Grind together a variety of dried fruits, adding some chopped nuts, and bind the ingredients together with honey. Form little balls and roll them in coconut or sesame seeds. For trail use, the fruit balls should be air dried. Chill them if they are to be eaten at home.

Trail Snacks

Try these combinations of dried fruits and nuts or vary them to suit your taste.

Variation #1:

½ cup each of dates, raisins, dried
  bananas, dried apples, almonds, sun-
  flower seeds, and sesame seeds
¼ cup honey
½ tablespoon almond extract
½ cup flaked coconut

Combine ingredients and spread on a cookie sheet covered with plastic wrap. Cover with waxed paper and use rolling pin to flatten the mixture. Remove waxed paper and dry like fruit leather (in a 150-degree

F. oven with door ajar), turning once so that both sides are dried equally. It should be leather-like but pliable enough to cut into bars. Cut into bars and dry some more until no longer sticky to touch.

Variation #2:

3 cups figs, sliced
1 cup walnuts, chopped
½ cup soy or whole wheat flour
½ cup dried milk

Combine ingredients and knead. Roll into balls. Roll in shredded coconut.

Variation #3:

2 cups each of raisins, dates, dried
  apricots, and dried pears
1 cup nuts

Mix ground fruits and nuts and roll into balls. Roll in shredded coconut.

Main Dishes

Pocket Stew

2 pounds hamburger
2 onions, sliced
2 potatoes, sliced
2 carrots, sliced (optional)
1 cup peas (optional)
4 strips bacon
salt and pepper

Place a hamburger patty in center of a 12 by 18-inch square of heavy-duty foil or a double layer of regular foil. Cover with thinly sliced potatoes, sliced onions, carrots, and peas and top with ½ strip of bacon. Season with salt and pepper. Wrap the stew in foil, forming thick handles for turning on both ends of the package. Place directly on coals for 15 to 20 minutes. Slit open and serve. Serves 8.

Note: Easy to serve to large backyard crowd, or can be made at home, frozen after wrapping, and taken on the trail for cooking the first night out.

Hearty Green Pea Soup

6-ounce box of dried hash-browned potato
   mix (potato and onion shreds)
2- to 3-ounce box of mixed dry soup
   vegetables
pinch of herbs
8 cups water
2 3-ounce packs of dried green pea soup
9-ounce can of *Vienna* sausages
1 tablespoon margarine

At home, combine the contents of both
boxes of dried vegetables and the herbs in
a plastic bag. In camp, cook them in the
water about 20 minutes or until tender. Add
the pea soup (very gradually to prevent
lumping), sausages, and margarine. Cook
about 5 minutes or until thick. Serves 6.

Deluxe Macaroni and Cheese

7¼-ounce boxed mix of macaroni and
   cheese
⅓ cup dry milk
6 cups water
2 tablespoons margarine
1 can tuna or *Vienna* sausages

Bring water to boil and add all ingredients.
Cook 10 minutes or until tender. Serves 4.

*Note: May top with grated parmesan cheese
for added flavor.*

Baked Ham and Cheese Buns

1 pound ham
1 pound cheddar cheese
2 onions, chopped
sweet pickles, chopped, or relish (optional)
4 hamburger buns

At home, put ham and cheddar cheese
through a food chopper and add chopped
onions and the pickles or relish. Mix together. Spread mixture on hamburger buns.
Wrap in squares of foil. Keep refrigerated
until you leave for the campground or first
night on trail. Bake 15 to 20 minutes over
hot coals. Serves 4.

*Note: Easy to serve to large backyard crowd
or on overnight Scout campout.*

Trail Rice Italiano

2 tablespoons dried onion flakes
4-ounce pepperoni sausage, sliced
3 cups water
4 ounces instant rice
2 tablespoons dry milk
2 tablespoons margarine

Soak onion flakes in ½ cup water for 5
minutes. Add pepperoni slices and 2½
cups water and simmer together for 10
minutes. Add rest of ingredients. Cover and
let stand for 5 minutes. Serves 4.

Deluxe Campground Pork and Beans

1 pound ground beef
2 tablespoons shortening
1 cup sliced celery
½ cup chopped green pepper
garlic salt
16-ounce can pork and beans
16-ounce can lima beans
6-ounce can tomato paste

Brown ground beef in the shortening. Add
celery, onion, green pepper, and garlic salt
to taste and cook until tender. Drain fat.
Add pork and beans, lima beans, and tomato paste. Simmer 10 minutes. Serves 4.

Charcoal Grilled Pizza

2 cups biscuit mix
½ teaspoon salt
⅔ cup reconstituted milk
1 cup catsup
¼ pound pepperoni, sliced
¼ pound mozzarella cheese, shredded
1 teaspoon oregano

Combine biscuit mix, salt, and milk. Knead
8 to 10 times on a surface floured with
biscuit mix. Divide into 4 equal balls. Pat
each into an 8-inch circle. Place on grill
5 inches from coals. Cook for 8 minutes.
Turn grilled side up and spread with catsup. Add pepperoni, mozzarella cheese,
and oregano. Cook 12 to 15 minutes or
until the sauce bubbles. Serves 4.

Corn-Egg Scrambled Supper

4 strips bacon
1 green pepper, chopped
1 onion, chopped
1 pound can cream-style corn
1 teaspoon salt
pepper
4 eggs, beaten (or dried egg equivalent)

Fry bacon until crisp. Discard all but three
tablespoons of fat. Saute green pepper and
onion in fat until tender. Add rest of ingredients. Cook until thick but moist.
Crumble bacon on top and serve. Serves 4.

HOW TO CLEAN FISH

1. Wash fish. Scrape off scales from tail to
   head (with dull edge of knife).
2. Slit from neck to vent with a sharp knife.
3. Remove entrails and gills.
4. Scrape out kidney tissue with knife or
   thumb.
5. Remove head and tail if desired.
6. Wipe out cavity with clean, damp cloth.

HOW TO STORE FISH

1. Fish should be stored dry and cool.
2. If iced, pack in plastic bag first with all
   air pressed out of bag.

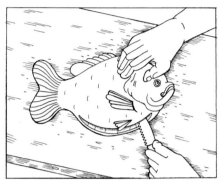

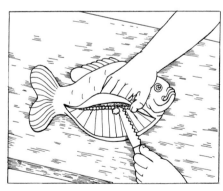
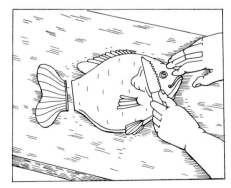

Fish and Game

Crispy Fried Fish

4 servings fish, cleaned
1 cup flour
1 teaspoon salt
¼ teaspoon pepper
4 tablespoons oil or bacon grease
salt and pepper
lemon juice

Roll the fish in a mixture of flour, salt, and pepper. Then add them one at a time to the hot oil or bacon grease. Do not allow the fat to smoke and don't cool it by adding fish all at once. Quickly brown the fish on each side. When done, the meat will be white and flaky. Drain the fish on paper towels. Serve with a sprinkling of salt and pepper and a squeeze of lemon. Serves 4.

Note: You may substitute cornmeal, pancake mix, or biscuit mix for the flour. Try dipping the fish in flour, then in beaten egg (fresh or reconstituted) or in canned milk and then rolling it in fine bread crumbs or cornmeal.

Fish Baked in a Paper Bag

1 fish, cleaned
salt and pepper
lemon juice
1 slice bacon and/or 1 small onion, sliced

Place cleaned fish on a double thickness of waxed paper. Season with salt and pepper and a squeeze of lemon juice and add bacon and/or onion. Wrap the fish in waxed paper and put it in a large, heavy-duty, brown paper bag. Saturate the bag with water and place it directly on the coals of your fire. Watch it closely, turning frequently and sprinkling with water as needed. The fish should be steaming, flaky, and tender in 10 minutes or by the time the bag is scorched and charred enough to concern you about a lost supper. Serves 1.

New England Trail Chowder

2 cups dried hash-browned potatoes
3 cups boiling water
1¼ -ounce package dried potato soup mix
½ teaspoon salt
dash pepper
1 teaspoon dried onion flakes
2 8-ounce cans minced clams

Cook potatoes in boiling water for 10 minutes. Add potato soup mix, pepper, and onion flakes to potatoes. Stir. Add clams and 1 cup of milk. Cook over low flame for 20 minutes. Then add 2 cups of milk and simmer for 20 minutes more. Serves 4.

Wild Stew

(A kitchen or campground recipe)
2 pounds wild game (venison, elk, caribou)
¼ cup bacon fat
6 carrots cut in chunks
1 bay leaf
1 teaspoon salt
½ teaspoon pepper
6 potatoes cut in chunks
6 onions
1 cabbage
¼ cup flour or cornstarch paste
water

Cube meat and brown in bacon fat in a Dutch oven. Add water to cover. Simmer covered for an hour. Add carrots, bay leaf, salt, and pepper. Simmer for 30 minutes. Add potatoes, whole onions, and water as needed. Simmer stew for 30 minutes more. Add cabbage, quartered, and cook until tender. Season with salt and pepper to taste. Thicken pan juices with flour or cornstarch paste. Serves 8.

Deer Speedies

(A backyard recipe)
3- to 4-pound venison roast
1 cup oil
1½ cups vinegar
1 teaspoon pepper
1 tablespoon garlic salt
1 tablespoon oregano

Cut raw venison into 1-inch cubes. Marinate in a sauce of oil, vinegar, salt, pepper, garlic salt, and oregano for 24 to 48 hours in the refrigerator. Put cubes on skewers and cook on a charcoal grill until brown. Serve on slices of Vienna or French bread. Serves 8.

Vegetables

Wild Greens

Edible wild greens
¼ cup vinegar
¼ cup bacon grease
salt and pepper to taste

The young, tender leaves of dandelions, lamb's quarter, pigweed, purslane, sheep-sorrel, nettles, Russian thistle, miner's lettuce, shepherd's purse, and violets can be cooked like spinach or used raw as a salad. Either way, combine the four condiments to make a dressing that complements the tart flavors of the greens. Flavor will also be improved if you change the water several times while cooking the greens.

Note: For creamed greens, cook and drain greens and add 1 cup white sauce.

Country Succotash

1 cup freeze-dried green string beans
(or lima beans)
1 cup freeze-dried corn
4 cups water
½ cup dried onion flakes
2 tablespoons dry coffee creamer
1 tablespoon margarine
salt and pepper

Bring 4 cups of water to a boil. Remove from heat. Add green beans, corn, and onion flakes. Cover and set aside for an hour. Bring vegetables and water to a boil. Cover and simmer about 20 minutes or until tender. Drain, reserving ½ cup of hot liquid. Add dry coffee cream to liquid. Add coffee-cream mixture, margarine, and salt and pepper to vegetables. Serves 6.

Hutspot

(Adapted from an old Dutch dish)
1 package dried potato slices or shreds
½ cup dried carrots
water
4-5 slices diced bacon
salt and pepper
margarine

Combine vegetables and bacon in a saucepan. Add water to cover, salt, and pepper. Cook about 30 minutes or until tender. Drain and mash. Serve with margarine. Serves 4.

Parslied Carrots

3 chicken bouillon cubes
3 cups water
½ cup dried carrots
¼ cup dried onions
1 tablespoon dried parsley
1 tablespoon margarine

Add bouillon cubes to 3 cups of water. Bring to a boil. Remove from heat. Add carrots and onions and cover. Set aside for 1 hour. Bring to a second boil. Cover and simmer about 20 minutes or until tender. Drain, sprinkle with parsley, and add margarine. Serves 6.

Drinks

Hot Chocolate Mix

25-ounce box dry milk
8-ounce jar of non-dairy creamer
¾ cup powdered sugar
1-pound can of instant sweetened choco-
  late mix that requires milk

Sift together dry milk, sugar, and chocolate mix. Add non-dairy creamer. Store dry ingredients in an air-tight container. To reconstitute, add ⅓ cup of mixture per cup of water. Makes 40 to 50 cups.

Note: For a mocha flavor, add ½ teaspoon instant coffee to ⅓ cup of the mixture.

Orange-Spice Tea

1-quart package sweetened orange drink
1-quart package sweetened lemon drink
4-ounce jar instant tea
½ cup sugar
1 tablespoon cinnamon
1 teaspoon ground cloves
1 teaspoon nutmeg

Mix ingredients. Add 1 to 2 tablespoons of mixture to 1 cup of hot water. Increase amount of mix if you prefer a fruitier drink. Stores well for home use, too. Makes 25 to 30 cups.

Trail Milk Shakes

1 cup dry milk
1 small package fruit jello or pre-
  sweetened fruit drink
2 tablespoons malt powder

Shake ingredients in a plastic bottle with 3 cups cold water. Makes 1 quart.

Breads & Desserts

Basic Bannock or Skillet Bread

2 cups flour
¼ cup dry milk
1 tablespoon sugar
½ teaspoon salt
2 teaspoons baking powder
2 tablespoons shortening
1 scant cup water

Put dry ingredients together in a plastic bag before you leave home. At camp, add 1 scant cup of cold water gradually and mix into a stiff dough. You can do your mixing right in the plastic bag or in a pan so the dough can be scraped out more easily. Melt shortening in a skillet until hot. Turn dough into skillet, patting it into a big, oversized biscuit. Brown over the fire. Turn when crusty and firm, and brown the other side. Then (to finish baking the inside) stand the skillet on edge before the coals, using it as a reflector. Turn bread frequently and adjust distance from heat to keep it from getting too brown. Bake until bannock sounds hollow when tapped. Break into pieces and serve with margarine and jam. Serves 4 to 6.

Biscuits

1 basic bannock recipe
2 tablespoons cooking oil or shortening

Roll egg-size chunks of batter into flattened patties. Fry in skillet on both sides. Makes 16 biscuits.

Dumplings

1 basic bannock recipe
1 cooked beef and vegetable stew
2 cups water

Mix up basic bannock recipe. Drop dough by spoonfuls into the boiling meat and vegetable stew to which the extra water has been added. Cover and steam for 10 minutes. Remove lid and cook stew, about 10 minutes or until dumplings are done. Serve at once. Makes 16 dumplings.

Pancakes

1 basic bannock recipe
2 dried eggs (1 pack usually equals 2 eggs)
1 cup water
1 cup fresh berries (if available)

Add dried eggs to basic bannock recipe and add about 1 cup more water—enough to make a thin batter. Add berries. Fry as usual.

Note: To avoid carrying pancake syrup, make 1 cup by adding ½ cup white sugar and ½ cup brown sugar (packed in one bag) to ½ cup water. Boil until it thickens to desired consistency.

One-Pot Cobbler

1 cup water
1 cup sugar
1 package diced dry apples
1 teaspoon cinnamon (optional)
½ basic bannock recipe

Combine water and sugar in a saucepan and bring to a boil. Add apples and cinnamon and set the mixture aside for 30 minutes until the apples are plump. Reheat, adding extra water if needed, and drop bannock dough by spoonfuls on the top. Cover and steam for 10 minutes. Turn dumplings and cook 10 minutes more. Serves 6 to 8.

Note: Fresh berries or other dried fruit such as apricots also make good cobblers. Another option is to substitute ½ package of gingerbread mix for the bannock mix, adding just enough water to make a stiff dough.

Drop Doughnut Balls

1 basic bannock recipe
½ cup sugar
1 teaspoon cinnamon
½ cup shortening

Drop batter by spoonfuls into hot grease in skillet. Brown on both sides. Roll in cinnamon-sugar. Makes 16 to 20 balls.

Fruit Fritters

1 basic bannock recipe
½ cup dried fruit, chopped
  (apples, dates, raisins, or apricots)
2 tablespoons shortening

Make basic bannock. Add dried fruit. Drop by spoonfuls into hot grease in skillet. Brown on both sides. Makes 16 to 20 fritters.

Cookies

1 basic bannock recipe
1 tablespoon dried egg powder (or 1 egg)
½ cup leftover gorp or a combination of
  nuts and raisins
1 teaspoon cinnamon (optional)

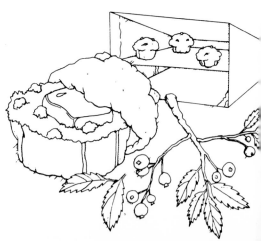

Make basic bannock dough, adding egg and cinnamon. Add left-over gorp or a combination of nuts and raisins. Drop by spoonfuls into hot greased skillet. Brown on both sides. Makes 24 cookies.

Corn Bread

1 cup corn meal
1 cup flour
¼ cup dry milk
1 tablespoon sugar
½ teaspoon salt
2 teaspoons baking powder
1 tablespoon bacon grease
2 tablespoons shortening or bacon grease
1 cup water

Combine dry ingredients in a plastic bag before you leave home. At camp, add cold water and bacon grease. Melt shortening in a skillet and bake like basic bannock. Serves 6.

Fried Pies

1 pastry stick
½ cup jam
2 tablespoons shortening

Mix up pastry stick as directed on package. Roll out egg-sized chunks into 8 flat patties. Place 1 tablespoon of jam in the center of each pattie. Fold pastry over and press edges together. Fry in lightly greased skillet on both sides. Serves 8.

Doughnut Sandwiches

4 cinnamon doughnuts
4 pineapple slices
butter

Slice doughnut in half horizontally. Butter halves and place a pineapple slice between them. Wrap in a square of foil and heat over coals or near the edge of a fire. Watch closely; the sandwiches scorch easily. Serves 4.

Fruit Compote

1 cup dried pears
1 cup dried apricots
¾ cup sugar
2 tablespoons lemon juice
   (from plastic lemon)
2 cinnamon sticks
10 whole cloves
5 cups water
1 cup pitted dried prunes

Add pears, apricots, sugar, lemon juice, cinnamon sticks, and cloves to water. Bring to a boil. Reduce heat, cover, and simmer about 15 minutes or until almost tender. Add dried prunes. Cook 5 minutes. Remove from heat and cool. Serves 6.

Gelatin

3-ounce box fruit gelatin
½ cup dried fruit, reconstituted
1¾ cups water

Prepare gelatin by dissolving the mix in 1 cup of hot water, followed by ¾ cup of cold water. Add bits of reconstituted dry fruit. Put in a snow bank to jell. Serves 4.

Note: A package of dry whipped-cream dessert topping made with reconstituted dry milk is a delicious addition to the fruit gelatin. For salad, use lemon or lime gelatin. Add ½ cup reconstituted dry vegetable flakes or freeze-dried cottage cheese and reconstituted milk beaten to whipped-cream consistency.

Snow Cream

2 dried eggs (2 tablespoons, reconstituted
   in milk)
¾ cup sugar
1 cup reconstituted dry milk
1½ tablespoons vanilla
pinch salt
snow

Beat eggs, sugar, milk, vanilla, and salt together in a large pot. Add fresh snow stirring until thick and creamy. Serves 4.

Note: For a quick version of snow cream, mix a 3-ounce box of instant pudding, 1 cup reconstituted dry milk, and snow to thicken.

Marshmallow Treats
(Non-Campfire)

8-ounce package chocolate chips
small package marshmallows
ground nuts, Rice Crispies, or shredded
   coconut
large cocktail toothpicks

Melt chocolate chips in a pan and add 1 to 2 tablespoons warm water to thin them to a syrupy consistency. Spear marshmallows on toothpicks. Dip in chocolate, then in ground nuts, Rice Crispies, or shredded coconut. For variety, substitute butterscotch chips for the chocolate chips.

Fudge

1 cup sugar
3 tablespoons cocoa
3 tablespoons dry milk
1 tablespoon butter
⅓ cup water

Combine dry ingredients in a plastic bag before leaving home. At camp, stir ⅓ cup of water into mixture. Cook over low heat until syrup boils and forms a soft ball. Remove from heat. Add butter. Stir when cool and pour into a greased bowl or skillet. Add nuts if desired. Cut into pieces.

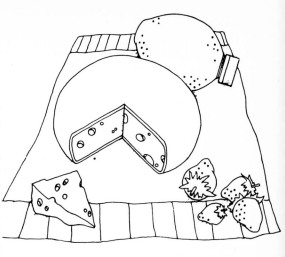

Sauces and Miscellaneous

White Sauce Mix

3 cups dry milk
1 cup sifted flour
1 cup margarine
1 tablespoon salt

Blend milk, flour, margarine, and salt with a pastry blender until it is the consistency of cornmeal. At camp, add 1 cup water per ½ cup mix, stir, and cook until thick.

Note: The mix will keep up to one month in a jar or in individual plastic bags. To store longer than a month, keep the mix in the refrigerator or on a cool, dry shelf.

Trail Jam

1 cup tart berries
⅔ cup sugar
1 tablespoon lemon juice
1 stick cinnamon (optional)

Combine all ingredients in a saucepan. Bring the mixture to a boil, stirring constantly until thick. Remove cinnamon. Serve with bannock, biscuits, or pancakes. Makes about 1 cup.

Trail Jelly

If a batch of fruit leather gets too brittle, turn it into a powder in your blender. On the trail add a *drop* of water to a spoonful of the powder for a quick fruit jelly.

Dried Cheese

Grate cheddar cheese coarsely. Spread on paper towels on a cookie sheet. Dry in a 150-degree F. oven with the door ajar until dry and crunchy—about 5 hours. The fat will melt out of the cheese so change the towels frequently. Store crisp cheese shreds in the refrigerator until ready to leave on your trip. Add to bannock or casserole-type dishes.

In search of winter wildlife

Kent Dannen

Despite occasional spills, the author (opposite) and his wife, Donna (above), were pleasantly surprised at how quickly they acquired their ski touring skills. As wildlife photographers, the Dannens now use cross-country skis to explore formerly inaccessible winter forests. They find the woods alive with creatures who leave tantalizing clues to their whereabouts and adventures in the snow. Cross-country skiing has also added a new dimension to the Dannens' personal lives. They think of it as serendipity, the gift of finding valuable or agreeable things not sought for. "We never know," says Kent, "what joys our skis will take us to."

Even falls are fun when my wife, Donna, and I are off on one of our ski touring adventures. That is just one example of how our outlook on life in winter has changed since we took up cross-country skiing. As we slip into the easy kick-glide-kick-glide rhythm of our newfound sport, something like a magic spell comes over us. Just as a blanket of snow simplifies the outlines of trees and shrubs, skiing seems to simplify the complex outlines of our modern lives, bringing us into spiritual harmony with nature during its time of rest. We live in the Rockies, and their forested slopes give us unforgettable moments of gliding down long, white aisles formed by snow-laden spruce and fir opening on vistas of extreme beauty and peace beyond thought.

Yet we find we are not alone. When we leave behind the plowed roads and shoveled walks around our home in Estes Park, Colorado, we enter winter wildlife country. There wilderness creatures write the adventures of their lives with tracks in the snow. As wildlife photographers, our instincts are to follow each one. Tracking animals often leads to surprise endings, but there are times when the trail grows very long.

My first surprise from cross-country skiing was learning how simple it is to get started. Despite the seemingly bewildering array of equipment for this mushrooming sport, we found it fairly easy to choose once we got it all sorted out into four basic types. I chose the heaviest kind, mountaineering skis. They are broad with metal edges to bite hard snow, and cable bindings to stabilize my heels while traveling the difficult terrain over which photography often takes me. My boots resemble hiking boots, cut high with lugged soles, double-layered for warmth during those cold hours of standing in snow, waiting for a picture opportunity.

Donna prefers general touring skis. They are lighter than mine, but heavier and wider than the light touring skis favored by most cross-country skiers who go out for recreation only. Her boots are nearly as heavy as mine, but are fastened to the skis only by light toe bindings. We haven't tried racing skis, which are lighter still, even delicate, and are designed only for use on prepared tracks.

But regardless of what equipment you choose, anyone who can walk can ski tour. In fact, Donna and I had had only one day's instruction and one day of practicing on our own when an opportunity arose to visit Yellowstone Park in winter for the first time. Undoubtedly we were overreaching in assuming that we were ready to ski and concentrate on wildlife photography at the same time, but the chance to see the herds of bison, deer, elk, and other wildlife that winter in the Park's geyser-warmed valleys was too much to resist.

On our first morning there it was 15 degrees below zero as we slipped on our skis at Snow Lodge near Old Faithful and set off on Upper Geyser Basin Trail. As we hurried along, hoping to catch the big game animals at breakfast, we felt that Yellowstone's flat plateau country must be one of the nation's best areas for ski touring. Thickly falling snow was adding to the four to six feet on the ground. The dramatic contrast between boiling hot geysers and icy cold air creates an awesome and steamy landscape.

In most places that February morning the dry and fluffy snow made skiing effortless even for novices like us. But frequently we skied over snow that had been partially melted by the boiling mudpots and hot springs below. The wet snow over these hot spots stuck in thick layers to the skis, slowing us to a dead stop until we had scraped it off. However, our slow progress was our protection. It made us less likely to slide accidentally onto hidden pockets that could collapse under our weight and dump us into scalding water.

I had blundered onto the sticky snow of yet another thermal area and was trying vainly to shake my skis clean when across a stream flowing from a hot spring I saw two bison bulls. A line in a Park Service brochure came to mind: ''Bison have a very uncertain disposition and should never be approached closely.''

I was not about to approach closer with several pounds of snow clinging to each ski. Nonetheless, I saw an opportunity to make some fine photos of bison during a lull in the storm. Donna, down the hill searching for a trail we had lost, was in no conceivable danger. The bison seemed unlikely to cross the stream, and I had a telephoto lens to shrink the distance between us. By supporting the camera on my ski poles, I could shoot at a low speed to compensate for poor light caused by storm and steam. And the bison bulls stood out as strong dark shapes in their snowy setting.

Then, not seeming to notice the stream, the bulls crossed it, moving slowly toward me! Like one-ton plows, they forged through the snow. Their huge heads swung back and forth, sweeping masses of snow away from the grass underneath.

Intent on survival, Yellowstone bison ignore Park visitors. In winter the animals must find grass to supplement the fat they've stored from summer's plenteous grazing. Now small herds congregate along the Firehole River (bottom) where geyser-heated soil shrinks deep snows to a mere six-inch blanket over rich, well-watered grass. The midday siesta (below) also takes precedence over chasing curious skiers; the time is needed to rechew the hastily cropped grass before it can become hide, hair and muscle. Park managers do not pamper the scattered herds with hay. When the spring thaw comes, carcasses of the losers may relay the gift of life to eagle, hawk, raven, wolf, coyote, cougar, or hibernation-weakened grizzly.

"Just coincidence," I told myself. "Even if they know I'm here, they don't care. How could anything that big care about me?" But the thought of my smallness and their bigness, together with vaguely remembered stories of gorings and tramplings, prompted me to see if I could back up on my skis.

Reverse gear was not working; in fact, the wet snow plastered to the bottom of my skis limited movement in any direction. Even if I could have glided away, I was too nervous to turn my back on those bulls, though continuing to face them would do no good if they decided to charge. Since I could not bring myself to move, I switched to a shorter telephoto lens and continued taking pictures.

The bison kept coming. Just my luck to be standing above the finest grass in Yellowstone. Why were these bulls here anyway? They seemed remote from any herd. Had they been kicked out? Were they cantankerous? They grazed closer, and I put on my 50-millimeter lens. Their shaggy beards were coated with ice, formed as warm breath met cold air.

Suddenly, Donna came up behind me, shouting "Don't go so near those bulls! They're dangerous!"

I did not attempt to explain who was approaching whom. But I could see that neither bull had paid any attention to Donna's shouting. Perhaps they were oblivious of me, too. A kick turn would set me in a retreat direction. Slowly, I picked up my left snow-and-ski-laden foot and turned it part way to my rear. The same awkward move placed the right ski parallel to the left. I shuffled away like a chain gang escapee.

After a few yards, I risked a backward glance. No bison with flared nostrils and lowered horns was charging my rear. Both bulls continued their patient, methodical head-swinging to uncover buried grass. Donna and I were beneath their notice.

Back on cold, dry snow, Donna scraped my skis clean and we glided effortlessly back to the trail she had found. Snow was still falling, though less heavily now, adding to the exhilaration of smooth, swift skiing on a gentle, downhill stretch. We passed a whole herd of snow-blanketed bison grazing along the Firehole River. Grotto Geyser erupted nearby with a sudden whoosh and roar of boiling water, creating a dazzling white plume in the icy air. Riverside Geyser gave a similar exhibition over the Firehole, obliterating our view of the river.

After a hot lunch at the Lodge, we noticed that snowshoes could be rented there. We had seen several people using them on the trails, and Donna suggested that we should try them ourselves to see which mode of winter travel we preferred. So we left our skis at the Lodge and rented snowshoes for a trial run. Our goal was Observation Point above Old Faithful where we hoped to get a wider view of the concentrations of big game animals.

Snowshoeing turned out to be simple indeed, but very hard work. Even with my down jacket flapping open in the sub-zero temperatures, I was uncomfortably hot even before we started climbing the hill. As the slope steepened, we discovered that switchbacking across the hill to reduce its grade was not as effective a technique on snowshoes as on skis. Snowshoes lack the edges which allow skis to bite into snow. Consequently, we kept sliding downhill. Turning or changing direction was especially difficult, even though we had brought along ski poles, standard snowshoeing accessories in hilly terrain. I found myself clinging desperately to trees in order to keep from slipping.

Crampons (sets of spikes designed to clamp onto the bottoms of snowshoes) would have solved our sliding problem, but these handy devices were not available for rent. Anyway, I would have been reluctant to add even their few ounces to feet which already seemed over-burdened.

We shuffled back to Snow Lodge and thankfully set out again on skis. As we passed over a small stone bridge that crossed the Firehole just above Riverside Geyser, two bull elk strolled out of the clearing vapor. They were using the warm river as a highway, avoiding the killing labor of fighting deep snows. The elk focused all their attention on foraging for food beneath the relatively shallow snow at the river's edge. Unlike bison, they use a front foot to dig through the snow.

On their Yellowstone visit, the Dannens tried snowshoeing for the first time, and found ski touring more to their liking. Donna (above) rests from her tiring first efforts. Her rented Michigan-style snowshoes are made of white ash with rawhide webbing. The "slippery noodle" leather binding holds the snowshoe securely to her boot, yet allows flexibility. A favorite trail for both snowshoers and skiers loops around Castle Geyser (opposite), named for its rampart-like shape. It is one of a cluster of 200 or more geysers that make Yellowstone the world's leading area of geyser activity and therefore one of its most spectacular winter wildlife havens.

Since the elk seemed oblivious of our presence, I pulled out my camera and Donna the drawing pad and pencils she always carries. For nearly an hour we made the most of this rare opportunity to capture the beauty of these animals, photographing and sketching to our hearts' content. Donna even became bold enough to shed her skis in order to crouch comfortably and concentrate on her work. One of her sketches became a watercolor which she later sold.

Excited and encouraged by the success of our Yellowstone efforts at both skiing and photographing wildlife in winter habitat, we decided on the way home that our next project would be to photograph the white-tailed ptarmigan in its winter plumage. The ptarmigan is a tough little grouse that lives its entire life above timberline on the mountains near our Colorado home. In summer the brown-and-gray feathered bird is easy to photograph once you catch on to its habit of sitting still in order to look like a rock. In winter, ptarmigan grow white feathers, perfect camouflage in the snow. They also have their own snowshoes—oversize feet with feathers covering each toe.

Reaching ptarmigan habitat is not easy once snow has closed most of the roads above treeline, and locating the birds is even harder. But the odds are challenging. Since ptarmigan gather together from their scattered summer territories, finding one means finding a flock. On the other hand, that leaves many square miles of alpine tundra as empty of ptarmigan as of trees. It's an all-or-nothing gamble, for in addition to being almost totally white, ptarmigan often roost *under* the snow to get out of the wind and stay warm. They may stay there up to 12 hours, eating snow for water. There is literally no sign of their presence unless a skier passes within inches and flushes them from under their cover.

Donna and I did not know all this when we set out to get our winter photos. It would be simple, we thought, to snap on our skis, climb above timberline, and take the pictures. To make it even simpler, we joined ptarmigan expert Dr. Clait Braun on a Christmas bird count to look for and count the white grouse in Rocky Mountain National Park. The climb was tiring, and the weather was awful. One-hundred-mile-per-hour winds whipped the snow, creating whiteouts that forced us to stop because we couldn't see the terrain. However, Donna and I accept bad weather as a vocational hazard and are prepared for it. In spite of it, Clait showed us the birds. Unfortunately, the wind and whiteouts made every living thing jumpy—ptarmigan, birdwatchers, even the tortured, twisted timberline trees. It was impossible to get the quality photos we wanted, photos in which every vein of each feather covering every ptarmigan toe could be counted. We would have to try again.

With magnificently antlered elk parading and posing before them for a full 45 minutes, the Dannens reap the benefits of 90 years of protection which have made some Yellowstone elk unafraid of man. Elk can use the Firehole River (opposite) as a snow-free route to grass, twigs, and other food along its banks because its water is warmed by the boiling eruptions of Riverside Geyser and other thermal features. A regal bull chewing his cud in the midday sun enables Donna to fill her drawing pad with sketches for watercolors she will complete in her studio at home. For such chance encounters, she carries pencils, eraser, and drawing pad in her belt pack. Her obliging model is one of about 16,000 elk driven by deepening snows from vast summer ranges to limited wintering areas at lower elevations. Most of the herds migrate outside the Park, but nearly 1,000 elk crowd into its valleys. Like the bison, they are not given supplemental feed; thus winter becomes a natural winnowing process belying the beauty of the snow-draped setting in which only the hardiest survive.

To get these photographs of white-tailed ptarmigan in winter plumage, the author (opposite) skied over 120 miles and his wife skied over 160 in the Colorado Rockies, in a winter-long search of the alpine tundra for the hard-to-see birds. In April the Dannens accidentally flushed these small grouse from their roost holes (shown in the snow behind each bird) above Guanella Pass near Squaretop Mountain, just before they began to molt. In winter ptarmigan flock together and feed on dwarf willows, but scatter across the tundra to nest in June. Their winter habitat is declining in Colorado due to reservoir construction, roads, grazing, and snowmobiles.

Try we did, again, and again, and again. Without Clait to help, Donna and I found no ptarmigan. We climbed time after time, in good weather and foul. We skied slopes we wouldn't have dared try for fun and found them not so tough after all. We found droppings. We found tracks. We found feathers. We found roost holes. But we found not one single ptarmigan.

By Palm Sunday snow was melting away from the lower slopes around Estes Park. Soon, if not already, ptarmigan would molt their white feathers. I was frustrated. I was mad. I was obsessed with photographing white ptarmigan. That morning Donna and I saw a black-and-white warbler, an unusual sighting in Colorado. "When you start seeing rare warblers," I growled (my only tone of voice by then), "winter's over. It's time to give up on white ptarmigan." So I did and felt better for having voiced my defeat.

Skiing only to get pictures had robbed me of the peace that had attracted me to the sport in the first place. It was time to retrieve that peace. Donna and I arranged to meet friends at Guanella Pass for a tour that Palm Sunday afternoon. Even at the high altitude of the Pass, over 11,000 feet, snow was melting fast. We inserted our skis into carrying slots on our packs and started walking up a ridge that still held snow near the top.

Cackle, cackle, cluck! There they were: pure white ptarmigan scurrying from under our very boots! The sun was shining brightly and our cameras were freshly loaded. Donna and I snapped ptarmigan from every possible angle as five birds popped out of the snow and began to peck hungrily at swelling willow buds. They seemed unafraid, as if confident that their superb camouflage made them invisible. On some of the birds we even spotted the bands Clait Braun had attached to study flocking behavior. It was like meeting old friends.

Had I known that all I needed to do to find ptarmigan was quit looking, I would have done it in January. Now I could really devote what remained of the season to enjoying cross-country skiing for its own sake rather than demanding specific rewards for my efforts. For our next tour we invited our friends Lance and Carol Bischoff to ski with us over Shrine Pass.

The snowbound Pass road was a perfect day trip—two miles up from Vail Pass and ten down to Redcliffe amid some of Colorado's most spectacular scenery. By the time we reached the top of the Pass, I was enjoying again everything about cross-country skiing. As we paused for lunch, storm clouds parted and sunshine poured over us like a warm benediction. It seemed very appropriate.

Even more than the others, I relished the lunch that Donna had prepared. For overnight winter trips we carry a small stove to cook a hot meal, but today she brought only a thermos of hot tea to drink with the fresh fruit and mountain bars she had made. The bars are delectable quick-energy treats made of raisins, coconut, walnuts, wheat germ and oatmeal held together with honey and melted butter-

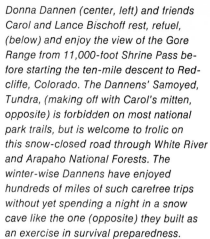

Donna Dannen (center, left) and friends
Carol and Lance Bischoff rest, refuel,
(below) and enjoy the view of the Gore
Range from 11,000-foot Shrine Pass before starting the ten-mile descent to Redcliffe, Colorado. The Dannens' Samoyed,
Tundra, (making off with Carol's mitten,
opposite) is forbidden on most national
park trails, but is welcome to frolic on
this snow-closed road through White River
and Arapaho National Forests. The
winter-wise Dannens have enjoyed
hundreds of miles of such carefree trips
without yet spending a night in a snow
cave like the one (opposite) they built as
an exercise in survival preparedness.

scotch chips. I thought back to my bachelor days when my eating on the trail would have sent a nutritionist into shock. Soon after we were married, Donna had put her booted foot down on such grim fare: "I don't *care* what John Muir ate. We can't live on scenery!"

After lunch, the others raced away from me with ease on skis made to run faster over easy downhill terrain. Only our dog, Tundra, breaking through the snow's surface with each step, stayed behind to keep me company. But Tundra and I caught up whenever the others stopped to listen to red squirrels scolding them from the spruces, make friends with mountain chickadees, interpret wildlife tracks, or examine unusual snow-draped branches. Endless items of interest appear to cross-country skiers.

Not even Colorado's unpredictable spring weather could dampen my spirit that day. The sun disappeared, the gray clouds turned black. Thunder echoed among the peaks. The temperature dropped and a fine, dry snow began to fall. The fresh powder covered the old compacted snow, testing our knowledge of the fine art of ski waxing.

The soft wax we had rubbed on the bottoms of our skis to climb up to Shrine Pass would not work well on the new, drier snow. Donna and the Bischoffs removed the soft wax from their skis with a wax scraper and substituted hard wax appropriate for the colder conditions. (Soft can be applied on top of hard wax without the bother of scraping, but hard will not cover soft.) Since the remaining miles were all downhill and the climbing benefits of wax would not be needed, I substituted ordinary paraffin, hoping it would give my skis a little more speed. It was a lucky guess, and I was the first one to reach the bottom. Poor Tundra finished last.

Near the end of the road, motorists were trying to drive up to cabins and homes above the town of Redcliffe. Snow was still falling heavily in the gathering dusk, and one steep place was especially troublesome. Cars were sliding all over the road. A few were stuck. The hopeless whine of spinning tires and the acrid smell of burning rubber filled the evening air. Relying on machines, these folks were getting nowhere fast.

We felt sorry for the stalled drivers, for it was just one more frustration in the series of stresses that plague us all in our machine-bound, technological society. As we skied toward our own car, parked in Redcliffe, it occurred to me that Donna and I had found in ski touring a way to leave our frustrations behind us for a time, buried, so to speak, under beautiful white snow.

We were going back to the problems, of course. They always wait for us as surely as last fall's unraked leaves emerge from spring's melting snow. But, refreshed by the serendipity of ski touring—its unexpected pleasures—we face the problems of modern living with fresh optimism. In other words, cross-country skiing keeps us from spinning our wheels in more ways than one.

LET MAP AND COMPASS LEAD THE WAY

Steve Netherby

It was early December in the Colorado Rockies and snow lay over the earth like a goose-down comforter. Our exhaled breath seemed to crackle in the minus-15-degree air as we slid our skis upward toward the Continental Divide.

Our packs were light. Tom, Harry, and I had left our tents and most of our supplies 2,000 feet below and miles behind us. Our food would last for two days, and my survival kit would provide emergency shelter and fire if we failed to find the cabin. It was an ancient log cabin, built by a miner or a trapper. A backpacking friend had told us about it, and we had found the tiny square symbol for it on our map. Finding it in the mountains might be something else again.

Heavy snows had long since buried the trail. Our compasses and our ability to read the land's bold features from the squirming contour lines of our map were our only guides. In late afternoon we ran out of water, and the need to travel to reach the cabin before dark kept us from stopping to melt snow for more. Dehydrated and tiring fast, we reached the top of what should have been the last ridge. Daylight was failing. Leaning against my ski poles, I glanced up to see black clouds crowding through a notch in the Divide.

"It should be down there," Tom said, "but I sure don't see it."

We S-turned down the slope. My mind had just begun planning a snow shelter when the dark timbers of the front wall came into view. We hadn't seen the cabin from above because the roof and three walls had been swallowed by a massive snowdrift. Now, if the thin blue line on the map was right, a stream should lie 100 feet beyond the cabin. I gathered canteens while Tom and Harry looked the cabin over. As my skis entered the woods, I began to hear the rush of water running free.

The storm clouds we had seen breaching the Divide moved in that night, loosing snarling winds and swirling snow. But we had shelter and water because our maps and compasses were good guides—and old, trusted friends.

Make your compass a fast friend. Learn to read the lines and colors of topographic maps as well as you read the expression on your best friend's face. You'll be rewarded with freedom of the wilderness, freedom to leave overused trails behind and head into the wild country. You'll find your cross-country skiing or photography, your backpacking or fishing, your hunting or canoeing, your birding or your day-hiking experiences enriched and enlarged. Each peak and creek and mountain valley will mean more to you as you learn to read its name from a map. You'll be able to navigate to trout lakes where only game trails lead and to wooded gullies where deer are likely to be found at midday. You'll be able to choose the easiest route around a hill or swamp, or to pick a campsite with shelter, scenery, and running water before you've even left home. And a map marked with your campsites, the meadow where you spotted a moose, and the snowshoe climb you named "Misery Mile" is a wonderful record of a trip.

There's also the obvious: if you can locate yourself with a map and compass, you can't be lost. In an emergency you can find your way to water or to the nearest road for help.

If you practice each step as it is presented, you should come away from this chapter knowing how to use a map and compass. Let's start with the map, a topographic map made by the United States Geological Survey. Check your telephone book's yellow pages under "Maps" for your nearest

A hiker enjoys the freedom of the wilds as he matches topographical map to terrain and plots a shortcut to his campsite and the meal stowed in his homemade pack.

TOPOGRAPHIC MAP SYMBOLS

Primary highway, hard surface . . . .

Light-duty road, hard or improved surface . . . .

Unimproved road . . . .

Trail . . . .

Buildings (dwelling, place of employment, etc.) . . . .

Index contour . . . .

Intermediate contour . . . .

Perennial streams . . . .

Intermittent streams . . . .

Marsh (swamp) . . . .

Wooded marsh . . . .

Woods or brushwood . . . .

Spot elevation . . . . x 7369

Water elevation 670

Topographic maps like the facsimile of one on page 85 diagram the lay of the land, showing its shape and elevations, its waterways and its man-made features. The illustration above shows a bird's-eye view of a stream flowing through a valley and into the ocean and how the same terrain is depicted on a topographic map. Notice that the brown contour lines are close together on the steep sides of the hills. Where the brown color is concentrated and the lines seem pinched together, there are cliffs. At the bottom of the valley, where the hills slope gently, the lines are farther apart. Walking usually is easier where the lines are less crowded. Memorize the map symbols above before hiking cross country.

Learn the lay of the land

dealer, or write directly to one of the map sources that are listed in the Appendix. Request a map in a scale of either 1:24,000 or 1:62,500 covering the wilderness area that you want to explore on your next trip.

A topographic map (opposite) is more complicated than a highway map because it pictures the *topography*— the shape and elevation of the land, its waterways, its man-made landmarks. That is what makes the map useful to the outdoorsman.

Look first at the white border around the map. In the top right corner is the map's identity—in our example, "Lake Luzerne Quadrangle"—after one of the landmarks in it. The name of the state containing the mapped area is also given there.

A *quadrangle* map is bounded on the sides by lines of longitude (running north to south; thus, the top of the map points to true north) and on the top and bottom by lines of latitude (parallel to the equator), measured in degrees, minutes, and perhaps seconds.

Those names in parentheses angling out of each corner are the names of adjoining quadrangle maps. The same is true of the names shown flush with the border at the midpoints of the four sides. So if your trail exits your map on the right side, you'll find it continued on the quadrangle named in parentheses at your map's right-hand border.

In the bottom right corner is printed the year the map was last updated. If the last changes were made 20 years ago, be skeptical about the map's less permanent features. Woodlots may have burned down to meadows since then, towns may have bloomed.

Above the mileage scales at the bottom center of the map, you'll find the scale of the map—most likely 1:62,500 or 1:24,000. The scale indicates that 1 inch, 1 centimeter, etc., on the map equals 62,500 or 24,000 of the same unit on the land. The 1:24,000-scale map shows terrain features in more detail and makes navigation easier. The 1:62,500 scale is quite usable, though,

and is often the only map size available (because of the U.S. Geological Survey's timetable in preparing and revising maps).

The ruler-like distance scales allow you to measure miles, feet, or kilometers. Lay a string along your route and then straighten it along the scale to read mileage or, better yet, cut a match or twig to a 1-mile length as represented on the scale and see how many lengths of it are needed to cover your route. Use shorter twigs for more accuracy in measuring winding trails.

Below the distance scales is the "contour interval," the number of feet of altitude between the map's brown contour lines. These lines (which look like the whorls of a fingerprint) give the topographic map its special character. They outline all but the flattest areas of a map and enable you to visualize how hilly and steep the land is.

All points on each contour line are at the same elevation above sea level. Each point along a contour labeled 1000, for instance, is 1000 feet above sea level. If the contour interval is 20 feet, each point along the next line closer to the mountain summit is 1020 feet above sea level. If the oceans were to flood to the 1020-foot level, the shoreline would follow this contour line exactly. Every fourth or fifth line, called an index contour, is darkened for easier reading and counting.

Look at any stream on your map. Where streams intersect contour lines, notice how the contour lines form V's (or U's if the stream banks are less steep). *The V's always point uphill, or upstream.* Valleys and gullies without streams also conform to this rule. A ridge is also indicated by contour lines forming a row of V's or U's, depending on the sharpness of the ridge. But *ridgeline V's and U's always point downhill.* Remember the difference.

If you're canoeing along a river and notice that the map shows contour lines crossing the river ahead of you, be alert. There's likely to be a rapid— or a waterfall—worth portaging around.

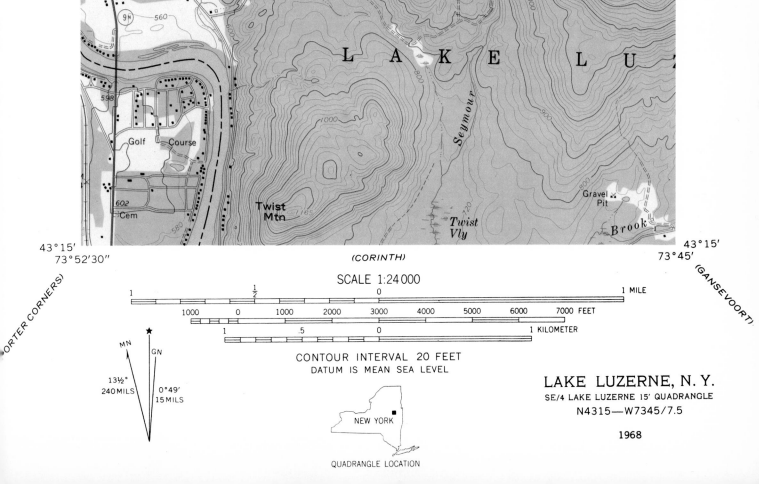

UNITED STATES
DEPARTMENT OF THE INTERIOR
GEOLOGICAL SURVEY

LAKE LUZERNE QUADRANGLE
NEW YORK
7.5 MINUTE SERIES (TOPOGRAPHIC)

(6270 IV NW
(TONY CREEK)

73°52′30″
43°22′30″

(WARRENSBURG)

73°45′
43°22′30″

(LAKE GEORGE)

Rockwell
Hill

Cemetery

S T A T E

Bullhead Pond
Mtn

Oak
Ridge

Bullhead
Pond

Lake
Luzerne

Cobble
Mtn

Constitution
Mtn

624

TOUR

ROAD

(CONKLINGVILLE)

Lake Luzerne

Brook

JEEP

TRAIL

Bartlett
Mtn 1535

Luzerne
Reservoir

(GLENS FALLS)

9 N

560

598

L A K E   L U

Golf   Course

Gravel
Pit

602
Cem

Twist
Mtn 1165

Seymour

Twist
Vly

Brook

580

43°15′
73°52′30″

(CORINTH)

43°15′
73°45′

(GANSEVOORT)

(PORTER CORNERS)

★
MN
GN

13½°
240 MILS

0°49′
15 MILS

SCALE 1:24 000

1   ½   0   1 MILE

1000   0   1000   2000   3000   4000   5000   6000   7000 FEET

1   .5   0   1 KILOMETER

CONTOUR INTERVAL 20 FEET
DATUM IS MEAN SEA LEVEL

LAKE LUZERNE, N. Y.
SE/4 LAKE LUZERNE 15′ QUADRANGLE
N4315—W7345/7.5

1968

NEW YORK

QUADRANGLE LOCATION

Now let's look at compasses. I am strongly prejudiced about them. In my opinion, wilderness trekkers should carry an orienteering type—either the Silva or the Suunto brand. Both are simple and quick to use and team up with a map better than any other compass system. For clarity, I'll be speaking the language of the Silva system here.

Let's begin by looking at your compass dial. North, east, south, and west are represented as N, E, S, and W. These cardinal points help interpret the language of *degrees.* Around the circular dial of your compass there are 360 degrees. Most compass dials are marked each 2 degrees, with a longer mark at each 10-degree interval. Beginning at N and reading clockwise, numerals indicate each 20 degrees, i.e., 20, 40, 60, etc. Note that north= both 0 and 360 degrees; east = 90 degrees; south=180 degrees; west=270 degrees. Since there's a 90-degree difference between these major points, you can see that to find, say, southeast —the midway point between 90 degrees (E) and 180 degrees (S)—you'd add 45 degrees to 90 and come up with a reading of 135 degrees.

If you could stand in the center of a huge compass dial and look out over the "W" on the dial's rim, you'd be looking along a *bearing* of 270 degrees from you. A bearing, then, is a line of direction from one point to another measured in compass degrees.

Two typical situations in direction finding are given on the next page. The compass work involved in them is surprisingly simple. There are just two steps: holding the compass level and waist high about a foot in front of you, with the direction-of-travel arrow pointing straight ahead, you *point* and *dial.* The same two steps are used in each operation; only the order changes. How these two operations are used in situations 1 and 2 is explained in the illustration on page 87. Before we can move on to situations that require us to use our compass with a map, we have to discuss *declination.*

The red "north-pointing" needle on your compass points north, but not necessarily to the North Pole. We

Get your bearings

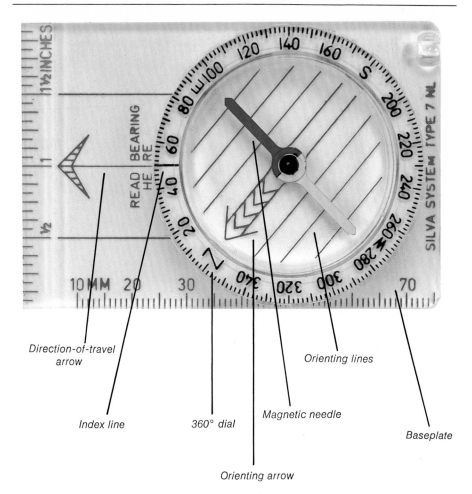

Direction-of-travel arrow

READ BEARING HERE

Index line

360° dial

Orienting arrow

Magnetic needle

Orienting lines

Baseplate

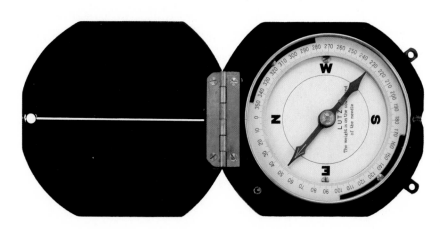

Which type compass should you buy? The Silva type (top) and the cruiser type (bottom) are suitable for outdoorsmen, though the Silva type is preferable for normal backpacking use. It is light, durable, and easy to use. Silva compasses have liquid-filled needle housings that prevent needle vibration and therefore reduce the amount of time needed to take a bearing. Some of the more expensive models have needles and direction indicators that shine in the dark. Their clear plastic baseplates make them ideal for use with maps, and their dial and index-line system reduces, if not eliminates, the need to remember the compass bearing. The cruiser compass usually is metal and is more finely graduated, but it is heavier, slower to use because the needle vibrates, and requires its user to remember or write down the bearing.

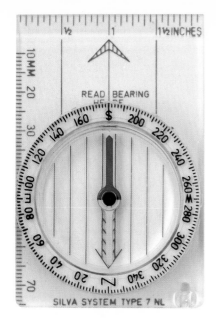

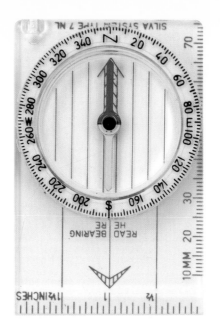

Situation 1: *Your friend told you he'd be camping 200 paces off the trail from the lightning-blasted tree on a bearing of 180°. You've reached the tree and need to find in what direction the 180° bearing points. First* **dial**, *then* **point**: *(1) Turn the dial until 180° and the index line meet. (2) Turn the entire compass until the magnetic needle points to N. The direction-of-travel arrow points to 180° S; walk 200 paces in that direction.*

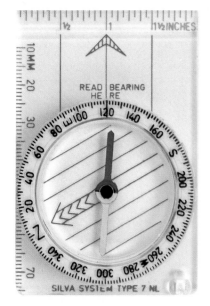

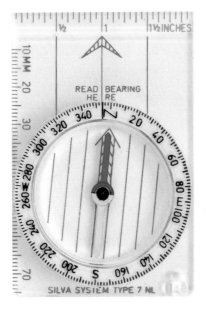

Situation 2: *From the top of a high ridge you spot a distant lake where you'd like to camp for the night. You want to find the bearing of the lone, tall tree near the lake's shore so you can navigate through the woods ahead. To find the tree's bearing,* **point** *first, then* **dial**: *(1) Point the direction-of-travel arrow toward the landmark. (2) Now turn the dial until the magnetic needle points to N. Read the bearing where the index line and the dial intersect. The tree's bearing is 354° N. Begin hiking along that bearing.*

learned earlier, however, that the sides of the topographic map are longitude lines and *do* point to the North Pole. They point to *True North.* At the bottom left of your topographic map there is a diagram containing a vertical line with a star atop it. That line also points toward the map's True North. The star symbolizes the North Star, Polaris, which shines above the North Pole and has guided navigators for centuries.

What *does* your compass' needle point to? To the North Magnetic Pole —an area of great magnetic attraction located around a thousand miles south of the North Pole.

If you were standing along a line that passed through both the North Magnetic Pole and the True North Pole, your compass needle, although attracted by the magnetic pole, would also point to the North Pole—toward True North. But if you moved to the west of that line, your compass needle, drawn by the Magnetic Pole, would fall to the east of True North. If you moved east, your needle would be pulled counterclockwise, or westerly, from True North. So, while your map is lined up with True North, your compass needle picks its own north—we call it Magnetic North—to point to.

The difference in degrees between Magnetic North (MN) and True North is called *declination.* On your topographic map, its value is printed above the horizontal line that intersects the MN arrow on the diagram. The declination of the map on page 85 is 13½ degrees west. If you draw a *compass* bearing on the map without correcting for declination, the bearing line will be 13½ degrees in error.

How can you avoid this error? What do you do about declination? Fortunately, the answer is simple: mark the map so that it is permanently oriented to MN. With a pencil and a straightedge, just continue the MN line from the declination diagram up into the map. Then, as shown on page 88, draw lines parallel to this one through the rest of the map about 2 or 3 inches apart (in the field I use the width of my compass baseplate). Once these MN lines are drawn on each of your maps you can forget about declination.

Now that we know how to deal with declination we can put map and compass together for use in more complex direction-finding situations. The illustrations on this page and on page 89 show several common situations and explain what to do when you are confronted with each one.

In the first basic compass technique, you dialed in 180 degrees, then turned to face in that direction. The next thing to learn is how to walk compass bearings. To get an idea of how to do this and to gain confidence in your compass' sense of direction, try a triangular compass walk (page 89, top).

The triangular walk teaches the basics of walking any compass bearing and also how to handle a series of changes in direction, including returning to home base. To walk a bearing, choose a prominent landmark along the bearing, put your compass away, and walk directly toward the landmark. In the wilderness you often cannot sight your goal for much of the walk, so choose an intermediate landmark (a lone pine, a large rock) that lies directly along the bearing and will be visible to you until you can reach it. Once you've reached that landmark, take out your compass (the bearing will still be set at the index line), sight again along your same bearing, pick another intermediate landmark, put your compass away, and walk to it. Continue this leap-frogging until you reach your goal. If you have a choice of good, visible landmarks, choose the farthest one for a more accurate overall course.

When you're planning the distance you'll navigate in a day's hiking, keep these figures in mind: without a pack, a good walker may average 4 miles an hour on a level road. With a pack, his speed may drop to 3 mph. On good upland trails a backpacker might average 2 mph. With a heavy pack and more frequent rest stops, the pace may slow to a mile an hour. A snowshoer in fairly gentle terrain can average 10 miles in a day, a competent cross-country skier about twice that.

Another factor to consider when planning your trip is the possibility of bad weather and its effects on your maps and compass. For trips where

Find your own way

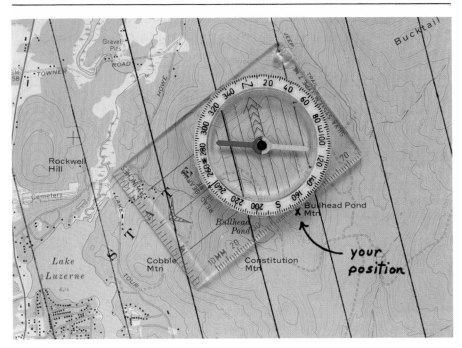

Situation 3 (above): *You wake up the first morning in camp and see a beautiful snow-covered peak in the distance. You wonder if it has a name. To find it on the map, you first use your compass to determine that it bears 247° from you. Then you plot the bearing on your map this way: Leaving the dial set at 247°, put the compass on the map so that either long edge of the base-plate passes through your position while the orienting lines parallel the drawn-in MN lines on the map. The orienting arrow should point to MN. The edge of the base-plate passes through the top of Constitution Mountain, 247° from you.*

Situation 4 (below): *Your map tells you the portage trail begins at the head of a small bay about a mile up the lake from your camp. In order to know exactly what direction to head to get there, determine the bearing between the two points on the map. 1. Put your compass on the map with the baseplate's long edge along your desired route. 2. Turn the dial until its orienting lines are parallel with the drawn-in MN lines and N points to north on the map. 3. Pick up the compass, turn your body until the needle points north, sight along the direction-of-travel arrow, pick out a tall tree in that direction, and walk toward it.*

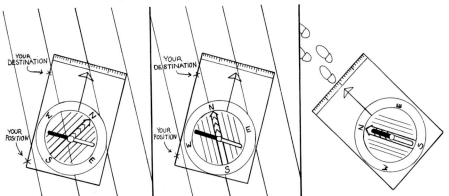

Situation 5 (not illustrated): *How to orient a map so north on the map corresponds to north on the ground. Hold the map in your hand and put your compass on the map so the orienting lines parallel the drawn-in MN lines and N faces the top of the map. Holding the map and compass in front of you,* turn your body until the needle points to N. The map's contour lines and terrain symbols should line up with the actual terrain. Merely sight from your own position on the map across to, say, a lake symbol and continue your gaze in the same direction to spot the actual lake.

Try a **triangular compass walk**. Go to the closest grassy park and lay a handkerchief down in the grass. Standing beside it, dial 0 (or 360) degrees into your compass and turn your body until the needle points to N. Sight along the direction-of-travel arrow, look up, and pick out something directly ahead of you—say a bench at the edge of the grass. Hold your compass at your side and walk ten paces toward the bench,

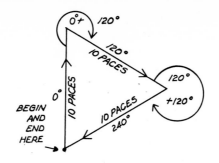

counting one pace each time your left foot hits the ground. At the end of ten paces, stop and dial in 120 degrees. Turn until the needle points to N, sight along the direction-of-travel arrow, pick out a landmark ahead of you—perhaps the bandstand—and walk ten paces toward it. Stop, dial in 240 degrees, and walk ten paces along that bearing. Your last step should place you next to your handkerchief again.

There will be times during your wild journeys **when you don't know exactly where you are**. Your map and compass can help you pinpoint yourself. If you know you're somewhere along a "baseline" (trail, ridge, stream, etc.), look for a landmark you can also find on your map. A mountain peak is ideal. Using the point-then-dial method, find the bearing from you to the landmark. Plot it on your map, making certain your compass' direction-of-travel arrow points toward the landmark's symbol. Draw the bearing line back from the landmark along

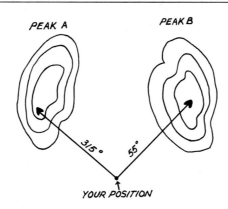

the baseplate edge until it intersects your trail. This intersection is approximately where you are. (The closer to perpendicular a bearing crosses your trail, the more accurate your charted position.) If you're not walking along a baseline that you can identify on your map, **locate your position by using bearings to two landmarks** that you can locate on your map. Find their bearings from you and plot them on your map, again making sure that the direction-of-travel arrow points at each landmark. Your position is where the two lines cross.

Save steps by "aiming off." You've set up camp on the shore of a large lake. Next day you set out to explore the country south of the lake. In late afternoon you decide to head back and you find out where you are by sighting on two mountain peaks. On your map, you read the bearing from your present position to camp—350 degrees. So if you start hiking along a compass bearing of 350 degrees you should go straight to camp; right? Probably not. If

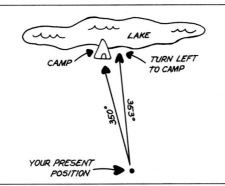

your estimated starting point is a little off, or if your navigation toward camp is slightly inaccurate, when you end up at the lake you won't know which way camp lies. The best plan is to deliberately aim off your inbound bearing by a few degrees at the outset. Walk a bearing of 353 degrees—3 degrees to the right. When you reach the lakeshore, camp will be to your left. For long walks, aim off 2 or 3 degrees. For shorter walks, aim off 5, or even 10, degrees.

When you run into an obstacle while walking a bearing, sight across it, choose a landmark along your bearing on the opposite side, and walk around to it. Or send a friend around to the other side, signal him onto the bearing line, then join him and continue to walk your bearing. If you can't see across the obstacle, **walk a right angle detour around it**. Say you're walking a bearing of 110 degrees when you come to a marsh. The best detour lies to the left. Subtract 90 degrees from your 110 bearing, for 20 degrees, and sight a landmark along the 20-degree bearing. Head toward the

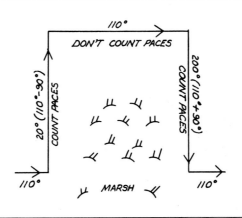

landmark, counting your paces, until you're past the marsh. Turn right and walk in your original direction—110 degrees—until you're past the marsh. No need to count paces here. Now, turn 90 degrees to the right, to 200 degrees (110 + 90), and walk the same number of paces you walked on the 20-degree bearing. When you stop, you'll be back on your original bearing line. Turn to 110 degrees. Always record the bearings and the numbers of paces in a pocket notebook rather than trust your memory. If counting paces seems tedious, time yourself instead.

A triangular detour pattern follows two equal sides of a triangle. In the example above, you might have decided that you'd save steps by angling away from your 110-degree bearing toward the point of the marsh, then angling back to your bearing. It looks as if a bearing of 70 degrees would be the easiest route, so you set your compass at 70° and take off. Count your paces or time yourself. When you've cleared the

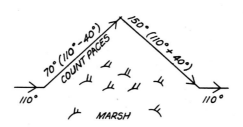

marsh and the walk back to your baseline looks clear, add the same number of degrees (40 in this case) to the baseline that you subtracted from it before (110 − 40 = 70 degrees; 110 + 40 = 150). Set your compass at 150° and walk the same number of paces or the same amount of time you walked on the 70-degree heading. You're back at baseline. Set your compass at 110° and continue your hike.

Everyone wins at orienteering

getting wet is a possibility, I spray my maps on both sides with a clear acrylic spray that can be found in most art or photo supply stores. This effectively waterproofs them. Also, some backpacking and sporting goods shops carry see-through plastic map cases. (A Zip-Loc plastic bag will do.) Or, put it inside your fishing-rod carrier.

If you buy one of the more expensive compasses, consider buying a belt case to protect the compass from getting scratched beyond easy reading after many years of use.

Don't store your compass near a strong electrical or magnetic influence. If, as rarely happens, your compass becomes "reverse polarized" so the needle points south instead of north, send it back to the manufacturer for remagnetizing.

If you enjoy fooling with a map and compass at all, you've got to give the "new" sport of orienteering a try. If you enjoy running, jogging, or just walking in the outdoors, you've got to try orienteering. If you want to learn to climb inside a map, to read all its meanings and subtleties, orienteering is your game.

Orienteering is racing from point to point, usually in a pleasant wild area, using map and compass as your guide. (It's also done by skiers, scuba divers, bikers, and horseback riders.) It's a wonderful way to get in shape, yet you don't have to be a superathlete to compete successfully at it. In fact, to call it a "race" is misleading. The tortoises very often beat the hares at this game because headwork—map and compass work—is fully half the challenge. Indeed, to "win" at orienteering you needn't even be fastest around the course. Since the earliest days of orienteering the tradition has been that anyone who completes the course successfully is a winner.

You can compete at any level you wish. At a meet there are usually beginning, intermediate, and advanced courses working simultaneously. If

you're just in it for the compasswork and a pleasant day in the woods, you can even stroll whichever course you choose. It's for persons of both sexes and every age group from grammar school to well past retirement. I remember my first "orienteering meet." My scoutmaster set a course in a familiar woodlot and started us on a "compass race." I was young and nervous and I wasn't sure I wanted to do it. But I did because I had to and I loved it. It was fun. And it sparked a love of working with map and compass that has stayed with me.

Orienteering got started in Sweden around the turn of the century, and its popularity and educational value are indicated by the fact that orienteering is a compulsory subject in Swedish schools. In 1977, the top meet there, the *O-ringen* (Swedish for orienteering), is expected to draw around 20,000 entrants from all over the globe. The sport was introduced to the United States and Canada in 1946 and 1948 by Bjorn Kjellstrom, former Swedish orienteering champion and co-inventor of the Silva compass system.

The first, modest American meet was held in Indiana in 1946. There were fewer than 50 participants. Today, there are over 50 orienteering clubs affiliated with the United States Orienteering Federation, a national organization (founded in 1971) that sponsors competitive orienteering in this country. Hundreds of people participate in weekend meets throughout the nation. Some American schools and colleges now offer courses in orienteering.

If you'd like to know more about this new sport write to the American Orienteering Service, Box 547, La Porte, Indiana 46350, or to the United States Orienteering Federation, Box 1081, Athens, Ohio 45701.

Like all races, orienteering meets (opposite) have starting (top) and finishing lines (bottom, right). But in orienteering meets, anyone can compete. Everyone who punches in at all the checkpoints that mark the course (bottom, left) is a winner.

Ride into the high country

Mel Baughman

Slipping away from his fellow trail riders to savor the sweep of Wyoming's flowered Teton Wilderness, Iowa student Andy Davis surveys the high country they will explore in the next 12 days. Through the mist of a waterfall (opposite) they enter Jay Creek Canyon just below the Continental Divide, near Parting of the Waters where Two Ocean Creek divides into Pacific Creek flowing west and Atlantic Creek flowing east. The pristine, timbered box canyon is typical of the spectacular scenery that lures hundreds of trail riders to the Tetons each summer from their desks in urban canyons across the land. With luck, they could glimpse one of the several dozen grizzlies or the occasional mountain lion that still prowls these youngest Rocky Mountains, the 8,000,000-year-old Tetons.

The first gentle breeze of the morning brought to my tent the stirring aroma of coffee and frying bacon. Suddenly I was ravenous. As I sat up to leave my sleeping bag, a gripping pain shot through my right leg, and I quickly lay down again. The pain subsided as I obeyed my body's stern signal to lie still.

Yesterday several of us were hiking miles above camp in the Grand Teton Mountains when we came upon a small snowfield. Unable to resist, I had placed my folded poncho on the snow, sat on it, and began a slow, controlled glissade down the snowfield. The glissading was great, but I was rapidly leaving behind the party I was supposed to be leading. Bringing my slide to a halt, I shifted my weight forward to stand up. Suddenly overwhelmed by a sense of dread, I felt the snow collapsing beneath me. Unwittingly, I had slid onto a snowbridge obscuring a 20-foot drop in the stream bed.

The rocks below were rushing toward me, barely giving me time to cover my face with my forearms. I landed on my chest and legs, and the impact knocked the wind out of me. After a time my breath came back to me, and as I cautiously got up, I realized that by some miracle no bones had been broken. I was severely bruised, however, and it was a struggle to remain conscious as I groped for a way out of the chasm. At last my companions reached me, hauled me to safety, and gave me some warm, dry clothes. One leg was swelling visibly, but, with help, I could hobble, so we started back to camp. It was a faltering, pain-filled, four-hour trek. Back in camp, Buffy Masten, a nurse from San Francisco, examined my bruises and prescribed 24 hours of bed rest.

In my tent at last, I watched the July night fill the valley. Lying with my leg wrapped in cold, wet towels, I could see the flickering campfire and hear the murmur of voices broken by an occasional ring of laughter as my friends swapped stories and recounted their day's adventures. Gradually the murmurs died away and the melancholy strains of a lonesome harmonica drifted through my canvas ward. I remember feeling very lucky to be alive, then drifting off to sleep wondering who was playing that haunting harmonica.

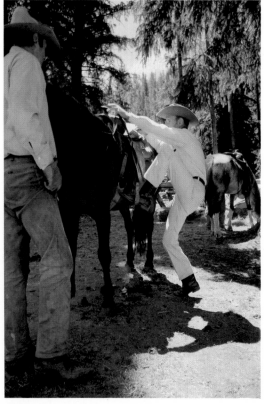

For 30 years George Clover, Wilderness Trails outfitter (above) has been guiding visitors along the hundreds of miles of trails that wind into Wyoming's high country. Here he leads part of his string of 36 horses and mules across the Soda Fork on the third day of the author's 110-mile trip for 20 guests and their gear. At left, Paul Wirth, a Washington, D.C., lithographer, takes the momentous step that will put him aboard a horse for the first time in his life. His first opportunity to dismount came unexpectedly—to help put out a small forest fire (opposite) for which Lynda May, a Toronto teacher, and Charlie Newton, an Illinois dentist, improvise a fire bucket out of a poncho.

Now, the morning after, I thought of the many times I had warned everyone else to be careful out here in the wilderness. There are no nearby medical facilities, and it takes several hours for a rider on horseback to get a message to the rescue helicopter pilot in Jackson Hole. And here I lay, the host of this trail ride, the only casualty of the trip. It was downright embarrassing. Why hadn't I scouted that snowfield before taking off so impetuously?

My thoughts were interrupted as Paul Wirth entered the tent and handed me a cup of coffee. Paul works with me in Washington, D.C., on the technical preparations of the National Wildlife Federation books and magazines.

"How do you feel this morning?" Paul asked.

"Subdued. Just a bit subdued. Thanks for the coffee."

"We all agree that you really know how to make a point and we promise to be careful. You don't have to jump off any more cliffs. If you think you can manage here, we're going to ride up to Crater Lake and catch a few trout this morning."

"Sure, I'll be all right. A little loafing will feel good for a change. Bring me a cutthroat!" From the tent I watched Paul stride to his horse, saddle it, and ride off with the rest of the group. Paul and I had been on this National Wildlife trail ride through the Teton Wilderness for five days, and now we both considered ourselves seasoned wilderness travelers. But I clearly remembered Paul's response when I first broached the subject of a saddlepack trip. We were in Paul's office at the time, deliberating over some photographs for a forthcoming issue of one of the magazines.

"Mel, the only horse I ever rode was a wooden horse on a merry-go-round. You are asking *me* to jump on the back of a real horse and ride off into the wilderness for two weeks?"

"Listen to me, Paul," I reasoned. "Instead of standing here looking at these color pictures of moose and trumpeter swans, we could be out there in the Rockies seeing the real thing. I know the outfitter running this trip. He's one of the best. He will size you up at a glance, point to a saddle, call for a horse by name, then put you all together and you will be a matched set. You will be custom fitted to horse and tack."

"But I'm telling you: I've never ridden a horse in my life!"

"We'll be riding along some of the finest cutthroat trout streams in the country," I coaxed.

I had dangled the right lure before this Maryland fisherman, for a few weeks later he was standing beside me at a corral in Turpin Meadow, Wyoming. With 16 other cowpokes-to-be we were watching George Clover, the outfitter, study each guest a moment, select a saddle, call for a horse by name, and unerringly create a perfectly paired horse and rider. Paul got an easygoing brown stallion named Ring; I was delighted to be reunited with Boots, the high-spirited roan I had ridden on my first trail ride with George three summers ago. Paul was relieved to learn that several other riders also had to be shown how to mount and dismount and how to start and stop a horse.

While waiting for everyone to be assigned a mount, we had watched the wranglers load supplies onto the pack mules. Heavy frying pans, cooking pots, tin plates, and cutlery went into large metal boxes called panniers. Beef steak, pork chops, other fresh meats, and groceries filled similar cases made of wood; canned goods, tools, and other gear went into canvas panniers. The wranglers balanced two panniers across the backbone of each mule and then strapped on the top packs of tents, bedrolls, and duffel. These hardworking cowboys would introduce us to a lot of the lore of the Old West before the trip was over.

At George's signal we had finally assembled, mounted our steeds, and rode single file into the wilderness. Following an ancient game trail worn by uncounted generations of elk, mule deer, bear, and mountain lion, our horses carried us into the cool shade of a stand of lodgepole pine and Douglas fir. Through the

"I always enjoy time in camp," says the author, "because that time is our own. It is a peaceful interlude to rest, reorganize our gear, or take an exhilarating dip in the icy meltwaters of a mountain stream." The first order of business for the wranglers, however, is to start a cooking fire, ancestral hearth of all wilderness homes. Although camp fires are permitted where blowdowns provide ample firewood, they are closely regulated by Wilderness Area managers of the Bridger-Teton National Forest. The use of chain saws is forbidden and the fire ring, like the temporary corral, must be cleared when the outfitter's seasonal permit expires. Trail riders often try their hand at the wranglers' skills of sawing logs, splitting kindling, and driving stakes to dry their boots on. But the skill they most admire is the lariat toss, legendary symbol of the West. Although George Clover assures beginners that it takes years of practice, Sue Cullom, a student from Baltimore (below), proves to be an exception.

trees we heard and occasionally glimpsed the sparkling South Fork of the Buffalo River 100 feet below as it rushed to join the Snake River at Jackson Hole. Soon our trail brought us out into a meadow aglow with a dazzling array of wildflowers. Indian paintbrush highlighted the green carpet with flashes of orange, red, and pure magenta. Swirling softly around the brilliant paintbrush were stands of blue lupine, lavender monkshood, reddish-purple elephanthead, and white mariposa lily. Columbine, my favorite, nodded in scattered clusters of delicate yellow, white, and translucent ice-blue blossoms. The wondrous fragrance wafting from these masses of flowers and the brilliance of their colors, surrounded by the sky-piercing grandeur of the Grand Teton Mountains, silenced our entire party.

I wondered that day if Paul were thinking, as I was, how good it was to be riding into such a scene instead of working with a photograph of it. In the presence of such beauty, what John Muir called "the galling harness of civilization" relinquished its hold on each of us. The immensity of the open sky in this land of no fences, no signposts, no shelters—so counter to the boundary-filled security of the world we had just left—evoked an exhilarating sense of freedom. It also awakened an acute awareness of our vulnerability. Leaning out from my saddle to see how Paul was doing, I heard a shout, "Smoke! There's smoke up ahead."

I gave Boots a nudge in the flanks, and we galloped across the meadow to where riders were dismounting and tying their horses to trees. Some of the riders were already emptying their canteens on a smoldering patch of forest floor. It couldn't have been more than 20 feet square, but it took our group of 18 riders and six wranglers almost an hour to put it out to the last spark. Fortunately, we had found a tiny spring—no more than a steady trickle. We formed a tin-cup-and-canteen brigade, augmented by a poncho that we filled to carry larger douses of water to the stubborn root-fed fire. Since there were no campsites around, we concluded that the fire had been started by a careless smoker. After refilling our canteens we rode on to our campsite and Paul's first night under Wyoming stars.

Five days later, at our second campsite, I crawled out of my tent, hobbled to the deserted campfire, and began sewing up the trousers I had torn in yesterday's fall. I hadn't brought much clothing and I would need those pants before the trip ended. Just sitting in the sun watching clouds form, grow, dissolve, and form again along the cathedral spires of the Teton Range proved wonderfully therapeutic for my mind and mending body.

Being forced to spend a day alone also allowed the magic of the wilderness to seep into my bones more deeply than ever before. I thought of the men who saw it first—men like Jim Bridger (for whom a nearby lake and the adjoining wilderness area are named), Jedediah Smith, Andrew Henry, and John Colter. The legendary exploits of these early 19th century trappers had captured my imagination as a boy. I felt the minor mishap that had grounded me yesterday helped me to understand their decision to spend their whole lives exploring the formidable Rockies—thereby earning for themselves history's title of "mountain men." Despite unimaginable hardships and chronic loneliness, they must have found their reward in the beauty and the wildness, the freedom and the peace, and the exhilarating challenge to survive.

The sound of hoofbeats announced the return of the fishing party from Crater Lake, with enough trout to feed the whole camp. Paul triumphantly laid his two largest cutthroat at my feet. With everyone helping, the catch was quickly cleaned and given to Priscilla Watkins to fry for our supper.

None of us will soon forget Priscilla. Time after time we watched her bake delectable corn bread and chocolate cake without an oven, cook blueberry pancakes in an iron skillet that required two people to lift, and fry fresh cutthroat trout to a turn—all for 27 people at a time. Priscilla could also pack a pannier, load a mule, and guide a mule train cross-country with the best of the cowboys. Through all this, she was first and foremost a lady. We were all fascinated to learn that

The early morning roundup of mules and horses from open meadow into makeshift corral is the first chore in wrangler/raconteur Jerry Roberts' day that begins at 5:30 a.m. and ends at dark. The clanking guard bell on the lead mule at left is a timesaver in locating the animals. Shoeing a horse is another skill many of the trail riders had not seen performed at close range. George Clover's son, Tom (below, center), uses a farrier's hammer to drive nails through holes in the iron shoe. He then clinches off the heads of the nails and files the rough edges smooth and even with the surface of the hoof. Both rocky terrain and mud can cause a shoe to loosen or be thrown. Depending on its condition, the shoe is then either reset or replaced. Normally each horse is shod "all the way around" at least twice during the season. Below, trail rider Tom Hadlow, a mortgage loan officer from Virginia, holds the halter of a pack mule while Tom Clover uses the traditional diamond hitch to cinch the 40-pound panniers so they can't slip during the 8- to 20-mile ride to the next camp. George Clover (opposite) sharpens his knife to repair a saddle. To keep all tack in top shape, he carries only a leather punch, rivets, rivet set, pliers, and strips of leather. Packing his saddlebags, the author (below, left) selects his photo equipment for a side trip.

Priscilla had also attended a finishing school in the East and graduated from Vassar before returning to her native West to cook and wrangle. Gathering around the campfire to enjoy the trout feast Priscilla set before us this night, we talked later than usual. Finally we said goodnight and headed for our tents, speculating on the adventures to come. Tomorrow it was on to our next camp, or so we thought.

I awakened next morning not at all sure my still-swollen leg was ready for a 12-mile ride. I hobbled to the breakfast fire where George told me that we could not leave at 8 o'clock as usual because several of his mules had run off during the night. On behalf of the other trail riders I acted diplomatically disappointed, but secretly I was thankful for the reprieve.

Most of the time the pack animals stay all night in the meadow where the grazing is good and do not need to be tied or hobbled. But mules being mules, these unpredictable animals occasionally slip away in the moonlight bent on adventures more in keeping with their wild ancestry. I kidded George a little because the same thing had happened at this very same camp on my first trip out here. That time, however, the mules took a mere 20-mile shortcut back to the corral at Turpin Meadow. This time the wiley critters had disappeared so mysteriously that, after a futile search of all their known escape routes, George resigned himself to losing a whole day's travel. He sent one of the wranglers back to Jackson Hole to hire a pilot to fly him over the high country to locate the animals. Twelve hours later, George and his posse returned with the truants.

The following morning I gingerly mounted Boots and was relieved to sense a marked improvement in my leg. I quietly thanked the errant mules. But most of my gratitude was reserved for Boots. I like saddlepacking because so much can be seen and enjoyed from the saddle and a lot of country can be covered in a limited time. I was well aware that my trip would have ended with my fall had I been hiking. And the trail we faced today was the most challenging and arduous of the trip. Boots seemed to sense my frailty as he fell quietly into line.

The first six miles were so steep they took us three thousand feet up toward a crest of the Continental Divide. After a brief stop for a drink at picturesque Crater Lake, the horses resumed the climb, now along a series of sobering switchbacks that clung precariously to the mountain's edge and tested the nerves of all the tenderfoot riders. At last the switchbacks ended in a high meadow, but even here the path led upward, flanked by fields of snow.

At the top of this long grade the country suddenly opened up before us as vast as the sky above. We were on the Continental Divide at fabled Ferry Lake Pass. The panorama of ranges was sprinkled with dozens of lakes and ponds, each mirroring a detail of the broad sweep of mountain grandeur before us. Just to have been at this one spot one time was worth the entire trip.

We used all of our brief rest time at the Pass taking pictures, then it was back into the saddle for the precipitous descent into Woodard Canyon which seemed even steeper than the uphill climb. It was five hours of tense zigging and zagging along switchbacks made slippery by melting snow, leaping over deadfalls blocking the trail, and fording swollen mountain streams. Our sleeping bags never felt better than they did that night.

After an early breakfast we were back in the saddle. It really was beginning to feel like home by now. Fording our first stream of the day we discovered some very large, fresh paw prints in the mud at the water's edge. George confirmed that they were bear tracks. He couldn't be sure whether they had been made by a young grizzly or by a mature black bear, but just knowing that the owner might be looking at us this very moment did wonders for our powers of observation. All eyes were on each clump of trees we rode past. But our next big game sighting was in the middle of yet another flowered meadow—a bull moose quietly grazing, the largest of several we had seen. Then we saw, wheeling in the sky above the moose, a seagull! It looked decidedly out of place soaring over a mountain meadow instead of ocean waves, but it seemed quite content, and we could understand that.

Charles Alexander (opposite), a student from New Hampshire, hauls in a fighting cutthroat trout from Crater Lake. Though the trout caught here ran smaller than the 16-inchers (opposite, top) caught in nearby streams, all are destined for the skillet. Tom Hadlow (opposite, bottom), cleaning fish with his economist wife, Pat, daily outfished everyone and proclaimed the Teton Wilderness a paradise he wanted never to leave. His enthusiasm moved women who were reluctant even to touch a fish to help clean the daily catch. Andy Davis (above) inspects porcupine damage to a lodgepole pine. The inner bark is an important winter diet item that tides the nocturnal, tree-climbing rodent over until spring buds appear. The porcupine's girdling of a few trees is ignored in the wilderness, but encounters stiff opposition from timber growers in commercial forests.

Wyoming wildflowers lure Wisconsin horse-woman Linda Burns out of the saddle and into the sunflowers (opposite) to try her hand at taking photos like those the author took of (left, top to bottom) blue columbine, whose nectar-filled spurs attract humming-birds; elephanthead, whose trunk-waving pink flowers are grazed by elk; the soil-enriching lupine, whose seeds and roots also nourish bears and mice; and the free-loading Indian paintbrush, whose roots parasitize the roots of other plants.

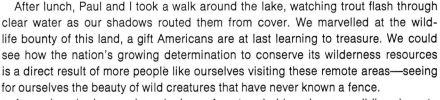

At our last camp George announced that he had saved the best for last, a trip to Bridger Lake. We packed a lunch and some extra film and set out on another long ride. The day was clear and shining. Only the creaking of saddle leather and the clop of the horses' hooves broke the stillness. At last we saw Bridger Lake glinting through the trees. George signaled us to ride up as quietly as possible. As we were tying our horses, Paul whispered, "Mel! Isn't that a trumpeter swan?" Everyone ducked and crept slowly behind trees and bushes to find a comfortable observation post where we would not disturb the rare white swan floating in the middle of the lake. Several other trumpeters glided onstage from a cove on the far shore. Looking as if their graceful movements had inspired the choreography of the Swan Lake Ballet, they glided toward us, wariness tensing their regal poise. They ghosted across the water in silence, but strains of Tchaikovsky welled up in my mind.

The splashing of a cow moose and her calf feeding at the water's edge broke the spell. The swans fled, winging low across the water, giving our photographers a chance at another prize shot. Then the camera buffs turned their attention to the ungainly moose, taking care not to get between mother and calf. We were ever mindful that there were no fences here, no safe places to flee to.

After lunch, Paul and I took a walk around the lake, watching trout flash through clear water as our shadows routed them from cover. We marvelled at the wild-life bounty of this land, a gift Americans are at last learning to treasure. We could see how the nation's growing determination to conserve its wilderness resources is a direct result of more people like ourselves visiting these remote areas—seeing for ourselves the beauty of wild creatures that have never known a fence.

A passing shadow made us look up. A mature bald eagle came gliding down to the top of a lodgepole pine and surveyed this magnificent domain that we shared for the moment. To me, his very existence bespoke a healthy land, a place where an eagle could go about an eagle's business of fending for itself, reproducing its kind, and rearing its broods with neither help nor hindrance from man.

On the way back to camp, everyone was in a jubilant mood. The horses, too, seemed more energetic than usual. As we approached our home meadow, the horses trotted, then moved into a full gallop—a race to the corral was on! I knew that Boots was the fastest horse, but I knew, too, that my leg was still too sore to grip the saddle tightly, so I reined him in, letting the others sweep by. The reproachful look on Boots' face as he turned to question this unthinkable command made me laugh. I couldn't help wanting to believe that he actually remembered what had happened three years ago in another race for the corral. He and I were leading the field that time, too, when Boots had bounded across a small creek and landed safely on the opposite side, riderless. He had left me in mid-air directly above the creek, clearly aware of my fate. As I waded out, Boots had looked back at me with this same expression which seemed to say that if he had had a decent rider, he would have won the race. This time I gave him an apple left from my lunch as an offering to carry me safely back to camp—and to hear George play the harmonica for the last time.

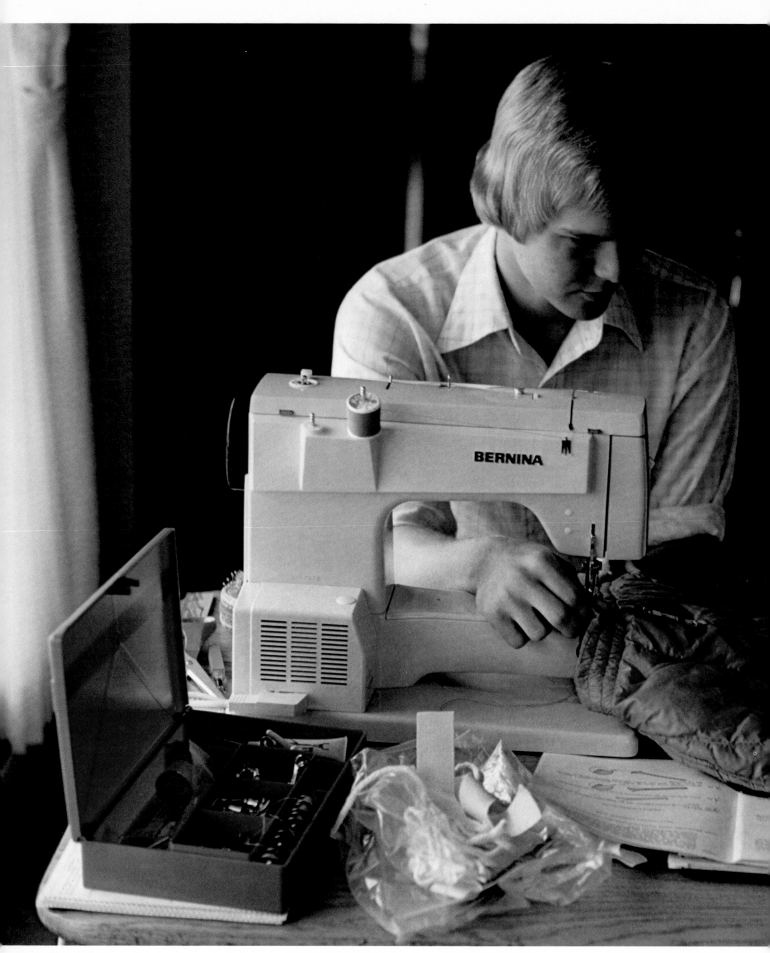

The desire for better camping gear at less cost motivates many a camper to master new skills.

MAKING AND REPAIRING YOUR TRAIL GEAR

Charlotte Bull

Campers by nature enjoy doing things for themselves, being self-reliant in the great outdoors. That attitude spills over into their ideas about camping gear. They often want unique gear designed to satisfy their personal styles of hiking and camping. In the past ten years, the explosion of interest in camping and the development of new materials for construction of gear have resulted in a great boon for do-it-yourselfers — the commercial production of kits that simplify making your own gear. Now, from kits that contain all materials and directions, anyone can produce (and modify) a wide variety of packs, tents, and down- or polyester-filled garments and sleeping bags. Even items like snowshoes and cross-country skis are now available in kits. (See Appendix for list of kit manufacturers.)

Using a kit is a gratifying way to create your own gear and save 30 to 50 percent of the cost of buying a similar ready-made item. Since you sew it yourself, you have the advantage of quality control: you can sear the edges of nylon fabric to prevent fraying, finish seams securely and evenly, and reinforce points of stress.

Kits have other advantages. By the time you complete one, you have learned the basics of good design and construction and thus know what to look for when shopping for ready-made items. Repairing and cleaning a garment is easier once you understand its fabric and construction.

But why buy a kit, you may ask. Why not start from scratch with a pattern and material of your own choosing? Putting kits together usually is both cheaper and more convenient. You do not need to spend time shop-

Sew it yourself with a kit

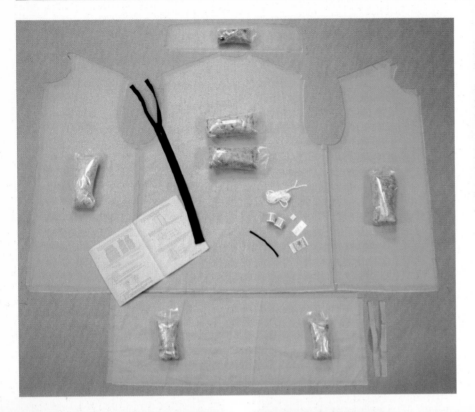

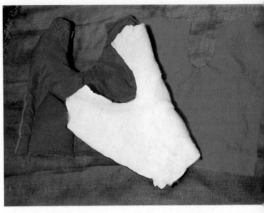

A vest is an excellent first-time kit project. Kits come with down (left) or polyester filler (above) and are conveniently replete with everything needed: thread, zippers, snaps, instructions, cloth, and filler. Polyester doesn't have to be quilted — it only needs to be sewn into the edge seams to stay in place — an advantage for the novice sewer. Down kits have ingenious ways to simplify inserting the down and sewing the quilting lines.

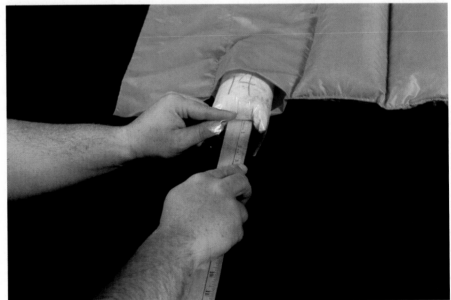

Sear the edges of nylon to prevent raveling. Trim off the long threads and melt the edges with a candle or soldering iron. The candle flame can burn into the fabric, so be prepared to blow it out quickly or to pinch the burning fabric with your fingers. Stretch the fabric tautly for greater control. Move the fabric past the flame at an even speed; going too slowly causes the fabric to catch on fire.

Down is inserted in three ways, depending on whether the manufacturer sends the down packaged in cotton sacks, plastic packets, or soluble plastic packets. If the down comes in cotton sacks, you carefully pull the down out and stuff it loosely into the tubes or quilted areas of the garment. If it comes in plastic packets, you use a ruler (above) to turn the packet inside out as you push the down into the tubes or quilted areas. If the down comes in soluble plastic packets, you insert the packets unopened. After the garment is completed, you pull the fragile plastic bag apart to release the down. The plastic melts away in the first wash. The author, who has equipped her family of five with gear made from kits (she made four down sleeping bags in one month), says that all the methods work well.

ping for materials and parts. You do not have yardage waste left from cutting since exact amounts of cloth are provided. Also, kits give you the benefit of tested and proven construction designs and techniques.

Even if you think you need to start from scratch because you want, say, a jacket with extra-broad shoulders or a unique design feature, you should still look into kits. Kit manufacturers are very competitive, and they have been quick to satisfy a wide range of consumer needs. Some companies send pre-cut fabric so the sewer needn't bother with cutting out the pieces, but others send uncut fabric with the pattern silk-screened on so the sewer can alter it to fit his personal needs. If you think searing the edges of nylon is a nuisance, you can order a kit designed to eliminate the need for searing. And you can buy extra fabric, fillers, and materials to adapt a kit in other ways.

You also have the choice of buying kits for making either down-filled or polyester-filled clothing and sleeping bags. Of course, you will want to consider the merits of each filler as an insulator (see pp. 35-36 — Ed.), but the type of insulation is not my major criterion when selecting a kit. I look at all aspects of the kit's design. For a parka kit, I would also find out how many pockets it has, whether it has snaps or Velcro to close the pocket flaps, and whether it has a hood.

If you do decide to buy a down kit, you'll want to know about the different methods of inserting down (see illustration). One method might be more suitable than the others for your needs. I have tried all three methods and have found all three satisfactory.

Here are some hints for handling the down and inserting it. Close windows and turn off fans before opening a packet of down. Many kit sewers fill their garments in a bathtub in a warm, humid room. Some use a clothes sprinkler on loose down to make it easier to gather up if spilled. Holding a garment between your legs rather than horizontally across your lap and inserting the down downward provides greater control.

Success with kits depends most of all on following directions. Read the entire set of directions before starting any project so you understand the entire process in advance. Otherwise, you may think some parts are done in an illogical order. Skilled seamstresses who skip ahead or omit steps out of overconfidence or from being accustomed to different methods of construction can have disastrous results. Beginners who follow directions exactly can complete good products.

If you want to create your own special designs instead of buying kits, it certainly is possible. Nylon fabrics are easier to find than ever before. Velcro, nylon zippers, and nylon sheath lining fabrics are for sale almost anywhere. Pattern companies offer a variety of good designs for windbreakers, jackets, and small day packs.

Sleeping bags are much more complicated than they might seem, if you plan to fill them with down. There is much to consider, such as the construction of the baffles that hold the down (see p. 37 — Ed.) You might want to rip up a worn-out down bag and use it as a pattern for making a new one. And it is possible, though messy, to use your own down from your hunting expeditions or from an old comforter as fill for a homemade sleeping bag.

If sleeping bags, parkas, and packs seem too ambitious for a start, there are many other items the outdoor family can make easily. Stuff sacks and utensil holders, small belt or day packs, map pockets, lens holders, and moccasins are fun to make and useful on the trail.

Whether you decide to put together a kit or to start from scratch, you'll be using similar fabrics, sewing techniques, and equipment. One valuable maxim is, if your sewing machine is lightweight, attempt only lightweight projects. I use a heavy-duty machine and strong needle because some of the tents and sleeping bags I have made have as many as six layers of fabric in some places. Packs are often made of heavy, coated fabrics and webbing with leather reinforce-

Seams Used in Kits

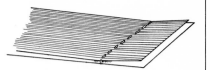

PLAIN: right sides together, edges even, sew seam ½" from edge

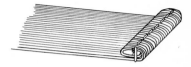

ROLLED: right sides together, edges even, fold back twice, sew in center

FELLED: wrong sides together, 1 edge longer, sew; fold long over short, sew

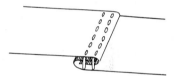

LAP FELLED: Interlock cloth by folding top down, bottom up; sew 2 seams

LAPPED: fold top so wrong sides touch, put over right side of bottom, sew edge

TURNED IN: wrong sides together, edges even, turn edges to inside, sew

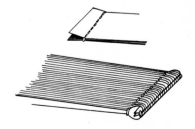

FRENCH: wrong sides together, sew plain seam; fold so right sides are together, flatten, sew plain seam

ment patches. I stitch the leather by hand and push the thick fabric through the machine stitch by stitch, operating the machine manually.

To make sewing easier, I clean, oil, and adjust the machine before each major project. I especially check for proper needle alignment, smoothness of the needle opening or throat plate, and proper thread tension. Some machines do not feed the thread smoothly when sewing heavy fabric, and you will want to watch out for that possibility, especially with coated fabrics, which create more tension problems than other fabrics do. If the pull on the thread causes the thread to fray or snap, loosen the tension and check to see if the needle is bent.

If you need more experience in setting thread tension and foot pressure (so the fabric doesn't bunch up in front of it), practice stitching in unobtrusive places first. Good places for this practice are the inside seams on separate pockets and on sleeves. In these areas, less-than-perfect stitching is acceptable since the piece is turned and top-stitched.

Kit instructions include such important advice as always to use a large needle (size 16 or 18, even size 20). A small needle or a ball-point one won't punch a large enough hole in the densely woven fabric. The friction caused by pulling the thread through a small hole makes the thread ravel and break. A large hole reduces friction. It is also important to know that nylon overheats the needle and must be stitched more slowly than other fabrics. Keep the fabric taut at all times, and hold the threads together in back as you start stitching.

If your kit comes with nylon thread, replace it with high-quality, sturdy polyester thread. Polyester thread is easier to use because it is less elastic.

Special stitching techniques help you turn out well-made projects. For example, using lap-felled seams (turned over and interlocked) helps the garment withstand strain (see p. 107 — Ed.). Backstitching two or three times at the beginning and end of each seam locks the threads firmly. For extra strength, try stitching several times

within the seam line at such points of stress as the armpits, pocket corners, and belt loops. Often, making more rows of stitching than the instructions call for will be worth the extra effort.

To reinforce areas where snaps are to be installed, add a piece of pressure-sensitive ripstop mending tape to the inside of the fabric. You can also put strips of pressure tape on the inside of the garment along the lines where the pockets will be stitched. The tape strengthens the seam, making it more difficult to tear the pocket. Zipper stops and pocket corners are usually bar-tacked in good products for added strength. You can do this with a zig-zag machine.

Searing the edges of nylon prevents fraying and raveling, common problems with nylon. The process is time-consuming and frustrating when you are eager to whip a kit together, but do not skip it. Allow time to sear all edges, including lacings, webbings, and slashes cut in neck and armholes to ease seam fitting. The only exception is the edges of coated fabrics, which don't ravel.

Basting is not needed in most kit construction. You simply pin the fabric together and sew. Keep pinholes within the seam and at a minimum, especially in coated fabrics. Masking tape is a good substitute for pins when holding thick layers of fabric together until stitched.

One especially satisfying aspect of making gear from kits is that you can add your own personal decorative touch to your products. One kit manufacturer sells a pamphlet filled with "customizing" ideas and instructions on how to incorporate them into your plans. Retail stores that carry kits often inspire their customers by displaying samples of completed, customized, kit-made gear.

Most customizing must be done before the construction stages. Yokes, for instance, are added to each piece of the body and then the kit is constructed as directed. The same is true for embroidery and applique designs; they are worked onto the pieces before the pieces are assembled.

To make a day pack useful to students, cyclists, and hikers, like the pack designed and worn by the author (opposite), follow the pattern on the next page.

For the basic pack (options 5a and 9a) you will need ½ yard of 36" wide **fabric** *(denim or nylon pack cloth);* **nylon webbing** *(one piece 24" long, 2" wide; one 55" long, ½" wide); 3½ yards* **cotton twill tape;** *heavy* **polyester thread;** *20" of* **cord;** *3* **buckles** *to fit ½" webbing; 2* **grommets** *and* **grommet setter.** *If you choose options 5b and 9b you will need 1 less* **buckle,** *12" more of ½"* **webbing,** *another* **grommet,** *10" more of* **cord,** *and a* **D-ring.**

The procedure is as follows:

1. *Lay out fabric; cut three pieces:*
   a. *pack sides — 2 pieces, 6" by 22".*
   b. *pack body — 12" by 44".*
2. *Cut ½" slits in sides, 12" up.*
3. *Fold top of each side down 5", right sides of cloth together, stitch ½" seams down to slits.*
4. *Turn inside out, stitch across.*
5. *Choose (a) a grommet-and-cord closing for side flaps or (b) a simple tie made of webbing. If (a), place grommet in top center of each side piece, ½" from end. Tie a 10" cord to each grommet. If (b), turn under ends of two 10" pieces of ½" webbing, and stitch one to top of each side.*
6. *Mark pack body for folding. Turn 5" flap under, wrong sides together, and stitch across.*
7. *With wrong sides together, pin sides to pack body, stitch ¼" seam.*
8. *Starting in upper front corner of pack body, encase all edges in 1" twill tape in continuous seam, catching both sides of tape in stitching.*
9. *Add fasteners, either (a) strap and buckle or (b) grommet and cord. If (a), attach buckles with webbing. Sear cut edge of webbing. Sew to front body and to flap; stitch as shown. If (b), set grommet in center of top flap and attach D-ring with webbing to lower center front of body. Add a 30" cord in a hitch knot.*
10. *Add shoulder straps (a) of webbing 2" wide and 12" long. You may wish to pad them. Attach to each shoulder strap a 15" length of ½" webbing (b) with a metal tip or seared end. Center the straps at top of pack back and set at a slight angle. Fit, pin, sew. Stitch reinforcing tab of leather or webbing (2" by 5") over straps (c). Sew buckles low on back of pack, 1½" from edge, with webbing extending over the edge and onto the bottom of the pack.*

How to make a day pack from scratch

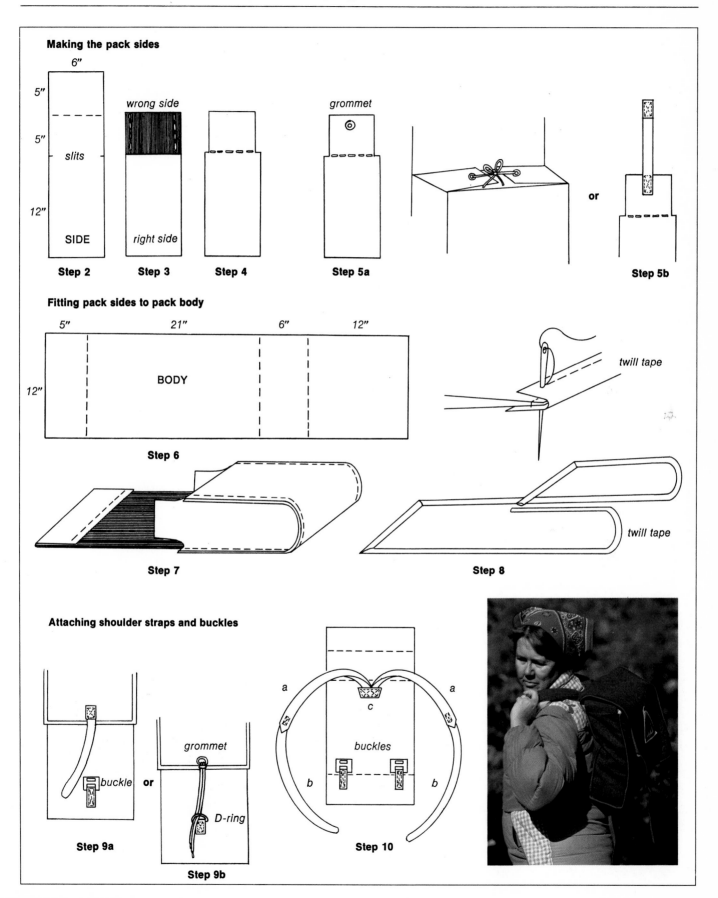

Making the pack sides

6"

5"

5"

slits

12"

SIDE

Step 2

wrong side

right side

Step 3

Step 4

grommet

Step 5a

or

Step 5b

Fitting pack sides to pack body

5"   21"   6"   12"

12"   BODY

Step 6

twill tape

Step 7

twill tape

Step 8

Attaching shoulder straps and buckles

buckle   **or**

Step 9a

grommet

D-ring

Step 9b

a   *a*

c

buckles

b   *b*

Step 10

In designing customized decoration, you must consider the kit's recommended quilting lines. To finish a yoke, for example, you may omit quilting the top lines and quilt along the yoke line instead. When adding stripes, remember that they will look best if the quilting lines and stripes coincide. Before cutting materials for decoration, plan carefully to include the required seam allowance, hems, and zipper turn-under.

Fabrics used for contrasting stripes, cording, and trim may need to be pre-shrunk. Carefully measure them so that they meet at the zipper. In all cases, you must consider the added thickness of the hem when the extra materials are folded over. Added bulk may make stitching very difficult. You may need to stitch from the middle of the bottom hem in order to get a power surge for stitching over a bulky place.

If you wish to embroider, choose fabrics like the firmer taffetas, not rip-stop nylon, which bunches easily and may catch and tear. Because down and cold air both can sift through holes, it is best to embroider a yoke made from extra fabric and sew it over the pieces of cloth the kit provides.

Aside from pure decoration, many useful additions and alterations can be made to improve kit products. Especially popular are extra pockets to help organize the small items everyone seems to carry. Try adding one to the inside of a jacket or parka. Add one to the back of a jacket you will wear when not carrying a pack. Pockets added to sleeping bags are handy for storing items removed from pants pockets at night. You might want to sew a pocket on your tent wall or add a map pocket to the flap of your pack.

For these pockets you will need to purchase extra fabric, thread, snaps,

*Most **customizing** is decorative and involves adding yokes, stripes made from bias tape, or colored cording in seams. Some kit users add intricate crewel embroidery or appliqued designs. Customizing is also done to increase utility, as in the jacket above, left, which has removable sleeves (held in place by Velcro). Adding synthetic fur increases warmth.*

110

Start with a kit, end with a flair

zippers, or Velcro. Kit manufacturers offer these raw materials so you can match the fabric in your kit. Many of the materials you will need are also readily available at sewing stores, although perhaps it is best to purchase fabrics themselves from the kit dealers. Many dealers do not sell less than a full yard, but, if you can visit a kit store, you may find a suitable small remnant for sale.

Another advantage of customizing is the opportunity to change construction details. You might prefer knit cuffs to elastic ones or want to omit that collar piece you will not need. You can omit the drawstrings at the bottom of a jacket and add an inch to its length. You can substitute a heavier zipper, or put short zippers in the side seams.

Sleeping bags can be customized with a pocket at the head for stuffing a jacket into, thus creating a down pillow at night. Parents of small children have substituted quick-drying polyester filling in the bottom of the children's bags to minimize the problems bed-wetting can create. One mother designed a bag connected by two zippers, so that the bottom could be separated from the top for washing.

As your appreciation for quality gear and quality upkeep grows, and as you learn to take better care of your gear, it will take better care of you. This ensures a better outdoor experience. I was really surprised on a trail ride to discover that I was the only one who had brought sewing equipment. It was borrowed constantly to repair ripped knees and holes in pockets. One person needed to sew up the entire side of a sleeping bag because the zipper had broken. Had it been winter, the broken zipper could have had dire consequences. No camper should ever go so unprepared into the wilderness. Accidents do happen, and a repair kit may be as crucial as a first aid kit.

My family combines the sewing and first aid kits in one large coffee can with a plastic lid and carries it in a special stuff bag. Our basic repair kit's contents are listed on page 113.

A much smaller repair kit will do for super-light, short trips. Our kit is made of felt and contains threaded needles, a button, a few pins, and several nylon tape patches. It also has a pair of boot laces or a hank of nylon cording. The complete kit for first aid and repairs just fills a band-aid box.

Whether we are going on short or long trips, before setting out we check the emergency kit to see that it is fresh and complete. For example, we replace the thread that was used on the last trip and check the matches to see if they have deteriorated.

Down-filled garments and sleeping bags are the items that most often need immediate repairing on the trail, and repairing them requires more care than repairing other types of clothing. Don't let a rip or burn hole in any down garment go unrepaired; you'll lose the down through the hole. Mend it immediately — and carefully. In real emergencies, scotch tape or masking tape works for short-term repairs. But it is best to use the special pressure-sensi-

Repair tears in nylon tents with ripstop mending tape. Either round the corners of the tape, or overcast around the patch with needle and thread, or both. If the tear is in an area of strain, apply an X of tape on both sides of the fabric.

tive tape made for repairing nylon. It is available in several colors at most sporting goods stores. You can also order it from camping equipment supply catalogs. Before putting on the patch, round off the corners so it will be less likely to pull off. Even then these patches do not always stick well; overcasting around the patch with thread and needle will keep it on for good. Remember not to bunch up the fabric or ruin it with too many holes through which down might escape.

Very small tears may be mended by simply bringing the edges together and overcasting them. Move all of the down out of the way, pinch the fabric together, sear the edges *very* carefully with a burning candle or match, *then* sew the edges together.

Scrap nylon is available at some stores and can be taken on trips or used at home to patch large tears. If you need to sew a large patch, be careful not to catch down on the needle or thread because the plumules may be pulled through the needle holes. A small curved needle is best for this job.

A very common problem in down items is the little bit of down that works its way through the fabric shell. Do *not* pull it out. You may extract a whole plumule or even several plumules. Either pull it back into the garment by pinching the down from the backside or clip it off close to the fabric.

Zipper failure is a fairly common trail nuisance. Stuck zippers can be prevented by rubbing a little candle wax along the teeth. Zipper repair kits are available at some kit stores. If you don't have one when your sleeping bag's zipper breaks or jams permanently, you, too, may have to sew your bag shut and squirm in from the top. Of course, the same is true of any zippered garment. The ones that have Velcro or snaps in addition to a zipper are excellent buys for that reason.

Any patched garment or bag needs more care during washing or dry cleaning. The nylon tape patches may not stay on during the cleaning. The safest measure is to replace the temporary patch before sending the item to be cleaned. At least sew down the edges of a tape patch.

Tents are patched in several ways. The photograph on this page shows how to mend a nylon tent. Larger, heavier tents of poplin or canvas will probably require a tent-patching kit. Sew together the cut or tear and then apply small patches to both sides of the tent with canvas cement.

Heavy carpet thread, large needles, and a thimble are necessary for some tent jobs where reinforcing tapes have been ripped out. Sometimes grommet-setting tools are needed to reset grommets that have been pulled out. On the trail, you can improvise a grommet by putting a small, smooth stone on the inside of the tent, pinching the fabric together around it from the outside, and tying it with a hank of nylon cord. Floors of tents need the appropriate rubberized or treated fabrics for patching. At home, all machine stitching should be back-stitched or bar-tacked, and all stitching areas should be waterproofed with seam sealant.

Mosquito netting tears easily. For patching, the best substitute for more of the netting is several layers of the nylon net used for making petticoats and veils for hats. It is sold in fabric stores. A few 12- or 15-inch squares of net can be useful additions to your repair kit. Pin the patch in place and then stitch around the edges of the patch and the tear.

On the trail, taking care of your equipment means not abusing it in the first place. Place your tent as far away as possible from an open fire. A few windblown sparks can ruin a good nylon tent very quickly. Tents have been known to go up in flames in just a matter of seconds. At times you will need to move your tent or douse your fire.

Obviously, tents should not be used as kitchens. The dangers of a tent's catching on fire from stove flareups and of carbon monoxide poisoning are very real. There are also the nuisances of condensation and spillage. If bad weather forces you to cook inside, take special care. Refuel and light the stove outside. Put a firm, level base underneath the stove to help keep the pot from toppling; keep the tent's vents

Good care adds miles to your gear

open to help control carbon monoxide and condensation. When you do spill soup or drop crumbs, clean up the mess immediately so it doesn't get tracked all over the tent floor, soiling sleeping bags and clothing.

Most campers insist that tents should not be washed, but there is no harm in carrying a sponge or rag to wipe up dabs of food. A small brush or whisk broom is also useful for such chores. Sweep the floor after setting up and before taking down your tent, as sand and dirt are very abrasive. It is common practice among tent campers to remove their boots before entering the tent. Hiking boots can easily tear a tent floor. That is one reason so many people carry a light pair of booties or soft moccasins to wear around camp.

Before putting up the tent, check the ground for sharp stones, pine cones, and sticks. Pine pitch is also a problem. Once it gets on the bottom of the tent floor it gets spread everywhere on the tent when it is packed. If possible, carry a plastic ground sheet to place under the tent. The plastic should be a few inches smaller than the tent floor. If it sticks out from underneath, it encourages water to seep under the tent. If your tent gets wet from dew, try to dry it in the sun before you pack it.

Heat is the most dangerous enemy of leather boots. Drying out wet boots by the campfire or standing too near the fire while trying to warm up your toes cooks the leather, causing it to shrink. The welts may eventually crack and break.

Dampness and mud are also hard on leather. When mud dries, it dries out the leather. Muddy boots, especially the stitching in their welts, should be cleaned immediately with a twig and dried slowly. Many hikers simply change into dry wool socks and allow the boots to dry on their feet. I have seen hikers remove their socks at a stream crossing, wear their boots across, and then put their socks back on and resume hiking.

To wash a down sleeping bag, prescrub dirty areas, put it in a tub of lukewarm water with mild, nondetergent soap or special down soap, and push the bag up and down gently. Never twist or wring the bag; doing so destroys seams, baffles, and down plumules. And don't pick it up by one end. The weight of the soaked down will rip out the delicate baffles. Drain the water from the tub without removing the bag. Add fresh water several times until it remains clean. You need to rinse out all the soap or the down will mat and lose its insulating capability. Drain the last rinse water and gently press the water out of the bag. Gather the bag to you, supporting all the weight in your arms.

To wash in a machine, prescrub, close the zipper, then put the bag in a front loading machine, not a top loading agitator. Use a fine fabric setting and half the normal quantity of soap. Repeat the rinse cycle twice.

A home dryer is too small for bags. Place the bag in a large net or mesh bag to drip dry for a while, then take it to a commercial laundromat. Put it in a large dryer set at low and add a clean pair of rubber sneakers to break up the down clumps and create static electricity, which increases loft. Occasionally stop the dryer and fluff the bag by hand, separating any clumps of down. When the bag no longer has clumps of down and fluffs as it does normally, it is dry. Take the bag out, give it another good fluffing, and then air it in the sun.

Repair Kit

Adhesive tape, for plastic and tarps
Ripstop nylon mending tape
Thread, 1 regular, 1 heavy duty
Needles, several sizes, one curved
Safety pins, assorted sizes
Buttons, 4 or 5
Nylon netting, to repair bug netting
Nylon cord, for lashing broken parts,
    boot laces
Light-gauge wire, for pack repairs
Zipper repair kit
Candle, to wax zippers, sear nylon
Small pliers
Small scissors
Clevis pins, for pack repairs
20-penny nails, for extra tent stakes

Sleeping bags are less durable than boots or tents and require the ultimate in considerate care. Again, preventive measures are best. It is helpful to put sheet-like liners in bags to absorb the body oils and moisture that otherwise would soil the bag itself. Wash the liners after every trip.

Trailside care begins with carrying the bag in a sturdy, waterproof stuff sack. Keep your down dry! It loses its lofting qualities when wet, and it takes an extremely long time to dry, perhaps several days. But remember, fires are not the answer to drying out a bag: campfire sparks can melt the nylon shell in seconds. On the trail, sun and air drying are the only solutions.

Handle your bag carefully at all times. Don't sit on stuff sacks with the sleeping bags inside; it compresses the down, perhaps damaging its loft. Unstuff a bag gently so as not to tear out the delicate inside baffles that separate the down into tubes. Shake and fluff up the bag and give it an hour or so to restore its loft before crawling into it. In the morning, open up the bag and air it out. Then carefully stuff it into the sack, foot first, allowing the air to escape out of the top of the bag. Rolling it compresses the down in the wrong way.

The care your gear receives at home is as important as the care it receives on the trail. Careless storing can ruin equipment as much as abusive use can. And it is needless! The proper methods of care are simple to learn and easy to carry out.

Tents should never be stored when wet because they become musty and mildewed; cotton tents may even rot. Your tent should be erected at home after every trip and allowed to dry thoroughly, even if this means setting it up in the garage or basement. This is the time to spot-clean and check for tears or worn parts.

You may occasionally want to re-seal the seams of your waterproof tent fly with a commercial seam sealer, especially if you have noticed any leakage. Cotton tents may be water-proofed by spray-on or paint-on compounds.

Tents are most easily stored in the compact, rolled form in which they are carried. Wrap them around clean tent poles and store them inside a tent bag. Do not store them in damp or hot places, as both conditions are hard on nylon. Pegs should be cleaned and counted and then stored in a small bag with the tent.

Once back home, clean your boots before storing them. Check for scratches, cuts, and gouges. Epoxy may be used to fill even deep ones. Many hikers apply a sealant to welts and seams and waterproof the uppers of their boots before storing them. You might also check for loose tongues, broken stitches, and worn soles. At the end of the season is a good time to have boots resoled for next year and to add inner soles.

Once the repairing and leather conditioning is complete, store your boots in a dry place. Heat from furnaces or hot water heaters is just as harmful as the heat from fires, so don't store your boots near them. Stuffing your boots with wads of newspaper or paper towels helps keep them dry, and inserting boot presses helps keep the toes from curling up.

Store down bags loosely, either hung on wooden hangers or folded flat on shelves. Some people prefer to fold their bags inside large pillow cases, sail bags, or boxes.

After a long season of use, your bag will be dirty inside and out, despite your carefulness. So you have to make the big decision. Do I send my bag to the cleaners or do I wash it myself? Actually, it really is not such a difficult decision, once you know the facts.

Down contains natural oils, and it absorbs body oils. How do you clean the latter without destroying the former? Dry cleaning *can* be done, but it is risky. Even mild fluids destroy the natural oils. There is also a very real danger in using a dry-cleaned bag without properly airing it first. You can develop a skin rash or become fatally ill from sleeping in an unaired bag just back from the cleaners.

Then, you may ask, why do some bag manufacturers recommend dry cleaning? Because, they tell me, too

many bag owners are afraid to wash a bag, and the manufacturers know that many of us do it incorrectly.

If you insist on dry cleaning, find the best cleaner in town who is experienced with down. Inquire at your camping store, or ask members of your local camping club. Do *not* just leave your bag at the nearest cleaners! Ask the person at the cleaners questions before you leave your bag. Be sure he will *not* use any chlorinated hydro-carbons, such as the common one called "perk" — perchloroethylene. Only leave a bag with a cleaner who will use a mild petroleum-based agent, such as Stoddard solution. On its return, air the bag for at least a week.

But, instead of worrying about how good a job the dry cleaner will do, why not wash the bag yourself? It's not such an ordeal. All you need are a large tub and a commercial dryer.

If you own a sleeping bag filled with polyester, your washing chores are much earier. Polyester-filled bags are machine washable — indeed, they must *never* be dry cleaned. Dry cleaning fluids harm the fibers. The washing instructions on the labels of polyester-filled bags urge you to hand wash the bag in warm water and with mild soap, being careful not to wring the bag. To wash and dry the bag in machines, follow the instructions given on page 113 for washing down bags, but omit putting tennis shoes in the dryer.

Taking good care of your sleeping bag and other equipment obviously has its practical benefits. The equipment lasts longer and serves you better, saving you from needless expense, inconvenience, and discomfort. It also has its subtler aspects. Caring for your equipment affects your attitude towards the rest of your environment. If you habitually keep your gear in good shape, you probably will be concerned to leave the wilderness beautiful for those who follow.

The Gene Garris family of Estes Park, Colorado reap the rewards of making camping gear from kits: saving money; knowing that their tent, packs, vests, parkas, and sleeping bags are of topnotch, best-quality construction; and having the satisfaction of saying, "We made them ourselves."

Float a wild river

Ed Park

Five adventurers (above) float down the Snake River on a raft named The Mug *to explore its 25-million-year-old course through Hells Canyon (opposite) which separates Oregon on the left and Idaho on the right. Relaxing after shooting a rapids in the deepest gorge in America, the adventurers take turns rowing toward the next white water. The extra oar lashed to the side of the rubber boat is just one safety precaution taken by Hank Miller (facing camera, far right), who abandoned an engineering career in nuclear safety systems to form his own outfitting business. The Mug* is one of four rafts he brought on this six-day float from Hells Canyon Dam to the Grande Ronde River. The 26 passengers, including the author and his wife, Lue, find it an exciting and unique way to explore wilderness without diminishing it for others.*

Look, two deer!'' Lue whispered. All eyes followed my wife's pointing finger to the rocky hillside above the river. A mule deer doe and her large fawn were browsing peacefully on some brush, and all conversation in the boat ceased as we broke out binoculars for a closer look. These were the first large mammals we had seen on our float trip, and for some of the guests from eastern states, the first-ever sighting of mule deer. The huge ears of this species amused those who were more familiar with the dainty ears of the eastern whitetail.

Until now on this first day of our trip down the Snake River through Hells Canyon the exciting moments had been provided by the river itself. We had shrieked our way through three rapids that buffeted our small rubber rafts, splashed us, and whetted our appetites for more.

As the current carried us away from the deer, I gradually became aware of a new sound from far downriver—a deep, distant, muffled roar. My first thought was of thunder reverberating against the Canyon walls. I gave Lue a puzzled look and noted she too, was straining to listen. The skies were clear, so it couldn't be thunder. Lue's eyes widened and my neck-hair bristled as we realized simultaneously that that far-off, ominous thunder was the next rapids. Obviously this one would not be a dancing, laughing riffle like those we'd already experienced, but a full-blown, white-water rapids of immense power.

A glance at the other three passengers in our raft told us that they, too, were aware that the mood of the river was about to change. Yet we could see nothing ahead except placid water. From the low viewpoint of a raft, rapids are not visible until you are right upon them. A deaf person could be swept into them before he realized they were there. A glance at Hank Miller, our boatman and outfitter, produced a knowing, ''I told you . . .'' smile. ''Wild Sheep,'' he announced, anticipating our question. ''It's a *good* one.''

For long minutes we all sat silent, straining to see what we could so plainly hear. For a good half-mile we floated without speaking, listening to the growing thunder of the unseen rapids.

Hank Miller (pointing at left) and his crew study Granite Creek Rapid, the roughest water of the 79-mile trip. Although they know the river well, the boatmen stop at each rapids to scout the safest route through the boiling waves and hidden rocks. Even minor changes in the water level can affect the way a rapids should be run. It takes time and experience to tell whether a "hole" in the white water is caused by a submerged rock, a fall in the river bed, or a back-curling standing wave. Besides identifying hazards, boatmen look for the V-shaped smooth tongue of fast water that indicates the path of the main current. Using a river difficulty scale of 1 to 10 known as the Colorado System, the boatmen rate the Idaho side (at left) 8 or 9, promising maximum excitement and some risks. To the relief of their passengers, the decision is to hug the Oregon shore below. Although the crew peg it at only 5 or 6, the safer route yields an exciting ride. Here the boatman backrows to slow the raft's progess into a standing wave.

Then there they were! River-swept boulders, boiling white spray, standing waves, and the awesome roar of powerful water in full turbulence. Since Lue and I were in the bow, we would be the first to catch the impact. We squirmed nervously, tugged at the safety ropes, tightened our life jackets, braced our feet, and prepared to hang on. Were we really about to plunge headlong into that seething, rock-bound chute?

Then with immense relief we realized that Hank was pulling strongly toward shore. He beached the raft just upriver from the first fast water, jumped ashore, and tied us up. The other boats pulled in above us in turn. As we all scrambled ashore, Lue shouted, "I thought we were going to shoot right through!" Hank shouted back that they always stop at all major rapids to look them over and decide how they should be run.

Grateful for our reprieve, we followed Hank and the crew along the bank to a point directly above the frothing river. When they had agreed on a plan, Hank explained it to the rest of us. "We'll head down just to the right of that huge flat rock, then pull hard to the right to miss those two big curlers coming out from that rocky point." I'm sure some of the more timid souls would have turned back right there, if there had been any choice.

We climbed aboard, slowly, and braced ourselves as best we could while Hank strained on the oars to propel us into the right position for a wild ride. Almost immediately we were sucked into the fast-water slick above the rapids.

We were in it! The crashing waves looked far bigger than they had seemed from the shore and the roar drowned out any other sounds, except our own shouts, as the raft was tossed about like a leaf. First spray, then solid, green water hit us from both sides, overwhelming us with a feeling of helplessness in the face of such power. We raced past huge rocks and walls of water, then plowed straight into the face of a standing wave. The bow seemed to be pulled under. We were completely engulfed as the wave crashed over the entire raft. I could dimly hear squeals, gasps, and excited screams, punctuated by Hank's whoops and hollers.

Then we popped free, sputtering and laughing and dripping. But now as we drifted free of the rapids, Hank pulled ashore with the aid of an eddy, giving us a grandstand seat from which to watch the others coming through. Somehow it didn't look nearly as fearsome from a safe sideline, but, judging from the squeals and shouts, those in the turbulence were as filled with fear and joy as we had been moments before.

During the rest stop some of the group dug into the waterproof containers for dry clothes and made a quick change. The rest of us just sloshed around in our wet ones, knowing the hot Hells Canyon sun would soon dry us out. We had been advised to wear old clothes and shoes that could take the soakings, and all such valuables as watches, purses, and wallets had been carefully stowed away. After a few more rapids none of us would worry about getting wet and would either wear rain suits if the weather was cool, or let nature take care of drying us.

We pulled ashore early that first afternoon to set up camp at an abandoned homestead on the Idaho side. Lue and I soon had our tent up and joined the others around the campfire. While Hank and his men cooked supper we began to learn more about each other. We had already enjoyed talking with the people in our boat—John Pier, a dentist, and his wife, Jane, and Jane's mother, Carye-Belle Henle, all from New Jersey. Riding in another boat were the Piers' sons, Jeff, 15, and Johnny, 13. Now we learned that our white-water initiation had also been shared with a nurse, two doctors, two occupational therapists, a psychiatric social worker, a chemical engineer, a radio technician, a salesman, a traffic manager, a student, and a retired submarine captain. We had come from all parts of the country just to ride an untamed river.

More guests, carrying apples they had picked from the trees, remnants of some homesteader's dream, joined the campfire circle. Hank commented that the ripe apples had attracted black bears here recently, but stressed that bears are infre-

quent visitors to Hells Canyon and that there is virtually nothing to fear from wildlife on such a trip. The most likely danger is from rattlesnakes, and he warned us to be careful when out collecting wood, scrambling around the rocks, or exploring in brushy areas.

Dinner that first night was broiled salmon steaks, potatoes and gravy, frozen peas, hot biscuits with butter and honey, dessert and coffee, tea or milk. It was the first of many good meals to come. We never solved the mystery of how the boatmen could produce such delicious meals day after day from the few food boxes they carried on our rafts.

During dinner we asked John and Jane Pier how they, from far-off New Jersey, had happened to choose a trip down the Snake River. "Well, technically, John and I are not on this trip," Jane laughed. Her husband and her mother exchanged smiles and John explained.

"Every year since our four boys were little, Jane's mother has taken them on some sort of birthday trip. She has taken them to the Museum of Natural History, a Columbia University football game, and professional baseball games. Four years ago she took our older sons, Greg and David, on a float trip down the Missouri River in Montana. Jeff and Johnny have been impatiently awaiting their turn ever since. When the three of them chose this trip, Jane and I were a bit apprehensive about such a rugged venture, so we decided to come along."

"The boys really objected," his mother-in-law put in, "but I calmed them down by promising we would ride in another boat and pay no attention to their parents." We were amazed at the spunk of Mrs. Henle who, at 76, took all the rapids, sleeping on the ground, and unexpected discomforts in stride. The explanation, of course, was that she has always been an active outdoors person, beginning with summers as a camp counselor, and then taking canoe trips through the Adirondacks' and in northern Maine and hiking trips in other regions. "Now," she said, "I no longer backpack or paddle, but I float very well."

On our second day afloat we made an early stop to look at some Indian pictographs. Back on the river at Dug Bar, Hank told us we were at the very spot where the famed Nez Perce, Chief Joseph, crossed the Snake River during his running battle with the U.S. Cavalry in 1877. We could almost see the great chieftain and his harassed followers, struggling desperately to elude their pursuers in the vastness of this immense canyon.

These frequent daytime stops gave all of us some time to do as we pleased. Some got out their cameras while others relaxed and drank in the scenery. Some sat in the sun to read while others went exploring. Lue and I proved to be the most

A chain line (below) moves a mountain of duffel from rafts to campsite (below, center). The visitors choose their own sites and pitch the tents provided by Hank. The leisurely camp schedule encourages swimming, fishing, hiking, or loafing until the supper bell summons everyone to the campfire. There they remain as darkness falls early, blotting out the harshly eroded volcanic landscape (left) that rises nearly 8,000 feet above the campfire's glow in the heart of the Canyon.

121

The campers are thrilled at the sight of a golden eagle (left) riding the first warm up-drafts and beginning its search for jack rabbits or for rodents such as the gopher or marmot also hunted by the rattlesnake below—and by the cougar (opposite, right) when larger mammals elude its stealthy spring. Early-rising anglers also find evidence at the water's edge (opposite, left) of nocturnal competition from the raccoon for its share of the Snake's bounty.

avid anglers of the crew. We did not catch so much as a glimpse of the giant white sturgeon, a 400-pound freshwater species that still roams the Snake, but the small-mouth bass and crappie that we and others did land provided fresh fish hors d'oeuvres for several meals.

Each day we switched around from boat to boat, riding with different boatmen and getting better acquainted with our fellow floaters. By the third day we were beginning to feel a little safer about running the rapids. Even though the hand pumps were in almost constant use unloading the gallons of water that cascaded into the rafts at each rapids, our confidence was growing that we *would* get through the trip safely. The seats in the bow which guaranteed the best soaking became the choice spots. In fact, we were beginning to anticipate the white water with more pleasure than fear until we came to Waterspout Rapids. There we saw the wisdom of all of Hank's safety measures, especially his uncompromising command that everyone wear a life jacket at all times on the river. Up against some rocks on the Oregon side, a jet boat lay wrecked and empty. All passengers had been rescued unhurt thanks to the life jackets they were wearing. But somebody had done something wrong and the power of the river had taken command.

Hank and his boatmen also had strong feelings about littering. At each campsite, every scrap of paper or other refuse, no matter how small, was picked up. Gradually everyone got into the act, even picking up litter left by former visitors and putting it in containers to go out with us. We left behind only our footprints in the sand—to be erased by the next rain.

In the quieter stretches of the river we did a good bit of birdwatching. Easterners were especially delighted to add the American merganser, chukar partridge, and canyon wren to their life lists. They were also pleased to find old friends—the robin, mourning dove, and crow. While running a small riffle the second day, an avid birder from the East suddenly exclaimed, "Did you see that bird? It fell in the water! He'll drown!"

Hank explained that it was a water ouzel and that it could swim. At that moment the chunky, dark-gray bird popped to the surface, swam around in tight circles a moment, then dove again. This amazing little bird, found mainly along fast-flowing streams of the western mountains, became one of our favorites. Also called the dipper, it perches on stream-side rocks, bobs up and down, then suddenly dives into the riffles to "fly" along the bottom in search of aquatic insects; its wings are partially spread to act as fins to hold its body down and let the current flow over it.

Our attention was pulled skyward one morning when a guest, shading his eyes with one hand and pointing with the other, asked "What kind of hawk is that?" A large, dark, majestic bird with a wingspread of about seven feet was soaring along the craggy Canyon rim; then it spiraled slowly upward, effortlessly riding a thermal updraft.

"A golden eagle," I replied. Not a word was spoken as everyone craned to see this great bird, the king of all North American hunting raptors. For several members of our party it was another first. The look on their faces told Lue and me that they felt they'd seen something very special.

Hank Miller catches boatman Don Ahlert off guard (below), and the ensuing water-fight drenches the innocent, including Carye-Belle Henle (far left) and her grandson Jeff Pier (far right, facing camera). Frequent waterfights provide relief from the 100-degree heat. In quiet waters (left) guests learn to use the oars. Some, like Barbara Sopp (opposite, far left), gain enough competence to man the oars through mild "face slapper" rapids.

At each campsite, we all helped gather wood for our evening fire. At the Robinson Gulch campsite, on our fourth evening, Johnny Pier was helping Mark the boatman when he suddenly called out, "Mark! Here's a snake!"

Mark dropped his armload of wood, grabbed a stick, and ran to Johnny's side. There, coiled a few feet from Johnny, was a three-foot rattler. Mark had evidently handled many snakes, for he deftly pinned the snake's neck to the sand with a stick, then calmly reached down and picked it up with a firm grip behind its head.

After everyone had a good look at the rattlesnake, Mark hiked off downriver with it. He released it well away from the camp area. Mark had no more than returned when other guests found a second rattlesnake in a pile of driftwood on the beach. This one was also hauled off downriver by Mark and released. Mark's philosophy seemed to be that it was we who were the intruders here. From then on, wood gathering was done with great caution.

By now everyone was feeling at home on the river and was ready to agree with Huckleberry Finn that you can "feel mighty free and easy and comfortable on a raft." Although a few people went swimming every day, eventually most of the party was jumping overboard for a swim now and then—always wearing their life jackets, of course. They'd drift along beside the boats, hang onto the trailing ropes and be towed, or even free-float through some of the less-violent rapids. In or out of the boats, we were becoming attuned to the rhythm of the river—calm, turbulent, then calm again.

We were also given an opportunity to learn to row the boats, mostly through the longer quiet stretches. This gave the boatmen welcome rests from the oars and gave each of us a new experience. Rowing is hard work, but there's nothing like being on the oars to feel the surge of the river in even the more gentle rapids and to gain a tremendous respect for its awesome power—and how little you can do to counter it. It was especially satisfying to see Jeff and Johnny Pier learning how to handle those big oars, to read the paths of bubbles in the water to follow the main current, and to use the eddy currents to help them pull ashore.

On the fifth day, we were floating through placid water in a narrow stretch where the vertical canyon walls rose more than a mile above us, when somebody spotted painted letters high on the rocks on both sides of the river.

"Those mark the proposed site of the High Mountain Sheep Dam," Hank explained.

"Here?" incredulous voices asked.

"Yes." Hank continued, "If we lose the fight to the power companies, this will be the site of one of two dams planned for this stretch."

This was August, 1975. In previous conversations we had found ourselves unanimously opposed to any more dams on the Snake River. (There were 17 already in place.) Indeed, it was the threat of another dam that had moved some of us to take this trip. But seeing the very spot where the dam might be built brought the idea crashing down on us with full force.

We'd just come through miles of spectacular scenery, wild rapids, and intriguing side canyons full of trees and wildlife, and had experienced the intense silence and solitude found only in wilderness. The thought of a colossal concrete

Indian pictographs challenge Lue Park (above) to decipher a message from the past. Conservationists rejoice that the message of the latterday graffiti below—engineers' markings for the location of a High Mountain Sheep Dam across Hells Canyon —never got through. A 1967 Supreme Court decision rescinded the Pacific Northwest Power Company's license to build, and in 1975 Congress established the Hells Canyon National Recreation Area instead. Visitors now may roam its 662,000 acres, and scientists have unhurried access to remnants of nearly 200 Indian villages and campsites. They may yet unravel the story of 8,000 years of human survival amid such rock-hosted beauty (opposite) as ferns, lichens, cheat grass (lower right), and miner's lettuce (lower left).

dam drowning forever all those miles of Canyon behind us—*our* Canyon—was impossible to comprehend or accept. How could anyone justify to himself the destruction of such a wealth of unique ecosystems? Many of us had helped fight for the preservation of Hells Canyon before, by writing letters to officialdom and attending protest meetings, but our involvement had been rather remote compared with our feelings at this moment.

Jane Pier said, "Whenever I have read about building dams out West, I could never understand what the commotion was all about. In the East, lakes are really desirable, and too often rivers and streams are polluted. I now see that the West is different. I'd feel as badly about damming this part of the Snake as I would about developing the last little corner of countryside in New Jersey." Later, in a letter to Lue and me, she wrote, "If I gained nothing else from the trip, I gained an appreciation of the wild rivers."

How much our few voices counted will never be known, of course, but five months after our trip, on December 31, 1975, President Ford signed the bill creating the Hells Canyon National Recreation Area and prohibiting any further dams in this, the nation's deepest gorge.

That afternoon Hank and the boatmen pointed out a mine entrance on the Oregon side that apparently had no access to it. Just a hole in the face of the cliff. "Bet you can't guess how they got to that mine," Hank challenged. Nobody could come up with a logical answer.

A quarter-mile or so below that point, we pulled ashore just above the mouth of Oregon's Imnaha River. As we beached, we were told to bring flashlights and wear walking shoes. A trail of sorts led upriver along the bank of the Imnaha. Several hundred yards above the river's mouth, we came to the entrance of an abandoned copper mine once owned by the Eureka Mining Company and actively promoted and explored at the turn of the century. The need for flashlights was obvious as we stepped from the bright noonday sun into the blackness of the tunnel. Immediately we felt a sharp drop in temperature.

Those without flashlights had to travel by groping. The tunnel had been blasted and dug through solid rock and appeared safe, though some people had an understandable uneasiness about being in such a place. We tripped over old, ore-cart rails on the floor, and deeper inside we found vertical shafts and hand-operated hoists. About 100 yards down from the entrance, we spotted a glow of light ahead. We stumbled on and found that glow to be an exit to the mine. It was high above the Snake River, where we'd just floated by, and Hank's puzzling question, "Bet you can't guess how they got to that mine," was finally answered. The mine tunnel had run completely through the ridge, forming a foot route between the Imnaha and Snake drainages.

Near the end of the sixth day we reluctantly pulled ashore for the last time, just below the mouth of the Grande Ronde River in Washington. Good company, excellent meals, and solitude had made it a trip we wished would never end.

In letters that have been exchanged since our trip, the amazing Carye-Belle Henle does not remember any hardships—she feels these were all borne by the staff. "Mud, rain, cold, and heat are all part of camping and make one more appreciative of the comforts of home," she wrote. She finished her last letter by saying she'd just been elected a member of the Kinnelon, New Jersey, Environmental Commission. I was not surprised that she would roll up her sleeves and dive into the hard work of protecting her urban environment with the same zeal she brought to enjoying a wild river. Jane Pier, on the other hand, recalls the trip as "luxurious —in not having to cook or plan anything, but just enjoy everything."

Lue and I feel we must go back to see the drama of seasonal change in the rich natural life of this remote and hauntingly beautiful canyon. And to enjoy again the three aspects of the trip which meant the most to 13-year-old Johnny Pier: "the wildlife, the feeling that all the things around are unspoiled, and the quiet, except for the steady sound of the river."

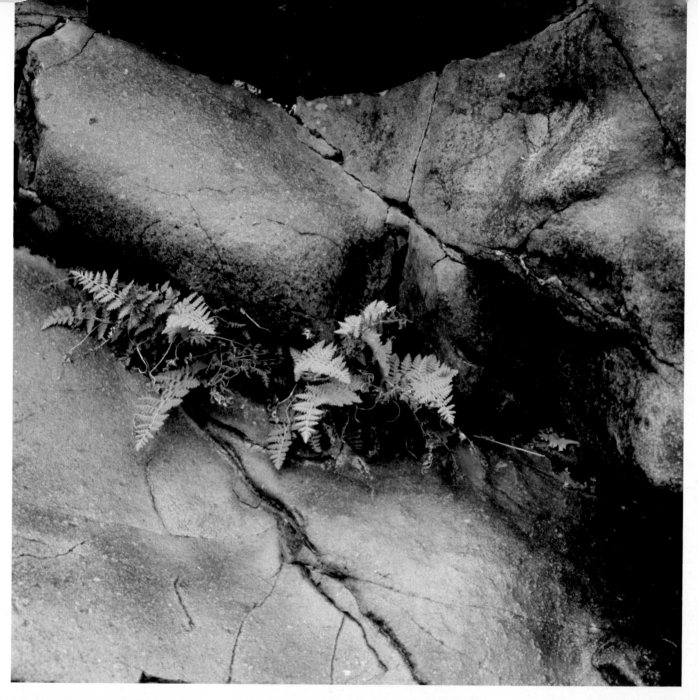

Weather can make or break an outing. Wise campers learn its warning signals.

BE PREPARED FOR THE UNEXPECTED

Anne LaBastille

One of the challenges of outdoor living is the element of the unexpected. Things *can* go wrong. You *may* become lost. Your companion *could* be injured. Weather *can* worsen. A bear *might* steal your pack. It's all part of the variety and excitement of being out in nature.

There are two basic requirements for staying safe and well in the wilds. The first is to be well-equipped and prepared, and physically and mentally ready for emergencies *beforehand*. The second is to meet whatever crisis arises with coolness and optimism. Dealing with outdoor problems is usually not a matter of muscle power, but of will power.

Before you leave on an outdoor trip, do four things. *First*, talk over with your companions all the things that could go wrong. Simulate injuries and act out first aid techniques. *Second*, camp in your back yard or a nearby public campground and try out equipment and food. At least one person in your group should be experienced in outdoor living and in first aid techniques.

Third, get yourself in shape. Jog, walk with your pack on, swim, do calesthenics. Any exercise that makes you huff and puff increases your lung capacity and strengthens your heart. Cut your toenails short and square.

Fourth, take medical precautions. Get tetanus and typhoid shots so you'll worry less about dirt in wounds and polluted water. Adapt your first aid kit so it is adequate to the area, season, and length of the trip. Tell your companion or the leader of your group if you are on any medication; if you are allergic to anything, such as bee stings; or if you are chronically ill with heart trouble, diabetes, or the like.

There are 12 major medical hazards that can occur outdoors and that someone in your party should know how to handle.

SEVERE BLEEDING: Immediately apply pressure with palm of hand over sterile or clean gauze or cotton pad, or press fingers on supplying arteries; elevate bleeding part above level of heart; keep pressure and padding on until bleeding stops; bandage securely. *Never* use a tourniquet except as a last resort and do not loosen it until hospitalized. (Write on patient's forehead the time it was applied.)

OPEN WOUNDS: Stop bleeding as directed above. If wound is only skin deep, wash with soap and water; if deeper, don't wash. Hold wound edges together; bandage.

FISHHOOKS: Don't try to pull out. *Push* barbed hook through and out skin; cut hook at either end with pliers; remove; treat as open wound.

BLISTERS: Wash with soap and water; prick at base with sterilized needle; drain fluid; apply antibiotic ointment, moleskin, and bandage.

BURNS: Relieve pain by submerging in cold water or applying cold packs; cover with moist bandage of clean cloth; give aspirin or pain killers; treat for shock; if not in shock, give sips of salt/soda solution (1 teaspoon salt, ½ teaspoon baking soda in 1 quart warm water) for deep, extensive burns. Do *not* use ointment, grease, spray, ice, salt, or any other preparation on burned area.

CHOKING, DROWNING, OR OTHER BREATHING FAILURE: See illustrations.

FROSTBITE AND HYPOTHERMIA: In frostbite, the skin of the extremities looks white or gray. Warm rapidly in warm water (102-105°F.); wash with soap and water; apply dry sterile bandage or clean cloth (only if transporting victim to medical aid); give victim warm liquids; elevate frostbitten part; keep patient indoors or in tent under warm blankets or sleeping bag, but prevent contact with frostbitten area. Do *not* rub or massage frostbitten areas. For hypothermia (subnormal temperature caused by the body's losing heat faster than it can generate it), see illustration on next page.

Know what to do

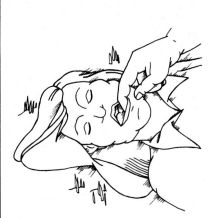

1. **When breathing stops,** act fast; in 4 to 6 minutes irreversible brain damage may occur. Place victim on back; remove foreign matter from mouth.

2. Tilt the head backwards as you lift under the neck to provide an open airway (keep the head in this position throughout); pinch nostrils shut.

3. Place your mouth around victim's mouth to form a tight seal. Blow in 1 breath every 5 seconds. Watch for chest to rise.

4. Turn your head sideways to listen for exhalations between blowings. Continue until victim begins breathing again or until you are exhausted.

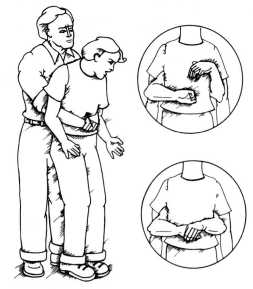

To assist a **choking person,** first strike victim's back four times with flat of hand. If choking continues, stand behind victim and wrap your arms around his waist above the navel. Make a fist with one hand and place its thumb side against the victim's stomach below his rib cage (near left, top). Grab your fist with your other hand (near left, bottom) and give 4 sharp upward thrusts (far left). This should clear the breathing passage. If not, repeat both procedures. If victim can't stand, lay him on his back; place your open hands, one on top of the other, below his rib cage; quickly thrust down and up toward the ribs.

First Aid Kit

Moleskin (for blisters)
Ace bandage, 4-inch (for sprains)
Bandaids, assorted sizes (for cuts)
Gauze bandages
Adhesive tape (two widths)
Eye cup (to dislodge particles)
Tweezers, needle (for splinters, ticks)
Kerchief (sling, constricting band)
First aid booklet
Padded board splints
Green soap or Phisohex (wash wounds)
Buffered aspirin or Tylenol
Empirin
Salt or salt pills (for heat exhaustion)
Baking soda (indigestion, stings)
Milk of Magnesia (laxative, indigestion)
Oil of cloves (toothache)
Syrup of Ipecac (to induce vomiting)

Water purification tablets
†Lomotil or Paregoric (diarrhea)
†Benadryl (allergic reactions)
Calomine (insect and plant rashes)
Rubbing alcohol (disinfectant)
*Snakebite kit
*Insect repellents
*Sunburn cream
†Neosporin ointment and opthalmic
   solution (wounds, eye infections)
†Antibiotics (pneumonia, bad
   infections)
†Pain killers (Talwin or Demarol)
†Tranquilizer or antihypertensive agent
   (muscle spasms, tension)

*Depending on country, climate
†Requires prescription

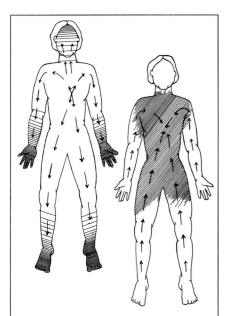

Normally, blood circulates to the extremities (above left). As the body chills, the blood vessels in the extremities constrict and blood concentrates in the body trunk (right). If the chilling continues, **hypothermia**—abnormally low body-core temperature—results. Untreated, it can cause death in 2 hours. Symptoms include fits of shivering, slowed mental responses, reduced coordination, and exhaustion. The treatment: warmth. If chilling is severe, have victim lie down between two warmth donors with bare skin in sleeping bag inside tent until normal temperature is restored. Give warm liquids (no coffee or alcohol). To prevent it, dress and eat properly, avoid overexertion, drink 2 quarts of hot fluids daily.

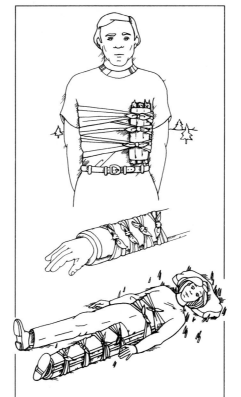

For **sprains, dislocations,** and **fractures,** elevate injured limb without disturbing injury. Don't wash, but cover open wound with sterile bandage. Don't set or align fractures or dislocations. Splint a dislocated or sprained joint to immobilize it. For a fracture, also immobilize the joints above and below the break with a padded splint made from tent poles or sticks. Treat for shock; give pain killers. Transport victim gently. Don't move suspected back or neck injuries.

FRACTURES, DISLOCATIONS, OR SPRAINS: See illustration at left.

HEAT EXHAUSTION OR STROKE: In exhaustion, skin is white and clammy, temperature is normal, victim is weak and dizzy. Lay the victim down; apply cool packs; give sips of salty water for 1 hour; rest for several days.

In heat stroke, skin is red and hot, temperature 105°F. or higher, pulse rapid. Undress victim immediately and cool body with cold water, rubbing alcohol, cold packs, or fanning until temperature falls below 102°F. Rest.

ANIMAL OR SNAKE BITES: Wash animal bite with soap and water or rubbing alcohol; apply antibiotic ointment and bandage. If infection starts, elevate bitten part, apply heat, give antibiotics, rest. If you suspect the animal is rabid, try to catch and confine to observe behavior or to kill and immediately take *undamaged* head and brain to nearest public health official for diagnosis. Rabies, after incubation period, is fatal.

Treat bites from nonpoisonous snakes as animal bites. For bites from poisonous snakes, kill the snake if possible. Have its victim lie down and keep calm. Keep bitten part lower than the heart. Apply a constricting band (not a tourniquet) 2 to 4 inches above bite to slow down venom absorption. Only if you can't get medical help within a couple of hours, make a straight incision just through the skin and never more than ½ inch long through each fang mark. Don't cut an X across each fang mark. To draw out venom, use suction cup from snakebite kit for one hour. Suck and spit out venom only as a last resort (you may have sores or cavities in your mouth). Cover area with cool compress. Treat for shock. Transport victim to hospital slowly—no running, alcohol, or stimulants. Reassure often. If you killed the snake, take it so the doctor can identify it for proper anti-venom serum.

SHOCK: Victim is pale, cold, clammy, weak; pulse faint and rapid (over 100); breathing fast; pupils may be dilated in advanced cases. Lay the victim down, keep warm but not hot, maintain an open airway by tilting head back and lifting neck. Stop bleeding; splint frac-

Cattail

Wild rosehips

Blueberry

Wild sunflower

Dandelion

Violet

tures; elevate extremities; give nothing by mouth. Reassure patient often. Get to doctor as soon as possible.

HEART ATTACK: If patient isn't breathing, give artificial respiration. Search patient for medicine or instructions about condition. If unconscious, give no fluids or food. Get medical help. Do *not* attempt cardiopulmonary resuscitation (CPR) unless trained.

Most of the foregoing medical problems could require transportation of the victim out of the wilderness. It's wise woodsmanship to know how to lift another person into the fireman and saddle-back carries; how to carry someone on two-handed and four-handed seats; and how to improvise a stretcher. Practice this at home. (See Bibliography for instruction books.) However, an improper evacuation can do great harm—especially with fractures. It may be best to leave the patient behind, resting in his sleeping bag inside a shelter with food and water, while you go for help. If possible, one or more people should stay with the victim.

Water is the most necessary of all requirements to sustain life. You can survive only two to four days without any in hot desert country. With water, you're good for ten days or more. Even in very cold climates, you need about two quarts per day; you need at least one gallon a day in the desert.

*These six **edible plants** are common in the wilderness. The young shoots of **cattails** taste like asparagus; their roots can be eaten raw or cooked, or dried to make flour. (Strip the outer skin off both shoots and roots.) The fruits of **wild roses**—rosehips— are ready to pick after the first frost. Super rich in vitamin C, rosehips have an apple- like flavor and are good eaten raw, boiled, or dried. The seeds of **wild sunflowers** can be roasted or parched and eaten or ground into meal. The more than 20 species of **blueberries** ripen from late June to Septem- ber, and all are edible. **Dandelion** greens and roots make a good-tasting, nutritious salad or cooked vegetable. Peel the outer layer off the roots first. You can use the leaves of **violets** in salads or stews. The flowers also make good trail snacks for a spring hike.*

No matter where you are, try to avoid dehydration. It confuses your thinking.

Since "a pint's a pound the world around," carrying several days' supply of water on your back is normally impossible. Where do you find water? Most rivers, lakes, and streams in the eastern United States below 1,500 feet (higher in the west) are potentially unsafe to drink untreated. Water must be boiled for 10 to 20 minutes (depending on altitude) or treated with water purification tablets for 30 to 60 minutes. Use only boiled or treated water for tooth brushing, dishwashing, and food preparation. At higher elevations, clear, fast streams are probably safe, as are recent rain pockets and true wilderness lakes and ponds. But usually it's wise to be wary of still waters.

Other sources of water are springs and seeps in dry stream beds or valley floors; under rocks and boulders at the bases of hills and in swampy or sandy depressions. Watch for birds flocking and for game trails that might lead to watering holes. Certain plants can help, such as large-leaved plants whose bases catch rainwater.

In snow country, water is everywhere. Clean snow can be eaten any time as a thirst quencher, but it will barely meet your body's requirements and will contribute to hypothermia if you are already chilled. Melting snow yields only about one fourth of the volume you start with. Water is best obtained from chopping a hole through the ice of a lake or stream. Throw in a wide-mouthed container attached to a cord (so *you* don't fall in) and pull it out full. Remember that just because it's freezing cold doesn't mean the water's pure. Heat, not cold, kills germs. Boil or treat the water.

Other emergency ways of finding water are squeezing body fluids from fish, mopping up rain or dew from metal surfaces or leaves, or collecting it in a plastic sheet. A solar still can be rigged up in the desert.

If you are without water, don't eat. Keep as quiet (and cool) as possible. Keep talking and panting to a minimum. In the desert, travel only at dawn, dusk, and night when it's cool and moist. Even in dire circumstances do

Nature's survival rations

Collecting dew is one way of getting water. Dew forms on the surfaces of cool objects at night. At dawn, use a piece of cloth to sponge up dew from leaves, pine needles, and rocks. Wring out the water into a container or your mouth and continue collecting. Or, scoop out a shallow pit, line it with plastic, and fill it with rocks cleaned of dirt (right). Dew will form on the rocks and collect at the low point of the plastic. At sunrise, remove rocks and drain plastic sheet.

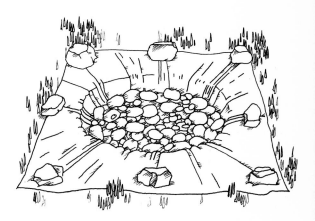

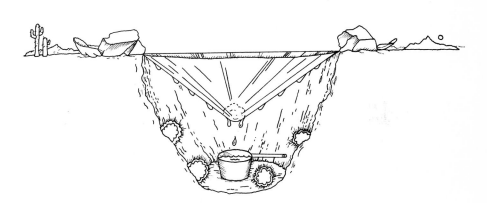

To make a **solar still,** dig a hole about 2 feet deep and 4 feet wide at the top. Put a container at the bottom and place chopped succulent plants along the sides. Drape a 6-foot-square, clear, plastic tarp over the hole, put a smooth rock in its center so that the rock hangs several inches above the container, and cover the edges of the tarp to form a tight seal. The moisture that evaporates out of the soil and plants condenses on the underside of the plastic and drips into the container.

A **barrel cactus** and parts of other succulent plants, like the pith in young stalks of agave, can help you slake your thirst if you are in desert country without water or the makings of a solar still. Slice off pieces of the barrel cactus and chew (but don't swallow) the pith. If you are walking out, you can carry slices with you. Another method (left) is to slice off the top of the cactus and mash the insides to a pulp with a stick. You then wring the pulp through some cloth—a clean bandana if you have one—to get the thick, drinkable juice. Some drinkable juice will collect at the bottom of the cactus. Be sure to use only green colored cacti; ones with areas of yellow may be infected with the larvae of moths and may be rotten inside.

Plants and animals to avoid

Rattlesnake

Copperhead

Water moccasin

Coral snake

*Watch for the **poisonous snakes** above. Keep hands and feet from burrows or ledges you can't see. Pit vipers hunt at night, using delicate heat sensors to home in on body heat. If you leave your tent at night, use your flashlight.*

not drink urine or seawater. The salt in them draws moisture from your body and increases dehydration. If you find a small, precious hoard of water, rather than taking a long draught, take little sips often.

A person can live for weeks without eating; however, one needs energy to be active. Even one meal a day is better than starving or nibbling. If you are lost and without food, nature can probably provide. Look for birds and eggs, porcupines, frogs and snakes, grasshoppers and dragonflies. turtles and lizards, crabs and mussels, termites and grubs. All are edible. Search along the high and low water marks of salt marshes, river banks, bays, and lakes. Also look along the edges of forests, fields, meadows, and fresh-water swamps. The best time to hunt is at dawn or dusk; the best locale, near water; the best weapons, a club, stone, or sharpened stick if you have nothing else.

With few exceptions, all animals are edible when freshly killed. Don't eat seafood or freshwater fish that is more than a few hours old. To catch fast game like rabbits and squirrels, place a snare or deadfall along a game trail or runway. (Consult the Bibliography for books having illustrations and instructions.) For fish and eels, use a simple hook and line, fish trap, or improvised net. You can use insects, worms, meat, bright bits of cloth, feathers, or metal scraps for bait.

There are many edible wild plants. Strips of the inner bark of birches, poplars, willows, and lodgepole pine can be chewed raw or cooked up in stews. Spruce needles can be brewed as tea for added vitamin C. Young twigs of evergreens are nutritious. Other nourishing wild foods or beverages include berries, rose hips, currants, cattails, waterlily and arrowhead tubers, wild leek bulbs, wild grapes, dandelions, young stems of fireweed, bamboo shoots, grass seeds, fern fiddleheads, cacti fruits, wild rice, boiled lichens,

and pine nuts. (See the Bibliography for identification guides.)

If you doubt a plant food, cook it, eat it sparingly, and watch for symptoms. If it tastes bitter or bad, spit it out or vomit it up. And avoid all mushrooms, puffballs, and plants with milky sap except dandelions and milkweed.

A wilderness meal can taste surprisingly good. As a registered Adirondack guide and instructor at wilderness workshops, I occasionally prepare a complete survival dinner for my students or clients. The most delicious we ever ate was gleaned from a swamp. It consisted of grilled bullhead and frogs' legs, roasted arrowhead tubers, boiled cattail stems, fresh raspberries, and Labrador tea.

The most sensible procedure, of course, is always to carry a small emergency food bundle with you when in the woods. In case you are lost or lose your pack, these light-weight, high-calorie tidbits can keep you fit for at least three or four days. Recommended items are: chocolate candy bars with nuts; beef jerky strips; space sticks; granola bars; gorp; small cans of pemmican or boxes of mincemeat; bouillon cubes or soup packets; tea bags; salted nuts; raisins; instant breakfast packets; powdered fruit drinks; salt; vitamin pills; and water purification tablets.

There are not many truly dangerous plants in the United States that can kill if eaten. Those that can cause skin irritation are few. The fly agaric and destroying angel *(Amanita)* fungi and toadstools should *never* be touched, let alone eaten. Water hemlock is also poisonous, especially the roots. The berries of ground hemlock, mistletoe, baneberry, moonseed, and buckthorn are *not* good for your tummy; neither are horse chestnuts. Steer clear of the fresh foliage of marsh marigold, horsetail, castorbean, wild cherry and plum trees. You should also stay away from the underground bulbs of fly-poison, death camas, and star of Bethlehem;

The common **plants that cause rashes** are fairly easy to identify. **Poison sumac** (above) is a shrub or small tree that grows in swampy places. Its leaflets have smooth edges and occur in opposing pairs (except for the end one). **Poison ivy** (center), to which approximately 50 percent of our pop-

ulation is susceptible, is noted for its clusters of three leaflets. In the fall, poison ivy bears small clusters of smooth, white berries, and its leaves turn brilliant red. **Poison oak** (right) looks much like poison ivy, except it is only an erect shrub, whereas poison ivy is also a climber and a trailing vine.

If you are exposed to any of them, the recommended relief is to remove contaminated clothing, rinse right away with lots of water, wash with soap for five minutes, and rinse again thoroughly. Apply rubbing alcohol, followed by Calomine lotion. Drink plenty of liquids. Don't scratch.

Many **inedible plants** look very appetizing. The poisonous fruits of the **moonseed** (top) look like edible grapes. You can tell moonseed by its single, crescent-shaped seed. The berries of **red baneberry** (bottom) and **white baneberry** look appetizing, but are

dangerous to eat. The foliage of some plants, like the **marsh marigold** (top), is poisonous when raw, but delicious when boiled in a couple of changes of water. Even a small bit of the white, gilled **destroying angel (Amanita Verna) mush-**

room may cause death. All parts of the **mayapple** (top, right) except its fruit are poisonous. The fruit is safe to eat once it has turned yellowish-green in late summer. The **bloodroot** (bottom, right) can cause muscular prostration, even death, if eaten.

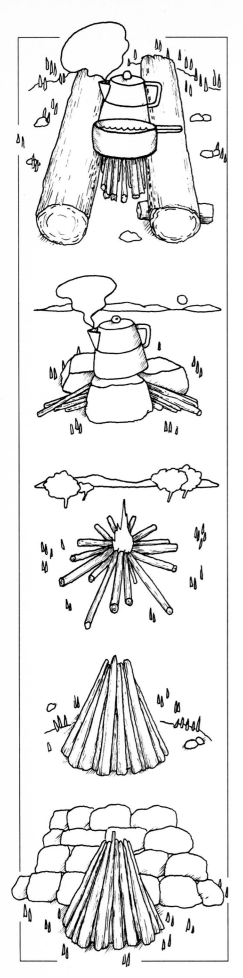

The most direct method of **starting a fire without matches** is to strike sparks into dry tinder—and hope it catches. Sometimes striking together the flat edge of a knife blade and a hard rock (right) or even two hard stones, will work. Hold the flint close to the tinder so the spark won't go out too soon.

The age-old method of friction makes use of a bow, a drill (dry stick), a socket that fits into the palm of the hand and holds the top of the drill, and a fireboard with a notch cut through it. Enough heat is produced by rotating the drill to make a spark fall through the notch and ignite the tinder.

Another method is to focus bright sunlight through a magnifying glass, camera lens, or eyeglasses—any convex lens—onto dry tinder. The point of light should be made as small as possible to increase heat. Carefully blow the spark into flames. This method requires the least practice for success.

Without matches, you have to have **tinder** to catch a spark and start a fire. Tinder may be made from finely shredded birchbark, dry moss, dry grass, dead pine needles, fuzz off pussy willows, fluff from cattails, lint from your clothes, beetle borings in wood, crumpled Kleenex, even dried animal dung shredded into tiny bits. Once the tinder flames up, put on **kindling** to nourish the small fire. Dry sticks "shaved" into thin curls (top, left) make good kindling. So do thin dead twigs (top, right), wood shavings (bottom, right), birchbark (bottom, left). Last, put on larger, longer-burning wood.

In an emergency, a **fire is needed** for cooking, signaling, and warmth. Above, left, are two cooking fires—low, with protection from wind and support for pots, using small pieces of fast-burning wood. The "Indian" fire (middle) adds cheer, the wigwam and reflector fires (bottom) add warmth.

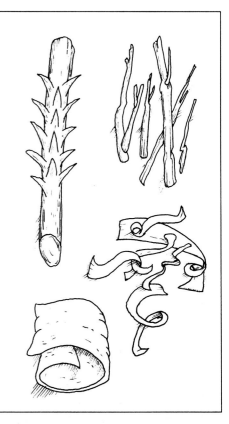

and the rootstocks of the mayapple, pokeweed, blue flag, bloodroot, and cowbane. Before attempting any wild food menus, it's wisest to go out with a botanizing friend or consult a good plant book.

Dangerous animals pose little threat to campers. All you need really worry about are rogue bears or bears with cubs, roving bands of peccaries or feral hogs, bull moose in the fall mating season, wild mammals with rabies, and poisonous snakes. Poisonous spiders are seldom met except in the desert or jungle. In general, no wild animal wants to attack humans unless it is molested, rabid, sick, or starving.

Your main protection is caution. Shy away from any animal that acts overly friendly, mixed up, or vicious. In bear country, bang metal plates together, sing, clap your hands, or wear a bell to give *them* fair warning of your presence. If you should unexpectedly meet a large animal on a trail or in a clearing, keep cool. Stand your ground and look at it for a moment, then walk slowly back towards where you came from. Subtle behavior at such moments will be carefully noted by any wild animal. Fleeing may be just the trigger that releases an attack. If rushed, climb a tree or play dead on the ground.

In all the animal kingdom, insects are probably the most annoying and threatening creatures. Consider the abundance of biting ants, bees, wasps, hornets, fleas, black flies, and chiggers —to name a few. You would be wise to prepare well for them, and pay less attention to reptiles and mammals. Be sure tent screening is intact or else carry a mosquito net, head net, gloves, and long-sleeved shirt. Always carry insect repellent in season. If you should forget or lose it, smear your face and hands with mud or, under extreme conditions, submerge yourself in water until dark. An excellent insect chaser is a smudge. Build a normal fire, then heap on green or rotting leaves, moss, punky wood, or any other smoke-producing material.

You should be aware if you are allergic to any specific insect before going to the boonies. I once almost lost a friend, a city dweller, who came to visit my Adirondack wilderness cabin during blackfly season. A few bites and her eyes swelled shut. A few more and her neck glands mushroomed and her lips puffed to twice normal size. We had to rush 25 miles to the nearest health clinic to obtain medical help. "Physician, know thyself" is good advice for the wilderness visitor.

When you find yourself without a tent, leanto, boat to crawl under, or wilderness cabin at hand, what can you do for shelter? Much depends on season and climate. In summer, there's seldom a life-threatening situation, unless severe thunderstorms or lightning prevail. But in late fall, winter, or early spring, making a shelter and fire take precedence even over finding water and food. They may be your sole protection against frostbite and hypothermia. In the desert, a shelter may prevent or retard dehydration, heat stroke or exhaustion, and sunburn.

A three-pole leanto is the fastest type of shelter to erect. Attach your poncho, plastic sheet, evergreen branches, bark slabs, grass bundles, or any other suitable covering to the framing. Larger and more elaborate leantos can be fashioned.

A word about sanitation around your shelter. Bury all human wastes. Merely dig 6 to 8 inches into the soil, or as deep as possible into snow, and cover with dirt, rocks, or snow. Also, burn sanitary napkins, tampons, greasy paper towels and dirty paper for sanitation and so they won't attract bears or raccoons. Pour soapy water and cooking grease into a hole in the ground and cover.

Before ever leaving on your outdoor excursion, you would be smart to practice using an ax, hatchet, and saw. Also learn to tie at least four basic knots— square, half hitch, slip, and bowline— and some simple rope lashing.

*Use a **downed tree** as a framework for a winter shelter. Add boughs and small trees.*

*Make **snow cave** entrance lower than main room. Poke hole in roof for cooking vent.*

*The hollow under a **conifer** can be walled in with branches, bark, or snow.*

*For **cold weather shelter,** be sure to face the door away from the wind and to ditch around the base if rain water could run in. Don't forget to cover the doorway. With just two human bodies and two candles, the inside temperature of a closed shelter will rise amazingly. It's best to sleep off the ground, if you can, on boughs, pine needles, dry moss, leaves, ferns, grasses, a plastic sheet or tarp—or on a crude cot made of poles in snake country. In summer, avoid swamps (wet and buggy), running water (flash flood risk), and tall, lone trees (lightning danger).*

137

Keep an eye on the weather

What To Do If Caught In A Lightning Storm

It Is Unsafe . . .

to climb on exposed rock

to stand on top of exposed hill

to swim or canoe or be in water

to wait under a lone tree

It Is Safer . . .

to crouch on foam insulation

to crouch between flat rocks

to be inside a deep, dry cave

to wait under a low clump of trees

Once your shelter is ready, a fire should be started on the side out of the wind or, in severe cold, on the inside. Avoid building it on moist ground or under snow-laden evergreen branches. A fire is very important: it provides warmth for cooking, melting snow, and purifying water; dries clothes and gear; repels insects; scares off animals; and serves as a signal and also as a psychological pick-me-up.

Without matches, a metal match, a flint and steel, or a cigarette lighter, making a fire can be extremely difficult and time-consuming, but it can be done by the ancient bow-and-drill method. Once your fire is going, seasoned hardwood gives the longest lasting results. The heavier the wood, the greater will be its heating power.

Be sure to start early enough in the afternoon to have both your shelter set up and plenty of firewood gathered before dark—including some stashed away in a dry, convenient spot for early morning use.

Unexpected bad weather can turn an outing into a frightening experience. It can kill. *Never* set out on a trip without checking both local and national weather maps and forecasts. Knowing the forecast will help you decide what clothing to take, the best menus to plan, which sleeping bag or tent to use. But you also need to be a bit of a weather prophet yourself. At the very least you should be able to recognize when a low front is moving in and to identify various types of clouds. Equally important is being willing to postpone or cancel your plans if things look bad.

Lightning kills between 90 and 150 people in the States every year, mainly in small towns and rural areas. Strikes on people are uncommon in the wilderness; nevertheless, you should stay away from mountaintops, ridges, and open fields. If in a canoe or boat (especially a metal one), immediately head for shore and get out. Look for flat places with young, bushy trees.

ostratus

Knowing how to detect thunder and lightning storms gives you time to prepare. The sequence of pictures at the right shows the **development of a thunderstorm.** Fair-weather **Cumulus humilis** clouds are shallow, scattered, and seemingly flattened, though ragged. As they progress into storm clouds, they increase in size and form **Cumulus congestus,** which have moderate to large domes or towers, with flat, level bases. The next stage is **Cumulonimbus**—thunderstorm clouds. In them, the domes stretch up to 40,000 feet or higher and often develop an anvil shape at the top. Set up camp in a protected place! More severe thunderstorms, high winds, hail, even tornadoes may accompany the less common **Cumulus mammatus** clouds. They resemble Cumulonimbus ones, except they bulge downward from their bases. Common fall and winter clouds are Nimbostratus (above)–which bring a dramatic drop in temperature, gusty winds, and rain or snow —and **Altostratus translucidus** (below)– which may be an early sign of snow.

ratus translucidus

Cumulus mammatus

Cumulus humilis

Cumulus congestus

Cumulonimbus

Avoid getting under tall, lone ones. Take off your backpack and anything else made of metal. Get off and away from your horse and crouch under a clump of low trees. In other words, do everything possible *not* to be a lightning rod.

When you hear a storm approaching, try to estimate how far away it is and how much time you have to seek shelter. Count the number of seconds between the thunder peal and the lightning flash. Divide that figure by five to get the miles of distance between you and the storm. Note the direction and apparent speed of the black clouds, and head for the most lightning-proof haven around.

The first commandment of going far afield is: never travel alone. Always tell a trusty friend, a local ranger, or game warden where your party is going, what route you will take, and when you'll be back. If you can't find anyone, put a message on your car windshield or at a trail-head, or sign the register often provided for hikers.

The second commandment is to double-check maps, compass, matches, emergency food and first aid kits, watch, and weather conditions just before leaving.

If you get lost, the ways to get found are to stay put or to try walking out. If you decide to wait for rescue, make a smoky signal fire, stamp SOS in the snow or spell it with rocks or logs, periodically fire a rifle three times, or flash your metal mirror at a passing plane. Remember that any pattern or sound of three means distress. In Morse Code, SOS is . . . - - - . . .

If you decide to start walking, take a hard look at nature's signposts and figure out which way is north and which way you want to travel. This assumes, however, that you studied both a road map and a topographic map before starting your trip, and that you've been paying attention to major landmarks and general direction of travel.

As you bushwhack your way out, go slowly and methodically. Save strength by going around obstacles, not over or through them. To keep from walking in circles, as human beings naturally do when finding their way intuitively, sight landmarks that guide you along a straight path. Mark your way so you can backtrack if the going gets too tough. Following a stream downhill will not *always* lead you to civilization in true wilderness country. In rural areas it usually does. Game trails may be deceiving because they twist and turn.

Whenever I go off on an outdoor trip, whether as a wildlife ecologist, professional writer and photographer, or vacationist, I plan on taking my very own life-support system with me all the way. In simple terms, this is a small, light, survival kit. Some of the things fit in my pockets, some in a canvas bag. They are in addition to my conventional backpack, sleeping bag, cookset, and tent. Some day my survival kit may save my life. And thus far the combination of that kit, an emergency food stock, and my first aid gear has enabled me to solve almost any problem when things go wrong.

As important as the equipment one carries is one's attitude. Always try to build your morale. As a leader or a good team member, in an emergency act as if you know what you're doing. Your air of confidence and optimism can convince you and others that everything will be all right. And it probably will be.

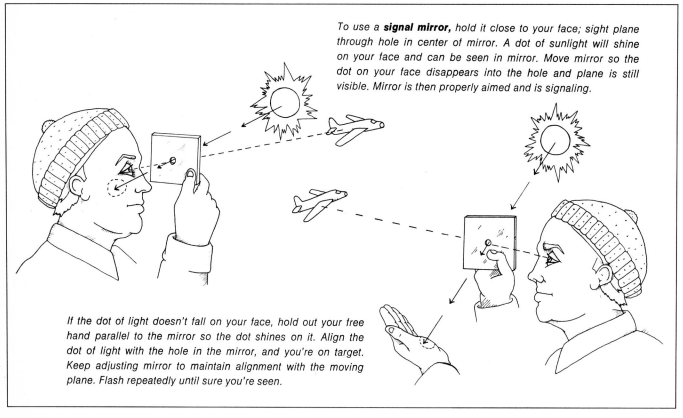

To use a **signal mirror,** hold it close to your face; sight plane through hole in center of mirror. A dot of sunlight will shine on your face and can be seen in mirror. Move mirror so the dot on your face disappears into the hole and plane is still visible. Mirror is then properly aimed and is signaling.

If the dot of light doesn't fall on your face, hold out your free hand parallel to the mirror so the dot shines on it. Align the dot of light with the hole in the mirror, and you're on target. Keep adjusting mirror to maintain alignment with the moving plane. Flash repeatedly until sure you're seen.

Lost? Signal and wait or walk out

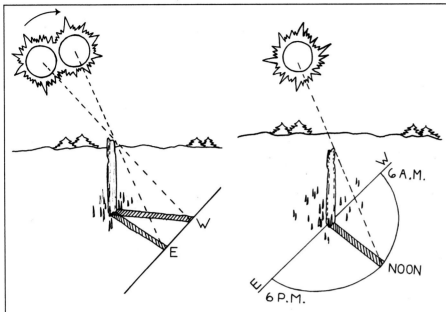

You can find north without a compass. *Plant a 3-foot stake in the ground and mark the tip of the shadow it casts, West. Wait 15 minutes, and again mark the tip of the shadow, this time, East. The line connecting the two marks lies on the East-West axis. A line through it at right angles marks North and South (not shown on the drawing). To make a sundial, you need only carry this process one step further. Move the stake to the intersection of the East-West/North-South lines. East is 6 P.M., West is 6 A.M., and North is 12 noon.*

If you're lost and decide to walk out, *mark your route for rescuers to follow. Use V's or arrows made with forked sticks (top), or rocks or sticks arranged in the desired shape. If necessary, blaze trees (bottom). A single long blaze means "straight ahead"; a short blaze to its right means "turn right"; one to its left means "turn left."*

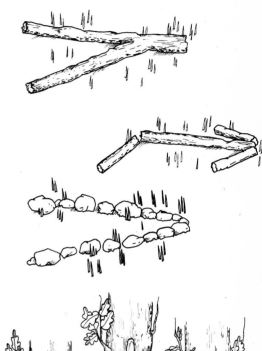

If there is no sun to make shadows, **use the stars to find north.** *All stars change positions, but the North Star, Polaris, always marks north and always stays in the same relationship to the Big Dipper. Sight along the side of the Big Dipper opposite the handle to see Polaris, the last star in the handle of the Little Dipper.*

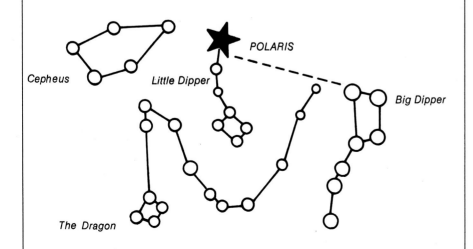

Cassiopeia

Cepheus

Little Dipper

POLARIS

Big Dipper

The Dragon

Survival Kit

Waterproof matches or metal match or steel and flint	Leader, 20 lb. test
	Wire for snares
	4 small nails
Pocket knife	Razor blade
Whistle	Salt in foil
Compass and map	Plastic tarp, 6 ft. by 8 ft.
Pen flashlite, switch taped, extra batteries, extra bulb	Space blanket
	Kleenex
Nylon cord, 30 ft.	Watch
Pencil and paper	Magnifying glass
Safety pins	Canteen
Needle and thread	Extra socks
G.I. can opener	Extra gloves
Candles	Eye glasses
Metal mirror	Medicine
2 snelled fish-hooks	Money
	Extra car keys

Ten great wildlife-watching spots

George H. Harrison

A flight of adult roseate spoonbills is one of many scenes of exquisite beauty that attract visitors to Everglades National Park, including the author and his wife, Kit. The Glades are also home to the young American alligator foraging in the spatterdock (opposite). The life-saving role of the alligator has earned it the title of "keeper of the Everglades." When dry spells come, the adult gator uses feet, snout, and lashing tail to bulldoze a bathtub-sized pond which it shares with tiny fish, turtles, snails, and other fresh-water animals. Attracted to the oasis are their larger predators which, in turn, become a meal for the hungry alligator. A breed stock of the small aquatic animals survives in these gator holes to repopulate the sea of grass when rains come again.

Where are the best places in North America to see wildlife? That question was asked me by the editors of this book, and it wasn't easy to answer. There are so many good places that anyone might have a different list.

In selecting my top ten, I used the following criteria: easy to get to; open to the public; masses and variety of wildlife that can be enjoyed by anyone regardless of background or experience; and timing, so that an exciting trip could be planned any time of year.

My wife, Kit, and I visited eight of these ten places in one year, starting in the Everglades in January and ending in late October on the Monterey Peninsula. It was a fantastic year, one that for sheer wildlife enjoyment will be hard for us to beat the rest of our lives.

In Everglades National Park we visited several excellent viewing spots — Coot Bay Pond; Mrazek Pond; Flamingo on Florida Bay, where we saw 56 roseate spoonbills fly over in 30 minutes; Shark River Valley, where we took a tram ride, and Everglades City where we took a boat ride. But, to us, the best of all was Anhinga Trail. This inviting footpath is not far from the park entrance 12 miles south of Homestead. From the Royal Palm Interpretive Station, it led us directly to Taylor Slough, where we immediately saw anhingas, alligators, great blue herons, green herons, and coots. A little pied-billed grebe was putting around the slough, while a long-toed purple gallinule walked across the lily pads. A water snake lay quietly in the warm sun. On the far shore, a snowy egret fluffed its plumes.

We walked the entire half-mile trail many times that week and each time we discovered new Glade dwellers. At the far end where the trail becomes a boardwalk over the water, we were delighted by crested flycatchers, palm warblers, mockingbirds, and red-bellied woodpeckers in the mangrove thickets only three or four feet away. Alligators lay motionless beneath our feet, only their eyes and nostrils above water. All of Anhinga Trail seemed to be alive . . . natural, unmolested, and unconcerned. A wildlife photographer's paradise, it captures the very spirit of the Everglades.

At the same time that the Everglades is peaking as a wildlife wonderland, Aransas National Wildlife Refuge in South Texas is entertaining its most famous visitors. Kit and I arrived at that well-known winter home of the endangered whooping crane on January 16. There at the refuge entrance, as if to greet us, was a contingency of three sandhill cranes, the whooper's common cousin.

The 54,000-acre tract, located just north of Rockport, on San Antonio Bay, is a mixture of salt marshes and freshwater ponds surrounded by live oak, greenbrier and red bay thickets. It is perfect habitat for the flock of wild whoopers, other wintering waterfowl, water birds, and songbirds.

The best way to see Aransas and most of its wild inhabitants is to take the 18-mile, one-way loop road which traverses all of the refuge's various habitats. On our first trip, Kit and I saw over 50 species of birds as well as herds of browsing white-tailed deer and wild peccaries (javelinas) scurrying for cover in the brush. Of the many trails leading off the loop road, Big Tree Trail was particularly productive. We were amazed by the huge wintering flocks of robins and cardinals flitting through the thickets. Farther along, we saw orange-crowned warblers, white-throated sparrows, white-eyed vireos, kinglets, and wild turkeys. In the undisturbed dust of the trail we noticed footprints of coyote, skunk, deer, and squirrel. At the end of the trail, we sat on an old log bench and watched gadwalls, northern shovelers, pied-billed grebes, American coots, and an alligator feeding in a pond. Later, in the picnic area, a nuisance fox squirrel jumped right up on our table looking for a handout.

From the observation tower, we observed many white water birds—great and snowy egrets, white pelicans, and snow geese—but no whooping cranes.

Finally, we learned that the only foolproof way to see whoopers at Aransas is to board Captain Brownie Brown's *Whooping Crane* boat, which sails out of the Sea Gun Resort Hotel north of Rockport at 1:30 P.M. every Wednesday, Friday, Saturday, and Sunday from October 20 to April 10. "We guar-an-tee that you will see whooping cranes, or your money back," was Brown's pitch. And he made good on it. Brownie's four-hour, 32-mile tour along the shipping lanes of the Intracoastal Waterway produced 20 whoopers for us, some of them as close as 100 yards. Brownie also showed us 60 other species of birds on the trip, including a caracara, white-tailed hawk, long-billed curlew, and, in the blue waters of the Waterway itself, several groups of bottle-nosed dolphins. It was a great trip and a must if you want to see whooping cranes.

Visitors to the Aransas Wildlife Refuge in Texas (above) often see only a few whooping cranes together because of each crane family's need for a substantial acreage, a foraging territory strongly defended by the tall, rare birds. In March, visitors may see the jumping, bowing, and flapping of the cranes' elaborate courtship dance; it precedes their migration takeoff with a bugling cry on the first fine April day that brings a good tailwind for Canada. March visitors may also greet the gaudy purple gallinule (opposite, right), laboriously flying in on short, rounded wings from wintering around the Gulf Coast or in South America. Elongated toes enable it to walk on aquatic plants. In nearby arroyos a caracara (opposite, far left), sluggish scavenger of the falcon family, hunts rodents and small turtles for its young, and the collared peccary roots for bulbs and tubers that it locates by its keen sense of smell.

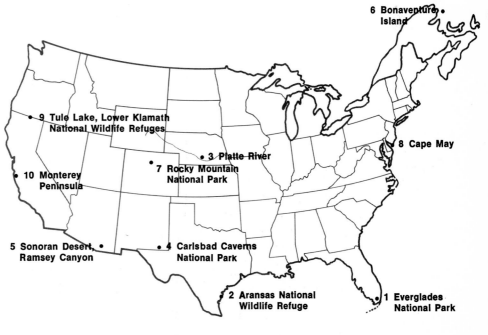

Ten Great Wildlife - Watching Spots

6 Bonaventure Island

9 Tule Lake, Lower Klamath National Wildlife Refuges

3 Platte River

7 Rocky Mountain National Park

8 Cape May

10 Monterey Peninsula

5 Sonoran Desert, Ramsey Canyon

4 Carlsbad Caverns National Park

2 Aransas National Wildlife Refuge

1 Everglades National Park

On to the greatest concentration of cranes on earth. In Texas, it was possible to see most of the world's population of the rare whoopers in a single day. Our next stop took us to a place in Nebraska where we could see most of the world's population of the most common crane, the sandhill, in one day.

There are perhaps 250,000 sandhill cranes in the world. Along the Platte River in central Nebraska in late March some 225,000 of them assemble in what is called a "staging area." Here they feed and rest up from their long flights from Mexico, Texas, and New Mexico and prepare themselves for still longer flights on to breeding grounds in northern Canada, Alaska, and Siberia. The staging area covers an 80-mile stretch of the Platte between Grand Island and Lexington and another 20-mile section of the North Platte River near Sutherland and Hershey. Most of the birds stay about a month, with the last ten days of March being the peak period.

Kit and I arrived in Grand Island on March 19. We found that the best way to see the cranes was to drive the secondary roads to the south of both the river and Interstate 80. Did we see cranes! We saw thousands of them in the air, in the cornfields, coming to the river and going away from the river — all of them bugling their mournful, beckoning call.

The birds had been feeding within two miles of either side of the Platte, but with thousands more hungry birds arriving each day, the search for food widens up to ten miles away from the water by the end of the month. Yet at sunset, all the cranes return to the river to roost in the broad, shallow waters of the Platte. We watched tens of thousands of them streaming across a brilliantly orange sky — calling as they flew.

The whoopers and the sandhills are North America's only two species of cranes. There are six subspecies of sandhills — the rare, nonmigratory Florida, Mississippi, and Cuban sandhills, and the migratory greater, Canadian, and lesser sandhill cranes. Perhaps one-fifth of the flocks we saw on the Platte were Canadians. All the rest were lesser sandhills — spectacular ash-gray birds with a six-foot wingspan. A red cap and a pompadour on the rump give the tall birds a touch of style. But they are too skittish to photograph easily. Without a blind, you'll need to use a telephoto lens — except for a car-window shot of a sky full of birds which you can get on most any road in the area.

With the wariness of true wilderness birds, migrating sandhill cranes choose a sandbar in Nebraska's shallow Platte River for their night's roosting place. Assured by scouts that the coast is clear, family groups of the stately birds come bugling in from a day of courting and feeding at this Central Flyway reststop. Thousands more arrive daily from marshlands in the Southwest and Mexico. In 30 days, both male and female must let the raw March winds toughen their 10-pound bodies for Arctic skies ahead and must accumulate the fat that will see them through weeks of shared duty on snow-covered tundra nesting grounds.

Working methodically outward for miles from the river banks, the foraging birds glean thawing cornfields and alfalfa fields and snap up the first crayfish and frogs to emerge from the warming mud. Lizards, snakes, mice, insects, tubers, berries, and weed seeds complete the menu that attracts sandhill cranes to this 80-mile-long ribbon of the Platte.

Thousands of bats pour out of Carlsbad Caverns nightly to consume 20 to 30 percent of their body weight in insects, mostly micromoths, an agricultural pest. Females return to nursery caves to suckle infant bats left hanging alone, while males rest in cooler quarters. At five weeks, the young join in feeding flights, fattening their bodies for the 800-mile October migration back to Mexico. There both juveniles and adults find mates and hibernate. In May the males return to Carlsbad, followed by the pregnant females to give birth in the caves' maternity ward.

Our next adventure was a cave in New Mexico where we rendezvoused with my father. Dad and I had received special permission from the National Park Service to stand down in a mouth of the Carlsbad Caverns at dusk to photograph the nightly exodus of Mexican free-tailed bats, a phenomenon that led to the caves' discovery in 1901.

First a few came out of the black depths, then a few more, then many more. Finally we were engulfed with bats, thousands upon thousands of them swirling up from the caverns below, passing within inches of us, and then up into the sky above the cave entrance. Dad ran his movie camera; I shot still photographs. Those 15 minutes were furious. There were unbelievable numbers of bats all around us, yet not one touched us. The one thing we hadn't counted on was the rain of guano (bat droppings) which had to be endured. What an experience!

The following night we watched the event the way most visitors do — in the stone amphitheater outside that faces the large, dark entrance to the cave.

"Here they come!" shouted a little boy. The first black shapes emerged from the cave. The trickle became a swarm that resembled smoke twisting and then melting into the evening sky. Before dawn they would all be back.

Following the exodus, a park ranger gave a talk about the tiny flying mammals and their role in the ecology of the cavern and the Park's surrounding 46,000 acres of canyon country. He pointed out hawk and owl roosts around the entrance where the bats' predators await their evening meal, and said that bats that fall to the ground may be snatched by snakes and ringtail cats.

As many as a thousand summer visitors gather nightly to witness the grand exit. Before leaving this unique wildlife habitat, they also get an unforgettable geology lesson by touring the gorgeous underground formations of Carlsbad in huge, well-lighted rooms that are quite apart from the bat roosts.

A saguaro cactus garden (opposite) cast the eternal spell of the desert over the Harrisons upon their arrival in the Sonoran Desert of Arizona. A home for red-tailed hawk nestlings (opposite, center), the 50-foot cactus also serves as a command perch for their parents' hunting strikes against horned lizards (opposite, top), other desert reptiles, and rodents. In the Arizona-Sonora Desert Museum a bobcat (below) peers from its den and a mule deer doe (bottom) thrives on shrubs in its desert habitat. The broad-tailed hummingbird (opposite, bottom) is one of many kinds seen at nearby Ramsey Canyon.

It's a short hop from Carlsbad to Tucson, where we explored the desert. Nowhere on the North American continent is there an area of more varied habitats than on the Sonoran Desert of southern Arizona. Like islands in a sea of hot sand, desert mountains rise 9,000 feet from cactus country through five distinct ecological zones to deep snow pockets and Canadian-type forests on top.

For those who want a prime sampling of two of these unique habitats, we recommend a visit to the open-air Arizona-Sonora Desert Museum and to Ramsey Canyon. On May 1, we drove 14 miles west of Tucson over Gate's Pass to the museum, which isn't a museum at all, but a living microcosm of the Sonoran Desert.

The walk-in bird area was our favorite display because there we could get unnaturally close to many of the shy desert species. A roadrunner in the display fell in love with Kit and she with it. The bird brought gifts — a flower blossom, cigarette butts, and dead leaves in return for gentle strokes on the back. While that was going on, I photographed at close range black vultures, Inca, white-winged and mourning doves, black-headed grosbeaks, and western tanagers.

The museum has a beaver dam with a cutaway view, a bobcat grotto, coati-mundi den, a chuckwallow haunt, and a rocky home for a desert bighorn ram.

Just outside the museum grounds we drove through a section of the Saguaro National Monument, where we viewed the greatest of all cactus gardens, with its awesome saguaros towering over lesser species. Here we recorded more desert birds: cactus wren, black-throated sparrow, brown towhee, gila woodpecker, curved-billed thrasher, black-tailed gnatcatcher, verdin, and an elf owl.

Seventy miles southeast of Tucson, in the Huachuca Mountains, near Sierra Vista, we drove up Ramsey Canyon to Mile Hi Ranch, also known as the "Hummingbird Capital of the World." Supplementing the nectar in the wildflowers that attract these tiny birds was the largest display of hummingbird feeders I have ever seen. Swarms of 12 different species of hummers consume an average of two gallons of sugar water a day! During our visit, we saw five species: black-chinned, broad-billed, broad-tailed, magnificent (Rivoli's), and blue-throated. But there were also other birds using the feeders: house finches, western tanagers, black-headed grosbeaks, and, a real surprise, a painted redstart.

Quebec's Bonaventure Island is white with snow in April when the gannets return from wintering at sea along the coast from New York to Florida, and white with the bodies of the large seabirds until August. Each pair of gannets returns to the same nest plot every year (below, left), until seniority admits them to preferred ledge sites. The birds incubate their single egg by holding it between their blood-warmed, webbed feet. The common puffin, or sea parrot (below, right), is another fascinating seabird that summers on Bonaventure.

With one big southwest to northeast leap across North America to Quebec, our next stop was Bonaventure Island, site of the largest gannetry in North America and one of the world's most spectacular sea bird colonies.

Only two miles off Percé, in the Gulf of St. Lawrence, Bonaventure is easily reached by ferry boats during the warm months. Most people go there to see the gannets, estimated to number around 18,000 pairs, but they also find thousands of other sea birds that nest in the same cliffs from May through August.

Kit and I arrived at Percé on June 24 and were on the first boat to Bonaventure the next morning. Preferring to approach the gannet colony first by land, we walked across the top of the island through deep, rich woodlands full of singing fox sparrows and Tennessee warblers. We knew that we were getting close to the gannets by the not-so-fresh odor of fish and the din which resembled the gobblings on a large turkey farm. Then, just ahead, the green grass ended where the carpet of snow-white gannets began and extended 50 yards to the cliff's edge.

We became so engrossed in the behavior of the gannets that we lost track of time. They are affectionate birds, courting, rubbing necks, talking, and bringing gifts to each other. They also fight and steal twigs from their neighbors' nests with enthusiasm. We admired the way they catch fish in power dives from great heights, find their way back to their mates among the mass of white, feed their young, and then become airborne again by hurling themselves off the cliff.

The following morning, to get a close-up view from the sea, Kit and I took the tourist boat that passes by the bird cliffs. Up and down the face of that 200-foot cliff we saw thousands of birds—gannets, common murres, razorbills, black guillemots, puffins, black-legged kittiwakes, and herring gulls. Birds in the air, on the water, at the base of the cliff, on ledges all the way to the top, more and more birds. This sight alone is worth all the effort to get to the tip of Gaspé. We will never forget it.

Back across the continent, we headed for the Rockies and the 13,000-foot peaks of Rocky Mountain National Park in Colorado. Kit and I like to spend a few days each summer on Trail Ridge Road, a 48-mile drive that crosses the Continental Divide between Estes Park on the east and Grand Lake on the west. Much of the drive is above tree line on the alpine tundra, the road remaining above the 12,000-foot level for more than four miles. On either side of the self-guided nature trails, great masses of tundra flowers — alpine forget-me-nots, miniature buttercups, sunflowers, sky pilots, narcissus anemone, arctic and moss campion, kings crown, and Indian paintbrush — grow as far as we can see.

Anywhere we stop along Trail Ridge, we find wildlife. The Clark's nutcrackers and Steller's jays are always on hand for a free meal of peanuts or crackers, as are chipmunks and fat little golden-mantled ground squirrels. These freeloaders make great photographic subjects, but we are very careful, knowing that they sometimes bite the hand that feeds them. More wary, but equally interesting, are the yellow-bellied marmots which sun themselves on convenient rocks near their dens. The haymaker of the heights, the pika, is there, too. If we are lucky, we spot a band of bighorn sheep grazing on the high country grass, but the elk have always proved too elusive for us.

One of the treats for bird watchers on Trail Ridge is the chance to see new species. It was here that I spotted my first white-tailed ptarmigan, the bird that perhaps best characterizes the alpine zone — white in winter and tundra-colored in summer. Roger Tory Peterson and I both added the brown-capped rosy finch to our life lists the same summer. They are often found among the tundra flowers along with horned larks, water pipits, and white-crowned sparrows. On lower wooded slopes, Kit and I have seen ruby-crowned and golden-crowned kinglets, ravens, and a female broad-tailed hummingbird that I photographed on its nest. Mule deer browse in the pines, and beaver enlarge their lodges at dusk.

All this flora and fauna, plus spectacular scenes with snow-capped peaks, glacial lakes, and endless spruce-fir forests, are hard to beat for a day's drive. And what kid doesn't delight in throwing a snowball on the Fourth of July?

Newcomers to Trail Ridge Road in Colorado's Rocky Mountain National Park marvel at the vastness of its mountain grandeur and at the intimacy of their encounters with the small wild things that live there. On their first visit, the author's children, Jennie and Peter (below, left), felt the tug of the wild as a Clark's nutcracker snatched peanuts from their fingers. Visitors may also see the pika (below) scurrying about with a mouthful of grass or spreading it to dry in the sun. The tiny mammal stores up to a bushel of the cured hay in the rocky scree for winter eating. The golden-mantled ground squirrel (bottom, right) prepares for winter hibernation by stuffing itself and by stashing food in its burrow. The omnivorous nutcracker trusts nature to provide. When wintry blasts drive it down the mountain, this scavenger lives on pine seeds and whatever it can find in backyards.

From mountaintop to seashore, Kit and I backtracked to the Atlantic Coast to be at Cape May, New Jersey, for the annual phenomenon that we call "days of birding madness." These are the days in September when migrating birds stack up on the peninsula in such numbers that they are "hanging on every bush and literally covering the ground," as one observer put it.

Many of the birds migrating south from northeastern North America follow the Atlantic coastline. When they reach Cape May, they must strike out over Delaware Bay, a flight of 18 miles across open water. If there is a strong northwest wind, crossing the open water may mean death because the wind could carry them out to sea. So the birds hesitate and mill around while more birds come down the flyway, creating a colossal mixup in birdland. If you are at Cape May when these unfavorable flight conditions exist, you may witness a "day of madness."

Although the weather was favorable for birds to cross the Bay at a normal rate on September 22, we could tell it was still going to be an exceptional birding day for us. By the time we had parked the car near Lily Lake on Cape May Point in the faint pre-dawn light, we were already trying to list species faster than Kit could write. "Rose-breasted grosbeak, redstart, scarlet tanager, mockingbird, red-breasted nuthatch, black-and-white warbler," I called to her.

The big problem was getting the binoculars on each bird before it moved on. Photographing them was impossible. To make identification more difficult, the fall plumage of most birds is duller or altogether different in color, and most have stopped singing or calling. Nevertheless, in 40 to 50 minutes, we had listed 46 species, including 14 warblers. At times birds were so thick and moving so fast that Kit and I were nearly hit by a Swainson's thrush, a common yellow-throat, and two tree swallows. Even monarch butterflies by the thousands were moving south along the beaches.

Even though we didn't experience a "day of birding madness," we were thrilled with our week on the Cape. We listed 105 species — song birds, birds of prey, waterfowl, and shore birds — 90 of them on that first fabulous morning.

156

In summer, the salt marshes of Cape May, New Jersey (left), are ideal habitat for visiting water birds like black-headed and laughing gulls and the snowy egrets stalking frogs, fish, mollusks, aquatic insects, snakes, and crayfish in the shallows. During low tide along nearby beaches, the willet below feasts on fiddler crabs, marine worms, and fish.

But in September, Cape May skies suddenly fill with millions of other migratory birds. Nudged by the first frost far to the north, ducks, geese, and shorebirds surge down the coastal flyway, joined by songbirds like the meadowlark (opposite, right) and birds of prey like the sharp-shinned hawk (opposite, left).

When certain weather conditions ground the southbound travelers on the tip of this narrow peninsula, frantic birds fill trees, thickets, marshes, and sky. Alerted by ornithologists like Roger Tory Peterson, who has written of seeing 10,000 robins, 5,000 flickers, and 1,000 sharp-shins at Cape May on one September morning, bird-watchers, too, wing in from faraway places, to see the rare assemblage of American species. When the weather lifts, the feathered tide moves on, sweeping with it the gulls, egrets, and willets back to their Southland winter homes.

From the Atlantic to the Pacific, I again crossed the country, this time from New Jersey to California. We have all read accounts of the early explorers who told of "wild fowl that blackened the sky." I could never be sure just how literally we should interpret that dramatic imagery until the day I drove along the Lost River inlet to Tule Lake in northern California. Kit missed this trip so I was alone as I came upon a great, shore-to-shore mass of ducks floating on the water. I stepped out of the car for a quick photo. For some reason the whole flock, mostly pintails, got up off the water in one great deafening whoosh and headed into the sun. At that moment, I believed the old explorers. There were so many ducks that they shut out some of the light, actually darkening the sky.

That was just a sampling of the experiences I had at Tule Lake and Lower Klamath National Wildlife Refuges on the California-Oregon border. It was early October and the waterfowl were pouring into the refuges. By mid-October, the refuge managers estimated there would be 605,000 pintails; 90,000 mallards; 109,000 American wigeons (baldpates); 19,000 gadwalls; 85,000 northern shovelers; 32,000 ruddy ducks; 9,000 teal; and 31,000 canvas-backs. When you add the geese, swans, and coots, the total is more than two million birds.

Lower Klamath is only 11 miles west of Tule and is made up of several bodies of water and marshlands filled with water birds such as American avocets, water pipits, ring-billed gulls, long-billed dowitchers, and white pelicans. Ring-necked pheasants by the hundreds dusted and fed along the edge of the 15-mile tour road. We spotted flocks of whistling swans, white-fronted and snow geese. I also saw my first Ross' goose. Because it was standing with two snow geese, the little Ross was easy to distinguish from its larger cousins.

The cliffs around Tule are inhabited by golden eagles, prairie falcons, ferruginous hawks, and great-horned owls. In the dry volcanic landscape nearby at Lava Beds National Monument, I called up a gray fox to within 30 yards by using a predator call. But my most vivid memory of Tule-Klamath is of the great masses of waterfowl, perhaps the greatest flock of that kind left in North America.

Like a scene out of Eden, the snowfields of Mount Shasta glisten behind a cloud of wild geese rising from Tule Lake, their wings whipping the crisp October air into a roar. Thanks to the insistence of Teddy Roosevelt that rest stops be set aside for the millions of waterfowl traveling the Pacific Flyway, both Tule Lake and nearby Lower Klamath National Wildlife refuges were established a half century or more ago. Like flocks that have preceded them down through eons of time, the white-fronted geese and Canadas at the top of the picture and the white snow geese below them have already flown 3,000 miles or more from Siberia, Alaska, and Canada, where the youngest were hatched only six months before.

Some of the 2,000,000 waterfowl that pass through this freshwater oasis each fall (and spring), including pintail ducks (right) and white pelicans (bottom, right), have only a few hundred more miles to go to their wintering grounds in the Central Valley of California; others must refuel for flights on into Mexico and South America. At Tule and Klamath, the birds find large, shallow, man-made lakes and marshes, and fields of grain and hay planted solely for them to harvest.

159

If you have never experienced the Seventeen-Mile Drive along California's Monterey Peninsula, you have missed one of the great drive-up wildlife attractions in North America. We turned off U.S. Highway 1 into the gate of the Seventeen-Mile Drive at Carmel Hill on October 23. It was a bright and warm day. Autumn is the best time to take the drive because the weather is usually good, birds are migrating through the area, and the marine mammals are relaxed on their favorite rocks. The time was 7:00 A.M., ideal for seeing wildlife and for photographing seascapes with the sun at our backs.

After paying the toll, we drove into Del Monte Forest, heading toward Pebble Beach. We immediately found orange-crowned Townsend's and yellow warblers flitting overhead through the Monterey pines. In an opening only 50 yards away, we watched three Columbian black-tailed deer browsing as a gray squirrel scolded us from the top of a boulder.

But we were eager to get to the ocean, so we continued on to beautiful Pescadero Point where we recorded our first seabirds. Sooty shearwaters, common murres, and red-breasted mergansers bobbed up and down on the swells. With the ocean on our left, we moved on. The smell of the sea and the sounds of the surf were our companions as we headed northwest through the only natural stand of Monterey cypress, each tree standing defiantly with its gnarled roots clinging to the rocks. At each stop, Beechey ground squirrels and California and western gulls came close to us, apparently hoping for handouts.

The highlights of the drive were at Seal Rock and, just beyond, Bird Rock, where we could see, though not closely, several hundred sea lions basking in the early morning sun. On rocks much closer, we identified black-bellied plovers, sanderlings, and a willet facing into the wind. And at last, we located our first sea otters, lolling carefree in the water.

The final stretch took us back through beautiful groves of Monterey pines and spyglass cypress. Though small, the Del Monte has to be one of the most unique forests in North America. Because there had been so much to see in such a short period, we decided to go back the next morning and do it all over again. Like our whole fabulous year in pursuit of wildlife, now drawing to a close, it had only whetted our appetite for more.

The bark of the harbor seal (right) and the many voices and amusing antics of the sea otter (left) draw wildlife watchers back again and again to the Seventeen-Mile Drive along the Monterey Peninsula of central California. Both of these marine mammals are usually visible from the Drive, the four-foot-long sea otter bobbing on its back in a kelp bed and the six-foot seal frequently sunning itself on offshore rocks. Neither animal migrates, but each mates in the sea — the monogamous seal in September or October, the polygamous otter, in any month. Both share a fondness for shellfish, mollusks, and squid, while the seal adds fish to its diet and the otter, octopus and sea urchins. But as a wildlife attraction, the sea otter has it all over the stolid seal. Grooming its baggy coat of fabulous fur (650,000 hairs per square inch), feasting on shellfish — often by cracking it on a rock held on its chest — and draping itself in kelp before falling asleep with forepaws shading its eyes, the playful creature has endeared itself to all as "the clown of the kelp beds."

HOW TO CAPTURE WILDLIFE ON FILM

Russ Kinne

Any family that goes camping is going to meet wildlife, at least momentarily. If Dad is in a stream fishing, he's the one who will most likely see waterfowl, an otter, or a mink. Back in camp, Mom may be amused by a chipmunk or a red squirrel filching blueberries out of the pancake batter. If the kids go berry picking, they are almost certain to see a rabbit, lizard, or butterfly — maybe a deer. But before anyone can say "Who's got the camera?", the wild creature will have vanished.

It is from such lost opportunities that a resolve to learn the secrets of wildlife photography often arises. Probably the first "secret" is that when photographers enter the animals' realm, we do so on their terms. Unlike family members who gladly pause to let us take their pictures — the kids helping Dad put up the tent or Mom proudly displaying the string of fish she caught — wildlife does not pose for us.

Since most birds and mammals feed at dawn and dusk, we adapt our sleeping and eating schedules to accommodate theirs. To catch them in natural, unguarded moments, we must be in the right place at the right time.

Since learning to move silently through the woods is one of the basic skills involved, and since dealing with photographic equipment and fast-moving animals demands one's full powers of concentration, serious wildlife photography is obviously not a family affair. However, the family's day-by-day schedule can be planned so that each photographer has an opportunity to go out alone — or at most, by twos — for several hours at a time. Success makes all the pre-planning worthwhile.

A 500mm telephoto lens brought Wendell D. Metzen safely face-to-face with this elusive bobcat in the Okefenokee Swamp.

Know what to expect from nature

To begin with, there is the challenge of catching wildlife unaware. Any wild creature's senses are so much better than ours that it detects us at a distance and usually moves away before we reach it. I doubt if we see a tenth of the animals that see us first. So our chances of getting good pictures will improve if we take our families camping in areas where animals feel safe from traps and the sound of gunfire. It also helps if they have become accustomed to the sight of humans and vehicles.

We Americans are enormously lucky to have hundreds of such places — for starters, 145 national parks, monuments, seashores, and recreation areas, and 384 national wildlife refuges, plus state parks and local wildlife sanctuaries. Here is opportunity for the most active photographer and a wide variety of activities for the rest of the family to enjoy.

Time of day and time of year are important in planning wildlife photographs. Birds migrate with the seasons, following food supplies. Mammals may have winter and summer ranges or follow a traveling food supply. Waterfowl and shore birds often move with the tides, and strong onshore winds may drive them from exposed beaches into lagoons. Deer and certain other creatures are seldom seen in full sunlight, and some, like bats and owls, are wholly or partly nocturnal.

The more we know about wild creatures, the greater our chances of getting good photographs of them. Learning in the field from experienced naturalists is perhaps the best method, backed up by our own study of nature books and magazines and field identification guides. The informal talks given by rangers in national parks are especially good because the informa-

tion is up-to-date, the reports on the animals' current movements often being just a day or two old. Many parks and refuges also have printed maps or leaflets that tell you where to look for which animals, and when.

Once camp is established and everyone has found something to do, pack up your camera gear and take off. Avoid heavily used trails and start practicing one of man's oldest skills — stalking wild animals. Wear neutral-colored clothes that won't flap in the wind or make scraping noises going through brush. Avoid quick motions and loud sounds. Leave the transistor radio and the cigarettes in your tent. Also the family dog. Walk into or across the wind so your scent won't alert the animals ahead of you. In general, try to pass slowly and quietly through the countryside instead of crashing along. Be flexible, gentle; it will pay off. Above all, don't hurry.

The habits and cycles of nature must become as familiar to the wildlife photographer as his equipment. To find snowy egrets in their nuptial finery (opposite), William J. Weber searched during the 10 spring days when their plumage is at its peak. Clyde H. Smith snapped the young raccoon (left) at dusk just before early snowfall drove it into hibernation. John Shaw caught the flighty dragonfly above at dawn when dew had stilled its wings.

The 35mm single lens reflex (SLR) camera
(1), basic element of the wildlife photographer's equipment, is lightweight and
compact. Its through-the-lens viewing and
focusing system lets the photographer see
exactly what his camera sees. Another
plus is its variety of interchangeable
lenses. A 200mm telephoto (2), 50mm
macro (3), and tubes (4) close the gap
between photographer and subject. An
electronic flash (5) completes the package.
With this setup, the photographer is ready
for whatever nature offers, such as George
Harrison's chance (opposite) to catch a
young squirrel pilfering a seed. His wife,
Kit, snapped the backyard picture.

Fortunately, the equipment we need
to carry is both compact and lightweight—good news for backpackers
who want to take high quality wildlife photographs, but don't want to
add much weight to their packs. Better still, even today's moderately
priced photographic equipment is de-
pendable and flexible, capable of
turning out excellent pictures under a
wide range of lighting conditions and
distances.

For a number of reasons, the 35mm
camera is the best choice for wildlife
shooting. This holds true whether you
pursue birds, mammals, herptiles, insects, flowers, or fish; whether you're
after scenics or close-ups; and whether
you use remote control, camera trap,
or telephoto photography. The 35mm
size has more lenses and more films
to choose from than other formats; it
has close-up lenses and attachments
as well as microscope and telescope
adapters. And since the equipment is
easy to carry, you can take it all along
every time.

There are two types of 35mm cameras, the viewfinder and the single lens
reflex (SLR). Many wildlife photographers—myself included—prefer the
SLR because its through-the-lens
viewing and focusing system enables
you to see exactly what will go on to
the film when you push the button.
However, if you have a viewfinder
camera, don't get rid of it. It is quieter
and lighter than the SLR, and it focuses more accurately in dim light.

If you have decided to buy your first
35mm SLR, you are still faced with a
bewildering number of brands and
models to choose from. I am asked
constantly, "Which camera should I
buy for wildlife shooting?" And my
answer is always this: if you can afford
one of the top four or five brands,
choose the one that looks best to you;
there's really not a lot of difference. If
price is a consideration, decide what
features you could do without (e.g.,
provision for motor drive) and select a
camera in the medium-price range. But
avoid cameras that are suspiciously
low-priced; they not only take poorer
pictures, they break down frequently
and spend many days or weeks in the

repair shop. You would be better off buying a good used camera, a name brand, even if it needs minor repairs. When in the field pursuing wildlife, you need *reliability*—and the lowest-priced cameras simply don't have it; they will let you down when you need them.

Good lenses are as important as the camera body for sharp, clear pictures; but the relationship of price to quality is slightly different for lenses than it is for cameras. For a high price, you will almost certainly get a good lens. But for a medium price, you may get just as good a lens, or you may not. The reason is that when a manufacturer asks a high price, he can afford to reject lenses that don't meet his high standards; when he asks a lower price, he is not able to maintain such high standards; he must sell all the lenses he makes. If you are willing to do some testing, you can try several medium-priced lenses and select the best one. (Better camera stores usually offer a 10-day trial period with a *money-back* guarantee.) Manufacturers may also economize in the quality of the mount and the mechanical parts of the lens; but if you are careful how you handle it, a medium-priced lens may last you as long as an expensive one.

Fortunately, competition among lens makers is very keen. Some independents offer excellent lenses at lower prices. These lenses are available in a variety of mounts to fit almost any camera on the market. Some lenses are made with a universal mount, which uses an inexpensive adapter to fit any camera, Thus, if you change camera brands in the future, you can still keep your lenses, buying only a new adapter to fit the new camera.

Another question that I hear regularly is, "What size lenses should I buy?" This must be countered with another question, "What do you want to photograph?" It does make a difference! The more retiring creatures—both birds and mammals—require a

telephoto lens of at least 200mm focal length (four power, if you compare it to the normal 50mm lens). A 200mm lens usually has an aperture of f/3.5 or f/4. The still longer 400mm lenses weigh and cost more and are slower, usually f/5.6, but produce twice as big an image. Shorter lenses produce a smaller image, but are faster; an aperture of f/2.8 is common for the 100mm. If you must make one telephoto lens do for everything, a 200mm or a 300mm will serve you best. Both are reasonably priced. Either one is light enough to carry and fast enough

for shooting even in fairly dim light (with the right film). It is possible to handhold both, but when the situation allows it, bracing yourself against a tree or car often produces a sharper image. Incidentally, telephoto lenses are usually thought of as distance lenses, but they are also superb for closeups of small, shy creatures, *if* they focus closely enough.

Wide-angle lenses, on the other hand, are of limited use in shooting wildlife, but they are fine for capturing scenic panoramas, sunsets, rainbows, or cloud formations. These lenses,

Lenses that bring nature close

usually 28mm or 35mm in focal length, often focus down to a foot or so and are useful in flower photography. And the ultrawide 20mm and 21mm lenses allow you to combine a close-up of a small object with a 90-degree view of its surroundings—and get a valuable "story-telling" picture. It can also be a useful teaching tool in wildlife photography when you need to depict an animal in its habitat. Their versatility makes these lenses great fun to use.

Another versatile lens that I do not recommend highly for wildlife photography is the zoom lens. Although its variable focal lengths are convenient, a zoom is heavier, more expensive, and less sharp than the telephotos with fixed focal lengths.

The only other basic type of lens for wildlife photography is the macro lens, which is usually 50mm to 55mm in focal length and has an aperture of f/3.5. It is superb for insect photography, thanks to a double-jointed mount that lets it focus from infinity to about four inches, where the image is half life-size on the film. Macro lenses come with a special extension tube for the lens that enables you to shoot from half life-size to full life-size. The macro lens is equally useful for plant photography and for such close-up work as the texture of rocks, lichens, or bark.

If I were limited to only one lens, I think I'd choose the versatile macro. Being designed for close work, it is superbly sharp. However, for close-ups, you usually must have a small flash to let you shoot at small apertures necessary for good depth of field.

As you become a more experienced photographer, this basic glassware may not meet all your needs. In my book, *The Complete Book of Nature Photography*, I discuss additional equipment, and you may want to look there for help with more sophisticated accessories and techniques.

Form the habit of carrying all your lenses when you go out shooting. You never know what you'll meet; and unless you bring them all, you will almost certainly need the one you left at home.

Using filters improves many pictures, there's no doubt about it. They add contrast, especially important in black-and-whites. For example, if I want darker skies, I use an orange or red filter. And for color shooting, I always carry a polarizing filter. This is the *only* way to control sky tone in color, and it works equally well with black-and-white films. You don't need many, but one that I wouldn't be without is a skylight or ultraviolet filter that screws onto the front of each lens and protects it from dust, scratches, rain, and salt spray. A damaged filter is cheaper to replace than a damaged lens.

An electronic flash unit is well worth the extra weight in your pack, even on a trip of several days. You're always prepared to shoot evening camp scenes or nocturnal creatures. At dawn and dusk, even when deer are too far away to be fully illuminated by the flash, it will make their eyes shine, which, in the opinion of many people, adds to the appeal of a picture.

You might not think of taking a flash unit along for use in broad daylight, but there are times when it pays off. You can light up a bird nesting in dense brush, or fill in deep shadows under a tree, or shoot close-ups of objects almost anywhere. A word of caution, however: most flash units are too strong for daytime close-up work, so it is sometimes necessary to move the flash farther away from the subject or to cover the flash with white cloth. By all means take spare batteries and avoid flash units with sealed-in batteries. Once they've been used, the whole unit is dead until you can get back to household current and the charger.

Telephoto lenses are almost essential for getting pictures of retiring creatures like the owls opposite. When it's impossible to move the camera close, these lenses shrink the distance between photographer and subject. For a first telephoto, the author recommends buying a 200mm (shown in author's right hand) or a 300mm of the best optical quality one can afford. The 200mm is usually faster by a full stop and easier to hand hold than a 300mm, but it isn't long enough in some situations. To shoot birds in flight, an even longer lens may be needed. The 400mm Novoflex (in left hand, above) is lightweight and well-balanced, and its follow-focus grip makes it invaluable in wingshooting.

The barn owl nestlings were photographed in their hollow tree nest by Lois Cox with a 300mm telephoto. An electronic flash not only illuminated the variety of textural details in the photograph but also highlighted the dark, penetrating eyes of the month-old birds.

There are not as many films to choose from as there are brands of cameras, but there are still plenty. Photographers seem to fall into two groups: those who use Kodak products, and those who don't. The latter usually have a favorite among the offerings of Agfa, Fuji, Perutz, or other manufacturers, which they swear by. This is fine. Whatever satisfies the photographer is the best film for him to use. Periodically, I test a roll of each major type, and at present I feel Kodachrome 64 is the sharpest and most stable color-positive film available. I *know* what it will do, and there's no noticeable difference between rolls processed a month apart. When I absolutely must have more speed, I go to Kodak's High-Speed Ektachrome, but I limit my use of it. The fidelity and sharpness of Kodachrome tend to spoil me.

The color-negative films, those which give you a negative and a print (instead of a slide), are fine for photo album buffs. But they are not nearly as sharp as the color-positive films, which give you a slide from which a print can be made, so I seldom use them; but, again, whatever gives *you* the results *you* like is the film for *you.* For black-and-white shooting, most photographers settle on Kodak's Plus-X and use Tri-X when the light is really dim. My choice is Panatomic-X, rated at ASA 100 and processed in Diafine; this is beautifully grained, has good contrast, and is fast enough for most daytime situations. But the films are all good, and each is a little different.

No matter what film you select, it's wise to buy all you'll need before leaving home. If you buy from an unknown store far from home, particularly in a remote area, you may get rolls that have been heat-struck or affected by humidity or dampness. And by all means take *enough.* Figure what you think you'll use, then double this amount. If you bring any back, it will last for months in the refrigerator or for years in the freezer. But don't get caught in a fantastic photographic opportunity with no film left.

Deciding on one film makes it simpler for you to perfect other parts of your technique, such as exposure of the film. This brings us to the final essential piece of equipment, the light meter. Since the meter is often built right into today's cameras, many people don't bother to carry a separate one. Tucking an extra in your pack is, however, a wise idea when going off on a shooting trip. If the camera's meter fails, you can still make good pictures; and even if the problem doesn't arise, it's good to know you can check the camera's meter against another one from time to time.

Built-in meters are very convenient, but all are of the reflected-light type that measure the intensity of light reflected *from* the subject. Furthermore, most built-in meters sense all the lights and darks in the entire scene and average the readings. Worse, they may "weight" the center of the scene's readings. I personally don't care for

this at all; I don't know how much the meter reading is being determined by that white cloud or that dark bush. However, even if you follow the meter blindly, you will probably get good exposure 80 to 90 percent of the time, and that isn't a bad average. Learning a bit about how the meter works and how light behaves should enable you to raise this percentage even higher.

Just remember that the meter built into most cameras doesn't know what part of a scene *you* consider most important; it strikes an average of the light reflected from the total scene and recommends an exposure for that. However, a flower standing in full sun requires a certain exposure, no matter what the background. If there is a dark green bush in the background, the meter will recommend one exposure; if the flower is in front of a white rock, the meter recommends another — and neither one will be correct. In a case like this, you should hold the camera close enough to the feature you want (such as the flower in the photograph at left) so that it fills the viewfinder, and take your exposure reading. Then back up to shooting position and use that camera setting to take your picture.

This is the only way to get really accurate exposure readings with a built-in meter; but of course it's impossible to move up close to most wildlife subjects, so you have to settle for the best you can do.

I much prefer a built-in meter of the spot type, which lets you measure whatever area you feel is the most im-

A passerby might not have noticed the spider (left) peering around a petal of a Turk's-cap lily, but Terry Ator captured the grandeur of its home with a 55mm macro lens. This type of equipment is ideal for projecting tiny subjects up to life-size on film. There are several types of accessories for such close-ups, all operating on the principle that the smaller the distance between lens and subject, the greater the image magnification. One system (opposite) adapts normal lenses by fitting an extension tube between camera and lens. These inexpensive tubes come in sets of 3 to 5 to be used separately or combined. Other kinds of close-up accessories are bellows and supplementary or plus lenses (discussed on page 187).

portant. With the telephoto lens this becomes a highly accurate long-range light-measuring device. Separate spot-type meters are available and they are good, too, but expensive and bulky, and one more thing to lug around. I also carry a separate exposure meter that measures both reflected and incident light (the light that falls *on* the subject). I read incident-light exclusively on snowfields, beaches, and other areas which are high in reflected light.

In any case, bracket your exposures if the picture is an important one. By this I mean take one picture the way the meter tells you to, open up one stop and take another, close down one stop and take a third. And whenever you have to make a choice, *under-expose* color, and *overexpose* black-and-white. Doing the opposite guarantees disaster.

Let us suppose that your photo-reconnaissance hikes have led you to a spot where there is a good possibility of shooting skittish creatures in a nest or feeding on the ground. If you can't figure out a way to get close yourself, your first thought may be to wish you had a tripod from which to operate your camera by remote control. But few campers carry one because a tripod is awkward to pack, noisy to lug around, and adds weight. So what is an alternative way to set up your camera so that it will be stationary and stable over a period of time? The solution is to take along a clampod, a small C-clamp affair with a camera screw on one end. It can be clamped to a branch, fence, or whatever is at hand; one model even has a woodscrew to be driven into a tree trunk. These are excellent little gadgets, well worth the few ounces they weigh. In just a few minutes, you can rig a remote-control device or get set for time exposures.

Another useful item for remote control work is a lightweight air-release. This little device permits you to set off a camera from 40 to 50 feet away by squeezing a rubber bulb. Using the clampod, you can position a camera near a bird's nest or some peanut butter or suet; you then bide your time at a distance and take close-up pictures of the bird's return. Make sure, though, that the air-release has *vinyl,* not rubber tubing; the latter has too much stretch.

A much simpler, effective remote-control rig, but one which has to be built and tested before your camping trip, is shown on page 175. It can be made from a few pieces of wood, some heavy black thread, and some tape. Experiment a bit at home, before the trip, to make sure your design works. It's wonderful for making good flash pictures of nesting birds — if you pull the thread slowly so they don't see any rapid motion and fly off.

Once you have devised a foolproof remote-control rig, you are ready for the next step — setting up the camera to go off automatically whenever an animal walks into a thread across a trail or picks up a bait with the thread tied to it. In other words, you are ready to create a camera trap that causes an animal to take its own picture while you're sound asleep in your tent. Use thin, easily-broken thread — cotton is fine. For night use, attach a flashgun rather than an electronic flash unit that will run down if left on a long time. Night or day, protect the whole set-up from rain and dew by slipping a plastic bag over the camera (as shown on page 179) with a hole for the lens to see through. (But don't try this kind of "trapping" in populated areas; you may lose a camera.)

Protecting photographic gear takes a little ingenuity, but it's worth it if you want to avoid expensive repair bills. Carry several large plastic bags to keep cameras dry when everything else in camp is soggy. Carry a supply of lens paper to wipe fingerprints from lenses and filters after you have blown off the dust. (Never use silicone-treated tissue paper on a coated lens — it forms an unremovable film on the lens.) In hot weather, wear a headband to prevent perspiration from dripping onto your camera; perspiration is so salty it rusts things rapidly. It's a good idea to put a tiny drop of shellac or clear nailpolish on all the screw heads on cameras and lenses; even then, I carry a jeweler's screwdriver to tighten the screws if they loosen anyway. Use caps for the front and back of every lens, and for the lens opening on the camera body as well. Screw-in filters can be "stacked" together, and a metal cap screwed onto each end.

Whatever equipment you're taking into the field, set it up beforehand, and make sure everything works. If it's a new camera, run a roll of film through it, have it processed, and find what if anything you're doing wrong before you go. Then you won't return with 27 rolls of blank film, ruined for some simple, preventable reason.

Now that you have assembled enough gear to work with, there remains the problem of carrying it all. Personally, I don't like the leather "ever-ready" carrying cases — they're really "never-ready" cases. I prefer to carry the camera around my neck and zipped inside a shirt or jacket. But the case that comes with the camera does protect it in a pack or duffel bag. For anywhere off the pavement, forget the over-one-shoulder gadget bag, too. Instead, wear clothing with many pockets, like trout-fishing vests and safari jackets, and extend your carrying capacity further by wearing belt pouches and round-the-waist carrybags. Lenses won't fall out, even when you run, and they are always close at hand.

If your neck gets sore, shift the cameras to one shoulder for a while. They will ride along surprisingly well. Lenses of 200mm and shorter ride comfortably on a camera around your neck if pointed up and a jacket is zipped over them, but longer lenses should be carried in holsters hung on a belt or on their own over-head-and-shoulder straps.

"Before leaving home, devise ways to carry your gear conveniently, safely, and comfortably on the trail," the author advises. His versatile outfit (above, right) consists of several home-made belt pouches and a quiver-like holster which distribute the weight of his equipment evenly and place everything within easy reach. The fanny pouch at right carries small accessories such as film, filters, and extension tubes. His belt pouches for lenses are made of imitation leather and stitched to a belt of the same material. Kinne carries his cameras on different length straps around his neck so that they don't bang against one another, and a camera with a long lens rests in a holster pouch at his side. To protect equipment from rain and spray when canoeing, he uses inexpensive plastic containers (above, left). With tight-fitting lids and bubble-wrap to keep the camera stationary, the containers even float.

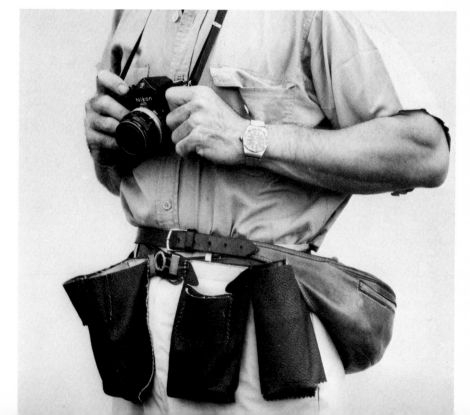

A candid camera for birds

There are hardly any creatures on earth more diverse, widespread, or fascinating than birds. They vary from two-inch midgets to ten-foot giants, from extremely shy ones to those you have to shoo out of your path, from flying experts to total nonfliers. And you find them almost everywhere, even at the poles.

Their allure is nearly universal, as attested by the presence of bird-watchers and birding groups in almost all communities. These people are a photographer's best friend when it comes to locating the best picture-taking opportunities, either locally or even within a few hundred miles.

If you share the birdwatchers' admiration and enthusiasm, it can be very disappointing to find that your first bird photographs consist of a group of small dots that you must interpret by saying, "See? *Those* are the birds." The problem, of course, is how to get close enough to shoot larger images of the birds on your film — and it can be solved in several ways.

The most obvious way is to move in closer, and this should be the first course of action. With practice, you can sidle up quite close. At times you may have to bend over, stoop, crawl, or climb. In every case, use whatever natural cover there is and, instead of walking directly towards them, come at the birds from an angle by facing a bit to one side and walking sideways as you approach. You will soon learn to detect their alert postures and stop your approach until they calm down.

Telephoto lenses are another means of getting a larger image, and they are a must for good bird photography. As mentioned before, the 200mm size is a very good choice because of its price, its light weight, and its ability to photograph in dim-light situations. However, longer lenses are often necessary for professional quality bird work. If you are willing to put up with the additional length and weight of a 400mm, for example, your chances of getting exciting bird pictures will be much improved. A few quite good 400mm lenses sell for about $60.

Another strategy is to move the *camera* close to where the birds are and use a remote-control device. A good tripod or clampod is essential, set up near the birds' perch, nest, or bait station. Birds will be suspicious of the camera at first, so set it up some distance away and gradually move it closer. Check your camera's instruction book, and if you can, lock up the mirror of your camera. This means less noise when you take a picture and doesn't startle the birds as much. Some shy species may take several days to get accustomed to the camera, so unless

Getting close enough to a subject like an anhinga (opposite) or a blue jay (above) to fill the camera frame with its image is dependent upon knowing the bird's habits, having the right equipment, and using special techniques. One method is to equip the camera with a remote-control device and station it close to a feeder, nest, or favorite perch. The remote-control rig above was set up by the author to photograph birds feeding. By placing peanuts just out of camera view, he lured the blue jay into position. When the bird was in focus, Kinne, hiding 30 to 40 feet away, tripped the shutter with an air release.

Kinne also devised a less expensive remote-control device (top) from some tape, two pieces of wood (one on the shutter release), strong thread, and a clampod.

A gentle tug by the photographer on the thread trips the shutter.

A blind (left) conceals the photographer as he quietly sets up his camera within shooting distance of a skittish bird. To get close to the anhinga as it perched just across the canal from the road he was travelling, Wendell D. Metzen used his car as a blind. The anhinga, with wings spread to dry after a plunge into Florida's Big Cypress Swamp to hunt for fish, remained unaware of Metzen as he snapped several shots with a 500mm telephoto.

Blinds can be a tent, a few yards of cloth that a photographer drapes over his shoulders, or even a shield on top of a tower. Whatever the design, it's important to select heavy fabric that can't be easily seen through.

you have this sort of leisure planned into your camping schedule, you may as well limit this kind of photography to your backyard. However, with luck, you can sometimes get a good shot in an hour or two.

A flash is often necessary for best results in remote-control work at nests and bait stations. In that case, arrange to have something in the near background — branches, grasses, or other natural material — or the distant background will be much too dark in the finished picture.

The air-release and pull-the-thread rigs both work, but by far the most convenient and productive equipment is the motor-drive camera. Each time you close the switch, the motorized camera takes a picture and rewinds itself. This saves you from having to charge up to the camera after each shot, disturbing the birds, and waiting for them to calm down again. Many people regard it as bird photography equipment at its finest.

Luring birds to a particular place where you want to observe them is an art in itself, yet millions of people do it daily — at their backyard bird-feeding stations. You can use the same strategy in your camping area or a little farther off the trail. The secret is knowing which birds like what foods. For example, sunflower seeds are universally liked by blue jays, cardinals, and other seedeaters; peanut butter or meat fats by woodpeckers, chickadees, titmice, nuthatches, and many other species. Look for natural cavities in tree trunks or branches and fill them with seeds or fat. Use cavities that are situated where they won't show in the picture.

Nest photography is really a field in itself, though similar to remote-control photography done at a perch or feeder. The essential thing is to avoid harming nest, eggs, or young birds in any way, including keeping the parent birds away too long or causing them to desert the nest altogether. Try to disturb things as little as possible. If it's

necessary to move branches for a better view, tie them back instead of breaking them off; when you leave, release them to their original position to resume their work of shielding the nest from sun or predators. To check on the progress of eggs or chicks, use a small mirror mounted on a pole. You can look with a mirror and slip away in 30 seconds, causing much less disturbance than climbing the tree. Be careful not to beat a path, literally, to the nest — that points out the exact location to passing humans, and to predators as well. Using a telephoto lens will let you set up at a slight distance instead of right on top of the nest. The 100mm and 200mm lenses are good for this.

Each nest presents slightly different problems in getting close. Nests on open ground, like those of gulls, terns, quail, pheasant, ducks, and geese, pose no difficulties other than getting the birds accustomed to a remote-control camera or camera blind.

A blind, yet another way to get close to birds, is usually an improvised cloth tent in which the photographer sits, stands, or lies, sticking his lens out through a hole in one side. Frequently the blind is set up at a distance and gradually moved closer until it is within good shooting range. The traditional material for a blind is burlap, also known as hessian. This rough fabric is inexpensive, but it stays wet forever once it gets soaked. Some of the lighter-weight fabrics blending cotton and nylon are much more pleasant to work with. Pure nylon is good, and a trip to a tent manufacturer or truck-and-boat-cover shop should yield you a number of choices.

One much-overlooked blind is the automobile. Most birds are used to seeing cars, and many will not shy away from them. Sometimes they will even be attracted to a parked car when they are seeking a windbreak on a blustery day. You simply stop your car on a dirt road, roll the window down,

Birds have such varied habits and habitats that photographing them requires a broad range of equipment and techniques. Nesting birds, like the Forster's terns at far left, are usually best approached in a blind. That was how Charles G. Summers, Jr. caught the male passing a tiny fish to his mate to feed their hungry chick. Despite the terns' reputation for launching fierce, screaming attacks on any intruder, including man, they will grow accustomed to a stealthily introduced blind. Summers set up a blind in his flat-bottomed duck boat and then slowly poled it within 15 feet of the Utah marshland nest of dead reeds. He caught the action with a 50mm to 300mm zoom lens.

The close-up of a cardinal above was taken by George H. Harrison using his Wisconsin home as a blind. After filling the feeder with sunflower seeds, Harrison retreated to his back porch, focused his 400mm lens on the feeder, and waited until the cardinal moved into a desirable pose.

To capture the alternately gliding and beating motion of pelican wings (left), David B. Marshall relied on a different skill, wingshooting. A good way to practice this type of shot is to focus a long lens on the point where one expects to catch the birds, find them in the viewer, and follow them with the camera until the image is sharp. Then shoot.

and wait; the birds will come and sit on the road in your lee. At other times you can inch along a road, beach, or field until you're within camera range. Convertibles are convenient for getting under birds on wires or high limbs.

Some people think it is sacrilege to use a blind to photograph a bird or to entice it with bait or to "control" it in any way. There's nothing wrong with this approach, of course, but if your objective is to get the best possible pictures, some sort of control is not only permitted, it is almost mandatory. Making bird-like squeaks by kissing the back of your hand, setting out seeds, suet, or other bait, and using commercial bird calls will help you get much better pictures than you would otherwise. I frankly see no harm in this, as long as you do not create an erroneous impression — drawing pine siskins into a flower-garden, for example, or chickadees onto a beach. That would make for misleading photographs, and can easily be avoided — especially if you've done your "homework" by studying the habitat and habits of the birds you are setting out to photograph.

One bird-attracting practice that is increasingly condemned by ornithologists is the use of tape-recorded birdcalls. Just because they are so true to life, the taped calls can cause male birds to desert a nesting territory. The female in turn may abandon young birds in the nest or be unable to feed them by herself.

Human beings naturally feel great kinship with other mammals because they feel, hear, smell, and see pretty much alike. The big difference is that they do these things so much *better* than we do, a challenge that creates most of the problems encountered by photographers.

Mammals come in nearly as wide a variety of shapes and sizes as do birds. There are mammals that are quite bird-like — bats, for example, which should be photographed using bird-shooting

techniques. Other mammals are decidedly fish-like, so underwater (or at least fish-stalking) methods are necessary. The majority of mammals are terrestrial, and they, too, require their own particular photographic approaches.

We usually think first of the larger mammals, more often than not the game species that are hunted in season in the fall. To get good pictures of them, as indicated earlier, it's better to go where they are *not* hunted, where they have no more than a normal caution towards man. A sanctuary surrounded by hunting territory is excellent. The game animals from all the surrounding areas will pour into the protected area and will be more concentrated than usual. They are no fools! Even if they feed outside the refuge at night, daylight will find them resting up where they've learned it's safe. Since such sanctuaries are usually open to the public, there are often free maps or visitor-orientation talks given that will inform you where (in general) to look for what, and when, and where you may not be allowed to go. Then it's mainly a matter of being where the animals are. Many times that means getting up before dawn and doing a little hiking to get to a desirable place for finding the mammal you want to photograph. When choosing your exact shooting location, bear in mind the direction of the light. The sun's first low rays are more likely to cause lens flare than the more nearly vertical rays of midday. Check also on wind direction, which can significantly affect the success or failure of your operations by alerting the animals to your presence. The wind is quite likely to shift just after sunrise — cool down-slope winds can change to sun-warmed up-slope winds within five minutes.

It is more important to keep noise to a minimum when working with mammals than when working with any other kind of wildlife. Avoid carrying anything that will clank, or put tape over it so it will clunk instead. Of course you should avoid white or bright clothing

and the strong smells of insect repellent, perfume, after-shave lotion, and tobacco. Even scented deodorants should be avoided if you really want to be serious about it. This also helps to make you less attractive to insects — which can be very helpful if you're in a blind for hours at a time. The mammals will know where *you* are much more of the time than you will know where they are — but they may still stay around if you don't do something that drives them off.

Using a hiding place of some sort, a blind or natural cover like clumps of bushes or a stand of trees, is beneficial in many kinds of large-mammal photography. Again, be careful about wind direction. Bear in mind that your silhouette is often more visible than your figure; make sure there are trees or something behind you to break up your outline and conceal movement. You may want to wear a head net for mosquitoes. It has the added advan-

The wariness of the cacomistle, or ring-tailed cat (opposite), typifies the highly suspicious nature that enables wild mammals to survive. Some species are so evasive that they can only be photographed with a remote-control rig (right, bottom) adapted for the animal to take its own picture. Here the author has turned a nonmotorized camera with a cable-release socket into a camera trap fired by a modified mousetrap (bottom of photo). The camera is mounted on a lowpod (shown on page 191 — Ed.), wrapped in plastic, and lashed with sync cord to a tree located on a game trail. When an animal either breaks the thread attached to the mousetrap, or picks up bait tied to the thread, the trap springs shut, pressing the cable release.

Because so many animals hunt at night, it's almost essential to go on a night prowl to photograph them. The author's simplest night rig (right, top) consists of a 35mm SLR with telephoto and flash unit, and a flashlight attached to the camera for spotting creatures and focusing. Willis Peterson had to have both nighttime and remote control equipment to get the shot of the startled ring-tailed cat as he turned to peer at the camera.

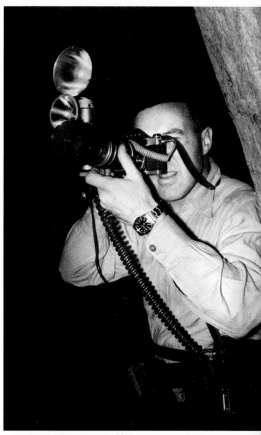

tage of hiding your face — often the most prominent feature viewed from a distance. Most head nets are green or olive-drab — perfect!

As to photographic equipment, the long telephotos are needed about 99 percent of the time, and carrying a small flash unit is a good idea, too. Many times, even at a distance that is supposedly too far, the flash will open up shadows a bit.

A challenging and suspenseful photographic technique is the camera trap, which is very useful for photographing elusive mammals. The camera is focused on a trail or on a bait station, and the animal takes its own picture by breaking a thread or walking through the beam of an electric eye.

In making a camera trap, a certain amount of improvisation is always needed, ranging from building a remote-control shutter release for a nonmotorized camera to setting up a switch mechanism for a motorized one. For example, you can improvise a simple remote-control shutter release for a nonmotorized camera by adapting a common mousetrap (as shown on page 179). Mount the trap separately, away from the camera, and use a cable release to absorb the vibrations. Otherwise, the trap jars the camera when it goes off. With a motorized camera, a rig that touches two wires together — paperclips or nails set up to touch each other when pulled by a thread — will set off the camera.

When using a camera trap at night, rig up a flashbulb gun. Any flashbulb gun will give enough light, and at 1/250th or 1/500th of a second you should stop most motion when your unsuspecting "victim" trips the shutter. However, it pays to run exposure tests outdoors at night before you leave home. Have a stand-in for the animal wear medium-dark clothing or even a fur coat to approximate the reflectance of the animal's coat. To get a better picture, use a second flash to backlight or rim-light the animal. Again, be sure to enclose gear in plastic bags, or rain, dew, and fog will raise hob with your equipment. Camera-trap work is fascinating, but fraught with frustrations. The suspense is high, but the

Whether portrait (opposite) or action shot (above), a good wildlife photo has something interesting to say about the way an animal looks or acts. Too often, a shot only bears witness to the photographer's ability to get close. Dean Krakel II's portrait of an elk is lifted out of the ordinary by the low light which halos antlers and body. Shallow depth-of-field softens the bands of light and dark, enhancing the elk's regal pose. Leonard Rue IV's dramatic sequence of embattled rams clashing horns to establish rank within the herd has the interest built-in.

rewards can be great. You may catch nothing but wind-blown leaves or a surprised Boy Scout, but you may catch a six-point buck or a bear.

The smaller mammals are a lot more common and often are much more approachable than the larger ones. For creatures like skunk, raccoon, or squirrel, the same basic techniques apply. Anything smaller than these requires special methods. You can set up a camera trap across the mouth of a den belonging to a mouse or chipmunk, but this is ticklish business and often unsuccessful. Sometimes you can put out food to entice a small animal to a photogenic spot, but you may have to hide yourself and watch for a long time before the animal will approach. Then the flash may spook him so much he will refuse to come out again. The deer mouse, is so flash-conscious that after one picture he'll sit with his eyes half-shut, looking highly suspicious and not at all deer mouselike.

Many of the large and medium-sized mammals are nocturnal, so you will have many more chances to get good pictures if you indulge in a night prowl. This is a fascinating activity, and I don't recall having ever been really disappointed in one. Since you can't always see where you are stepping, it's a good idea to wear waterproof boots in case you step into a bog or stream. You will need a flashlight, preferably two — a large one for mammal-finding and a smaller one for reading camera settings. The small one should have a red lens to preserve your own night-vision adaptation. It also helps to mount a flashlight on your camera or telephoto lens so that it illuminates whatever the lens is aimed at. Animals' eyes will shine in this light, enabling you to focus upon them easily. It's difficult to focus on anything except eyeshine, as the lens-mounted light doesn't throw any shadows you can use. A headlight that you wear like a miner's cap is even better because it frees both your hands.

By all means take as much photo gear as you can easily carry on a

night hike, because you may have opportunities to use all of it. Singing frogs require the plus or supplementary lenses; moths, which are most active at night, the macro lens. Waiting to catch a frog singing is tiring unless the camera is on a tripod or a clampod. In short, you never know what you'll find, but the hike is bound to be interesting.

For night photography, it's mandatory to let the landowner or game warden know what you're doing and where you'll be — with your light you'll look just like a poacher. Various calls — the commercial devices used by hunters to imitate the bleat of a lost fawn, the scream of a wounded rabbit,

and the sounds of other mammals — may attract hunters as well as the animal you're after. Even if you are not a hunter yourself, you need to be aware of hunting season dates. If you're out in the woods during the season, there are people with guns out there, too, and it's rather important to take steps to keep yourself alive. In or out of season, there *may* be poachers along the edges of sanctuaries and preserves. Not expecting any other human presence, they might mistake your movements or game calls for those of an animal — so exercise caution. By working closely with rangers and wardens you should be perfectly safe on your photography safari.

Creative use of the technical limitations of camera equipment is a challenge that faces all photographers. In this picture of a young white-tailed deer, Blair Pittman used the shallow depth-of-field of a telephoto set at a wide aperture to see his way through a difficult shooting situation.

With telephotos opened to a fast f-stop, the longer the lens, the shorter the distance in front of and behind the plane of sharp focus. In the setting above, Pittman turned that weakness into a plus. The tall grasses of Texas' Big Thicket didn't permit a clear view of the startled deer, but the telephoto lens captured a glimpse and softened the setting enough for an evocative shot. The deer's natural habitat became a hazy verdant screen that suggests the animal's elusive nature.

Photographing amphibians and reptiles

For dramatic and unusual photographs, don't overlook the "herps," reptiles and amphibians, whose ancestry goes back to the dinosaurs. From the 12-foot alligator to the frog no bigger than your thumbnail, they are a fascinating lot. And they're easier to find than you may think. Being cold-blooded creatures, herps become more active when they are warm and more sluggish when they are cold — an important cue for photographers: they're easier to photograph in cool weather.

If you go hiking or camping near a pond in the spring, you will almost certainly see and hear frogs, toads, salamanders, or newts. They must return each spring from their life on land to lay eggs in the water from whence they came. Look for frogs sunning themselves on a lily pad or rock. You should also find lots of them on a cool summer morning after a heavy rain. A telephoto lens is usually necessary to get a large enough image; try the longest one you have.

Children are fascinated by the way frogs develop from tadpoles. You could record the metamorphosis by taking some frog eggs (and pond water) home in a glass jar to photograph as they turn into tadpoles, into two-legged tadpoles, into tailed frogs, and into adult frogs. Of course, you can catch adult frogs and toads with a strong insect net and take them home in separate jars half-full of wet paper towels for photographing in a studio setting.

Lizards and turtles may be found sunning themselves, and a careful approach often brings them within range of a telephoto lens. Don't pass up cloudy days, however; they are good for dark subjects like turtles because the details show up better.

Using identification books adds greatly to the fun of photographing the amphibians you see, but it is absolutely essential that you study one before photographing snakes. You must know if you're dealing with a poisonous species. Remember that in the United States all poisonous snakes (except the tropical coral snake) have large, triangular heads that can be seen at a safe distance. By the time you're too close for comfort, you will also see that they have "cat eyes," eyes with vertical pupils. If you see a snake with a round head and round pupils, you can take your time in planning your shot. Remember, however, that this distinction does *not* hold true anywhere outside the continental United States.

Since most snakes prey upon amphibians, the pond is a good place to look for them also, on the bank or in the water. When you are photographing in any area where poisonous snakes are known to occur, carry a snake stick even though you plan to photograph only the nonpoisonous species. Use the stick to turn over logs and rocks without exposing your fingers.

If you do happen to come across a poisonous snake, I advise you not to risk photographing it, even if you have a snake stick. Many of the dramatic photos you see of poisonous snakes were taken by professionals who captured them, took them home in snake sacks, and cooled them down in the refrigerator before photographing them under controlled conditions with the aid of an experienced snake handler.

For indoor photography of captive amphibians or harmless snakes, the normal lens works well; but a macro lens will give you better details of feet, eyes, scales. A short telephoto with plus-lens enables you to do the same thing from a short distance — a necessity with shy subjects. The only real problem is shadows on the background. Position your lights to avoid this; sometimes adding rocks, branches, and plants will help, too.

Photographing a one-inch long spring peeper (opposite) can be a challenging outdoor or indoor project. Outdoors, a telephoto lens with extension tubes or a bellows attachment is needed, and perhaps a strobe unit. Photographers who capture their subject and take it home for a set-up aquarium shot usually take along some vegetation like the broken reed on which photographer Howard Kessler snapped this one. An atomizer is used to keep the frog's skin moist (for the frog's health, the photo's authenticity). Colored paper can serve as a background for the aquarium.

Turtles are sometimes easier to find than frogs. Photographer Alvin E. Staffan discovered the wood turtle at right on dry land, but they are also seen in and near water. Turtles move surprisingly fast; only high shutter speeds (1/125 sec. or faster) stop the motion of their feet.

Rachel Lamoreux's outdoor sequence of a monarch butterfly emerging from its cocoon (below) and the author's indoor shot of a salticid spider (right) both required knowledge of the creatures' life cycles, keen observation, timing, and perseverance. Though Kinne's indoor setup gave him more control of the shooting situation, he still had to wait to catch the spider in an interesting pose. To magnify its image to twice life-size, he attached a short extension tube and a bellows to a 50mm lens. An electronic flash provided the light and stopped the spider's movement.

Lamoreux's butterfly sequence required only a 90mm lens and consummate patience. Because of temperature fluctuations and other variables, she had to be ready to shoot at any time from the 9th to the 15th day of the maturation of the pupa (below, left). When ready, the adult frees itself from the pupal case (next two pictures) in 1½ to 3½ minutes. Pumping its body fluids into the wings takes another 10 to 20 minutes, followed by several hours of clinging vertically to the pupal case to dry before its first flight.

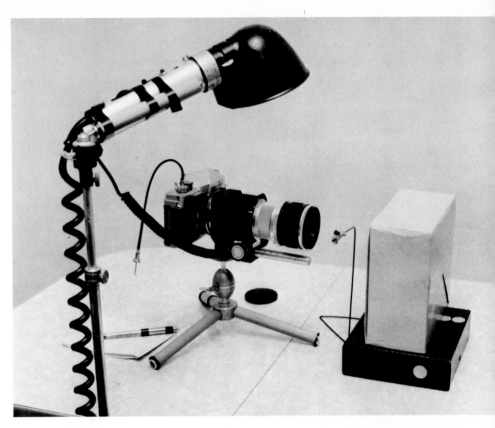

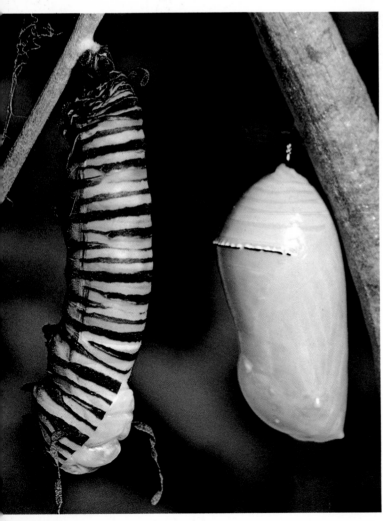

Picture the amazing world of insects

If you have ever been brought to the point of despair by hunting long and unsuccessfully for photographic subjects, turn to insects — there is almost *never* a shortage of specimens.

For a starter, a flower garden is an excellent place to work. After that, get a butterfly net or, better yet, a sweep net and go collecting in any field or vacant lot. Five minutes' work will give you enough specimens for a day's shooting. Another good source is your local beekeeper.

Since all insects are either small or tiny or nearly microscopic, you need close-up equipment for sure. And since insects are often shy, too, you may also need a close-focusing telephoto. In any case, try to shoot life-size or greater-than-life-size images on the film. The absolute minimum equipment for insect photography is a camera with a normal lens and a plus-three supplementary lens.

These are simple, inexpensive lenses, sometimes called plus-lenses, or portrait attachments. They screw onto the front of a regular lens, and in a pinch can even be taped in place. With the lens set at infinity, the camera is in sharp focus at a distance equal to the focal length of the plus-lens. A plus-one lens has a focal length of one meter, 39.37 inches. A plus-two is in focus at ½ meter, 19.7 inches, and a plus-three at about 13 inches. There are more powerful plus-lenses, up to plus-ten; but they degrade the image badly. Up through plus-three, you'll get good sharpness if you can stop down a little. With a plus-two or plus-three lens you can photograph butter-flies and damselflies, for example, if you spend a few minutes in a slow, careful approach; indoors, you can shoot any fairly large, captive insect.

The telephoto lens with a supplementary lens, extension tube, or bellows is excellent for close-up insect photography. Butterflies, dragonflies, and similar-sized subjects are best stalked with the 200mm, 300mm, or 400mm. The 100mm lens is best for smaller insects, down to half-inch in length. For even smaller insects, such as ants or ladybugs, special close-up techniques must be employed.

To shoot larger-than-life-size images of ants and other tiny insects, use a macro lens, the best lens commonly available for ultra-close-up photography. But reverse the lens so the back element faces the insect instead of the

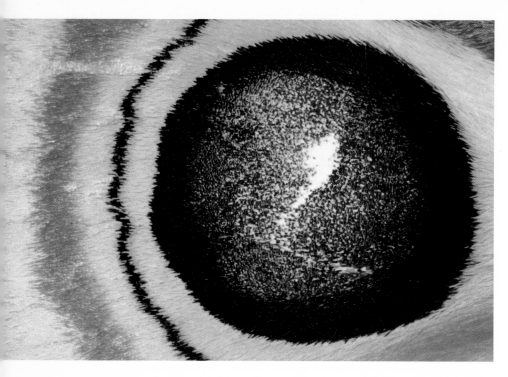

To photograph the mating activity of cecropia moths (opposite), David Cavagnaro approached the pair closely with a 55mm macro lens and filled the frame with their image. James Carmichael moves in closer still to explore the structural marvels of different insects. For the finely detailed close-up of a yellow jacket's head (below),

Carmichael used three extension rings with a 35mm lens. His four-times-life-size image of the eyespot on an Io moth's wing (above) appears to go beyond realism into sheer abstract design. To get that effect, he fitted a 100mm macro lens with three extension rings and used a strobe light to supplement natural outdoor light.

film. In the normal position, the deeply-recessed front element of a macro lens forces you to get very close when shooting life-size images. Reversing the lens gives you a couple more inches of room between the plane of sharp focus and the front of the lens. When rigged like this, the focusing mount does *not* change the focus. To focus, move the camera.

To reverse a lens, all you need is a simple reversing ring, which screws into the front of the lens like a screw-in filter and connects to the camera body or extension tube. Unfortunately, these rings are seldom stocked by camera stores. To purchase one, check the ads in a recent photographic magazine.

With the lens reversed, focus on a ruler and see how much area your camera takes in. If it's 1½ inches, you are getting a life-size image; if ¾ inch, a twice-life-size image; and so on. With extension tubes or a bellows, you can set any magnification up to about 5X. Beyond that, photographing through a microscope is in order. When you are doing close-up work, it's best not to twist the lens mount to focus; set the lens for the magnification you want, sight through the viewfinder, and move the camera back and forth. When the image is sharp, shoot.

In nearly all close-up work, electronic flash is needed. The depth of field is so shallow you will want to shoot at f/16 or f/22, and this requires a lot of light. The flash also stops motion. I find that with the smallest electronic flash I could find, having a Kodachrome 25 guide number of 30, I am shooting life-size images at f/22.

You can attract insects with bait, using different lures for different insects. Cut flowers, if they're really fresh, are good as bait for beetles, bees, and some other insects, but lose their appeal quickly. Drops of honey or maple syrup will draw bees, especially yellow jackets. Be careful around the latter, as they're the most short-tempered of all. The most docile of the stinging insects, by the way, are the brown *Polistes,* or paper wasps, that build their small nests under eaves and overhangs. They will tolerate all

In the outdoor "studio," a photographer has great control over stationary subjects like the Turk's-cap lily (right). Robert M. Butterfield wanted to show off the lily's colorful, pendulous flowers so he selected a shooting angle with an undistracting, dark background.

For settings in which lighting conditions are less favorable, Kinne suggests several techniques to obtain pleasing results. Immediately below, he uses gold foil (available in florists' shops) to throw a subtle, warm light on roses. He recommends foil whenever natural light doesn't adequately open up the shadows falling on a subject and he is reluctant to use fill-in flash because it may be stronger than the main light.

At right, below, he eliminates an overly detailed background by setting a self-timer to trip the camera while he waves a yard length of cloth just out of focus behind the plant.

Since many plant subjects are close to the ground, Kinne uses a "lowpod" (opposite, left), made by screwing a tilt-top head to a piece of plywood (perhaps 4 by 8 inches), and glueing rubber or foam to the bottom of the wood to steady the camera during long exposures.

To adapt an Instamatic-type camera with an added-on plus lens for close-up work, Kinne improvised the wire gadget opposite, right . The wire focal-frame shows what will be in the picture, yet stays out of the picture itself. The vertical tips of the focal-frame should be one meter (39.37 inches) from the lens for a plus-one lens, one-half meter (19.7 inches) for a plus-two lens, one-third meter (13.12 inches) for a plus-three, and so on. Says Kinne, "It works like a charm!"

Plants present a different challenge

kinds of close approaches without becoming alarmed. At night, a light beamed through a window will draw moths of all sizes, with luck even the beautiful pale-green luna moth. Photography under these conditions is easy, but a background of screenwire isn't too esthetic. Remove the screen and the moths will sit on the window-glass. They can also be captured and photographed later in an indoor setup.

Handling active insects can be a real problem. At home you can temporarily slow their movements by cooling them in the refrigerator. Don't overdo it — try 15 minutes for a start. Also put the *perch* you're using in the picture — rock, twig, or whatever — in the refrigerator. The cool perch slows the insect's warming up and gives you time for a few more shots before your subject becomes too active. In a camping situation, a shot of carbon-dioxide (CO_2) works well. You can buy a bottle from a scientific supply house. Put the insect in a small box, squirt in a bit of CO_2, and wait until he's "out." Then place him on a perch and wait for him to come to. You can get several shots as he wakes and begins to move. These tricks may seem like a lot of trouble, but if you do much insect photography, you will soon find they are worth it.

An intriguing, and motionless subject is a spiderweb. Spiderwebs are beautiful creations, true engineering marvels which are easy to photograph. Under natural light, they usually show best at dawn when they are dew-covered, which usually means rising early and prowling fields and gardens. At this time of day there is little wind, an important advantage. You may have to shoot through a small aperture to have the entire web sharp, and this means carrying a tripod so you can use a slow shutter speed for more light. If there is no natural dew, simply make artificial dew with an atomizer. Put it on slowly and gently, with the finest possible droplets. Sometimes at the break of dawn you can even catch a prismatic rainbow when the sun's rays strike a droplet. If the background of the spiderweb is cluttered or distracting, hang or have someone hold a coat or blanket behind the web, far enough away from the subject to be out of sharp focus.

Using flash for spiderwebs is often disappointing because the angle of the light is critical and you can't see what it will be. While looking into the viewfinder, shine a flashlight around on the web until you see the lighting effect you want; then place the flash unit in the same place and fire away.

No matter where you are in the outdoors, no matter how poor the animal tracking, the bird watching, or the insect stalking, you are still surrounded by good subjects for photography: plants. They are everywhere, and you can find attractive ones in any season. Even in midwinter there are lichens and fungi; evergreens with interesting needles, cones, and bark patterns; and naked hardwoods silhouetted against the sky.

Another appealing aspect of plant photography is that the entire family can take a part. The children are often better than adults at finding good specimens. And no one needs to keep quiet for fear of scaring off the subject.

As an extra bonus, just about any camera can be used for plant photography, though naturally some are better than others. Our old friend, the single-lens reflex, is nearly ideal, especially if it has interchangeable lenses, a built-in light meter (preferably of the "spot" type), and a macro lens. But twin-lens reflexes, rangefinder cameras, and even Instamatics can be used with good results. The simpler cameras often won't focus closer than four or five feet, but a quick-and-easy solution is to add a supplementary lens.

Sharp focus is particularly important when shooting close-ups. With the

SLR camera there's no problem, but with simple cameras and rangefinder types, you need a focusing aid like the one shown on page 191.

For flowers that grow in dark places, you must use a flash to get good exposures. For close-ups, the flash will be too close and cause overexposure; try covering the flash with two or three thicknesses of a white handkerchief. If photographing only by natural light, use the exposure meter in the usual way, but be careful since dark backgrounds will fool the meter and cause bad exposures. Move the camera in close so that the flower fills the whole viewfinder. Don't worry about focus; just set the exposure and back up until the image is sharp and shoot away.

Probably the biggest problem in this sort of work is the wind. With small flowers on slender stems, it can drive you to distraction. Wind shields are lifesavers, the most useful ones being of clear plastic as they can't throw shadows. Some photographers carry pieces of cloth (about three by four feet) that serve both as wind shields and as plain, out-of-focus backgrounds. But the clear plastic is much better. Sometimes you have to string up a miniature tent to block drafts.

Most tripods are 'way too high for flower photography. To make a suitable camera support, buy a small tilt-top tripod head from a camera store and a metal rod a quarter-inch thick and about ten inches long from a hardware store. Have one end of the rod threaded with a ¼-20 die, screw on the tilt-top, and have the other end sharpened. Now you can drive it into the ground and aim your camera. Another way of making a lowpod is illustrated on page 191.

When the camera is set up, look first through the finder to check for distracting twigs, branches, or rocks and to decide whether you want the background sharp or out of focus. It's often effective to throw a shadow on the background and leave the flower in strong light—or vice versa. To cope with a hopeless background, have someone hold a cloth out of focus behind the flower. If you can use an exposure of several seconds, and the

192

A red passion flower assumes new dimensions in James Carmichael's still life (opposite, bottom) through his choice of framing, lighting, shooting angle, setting, and equipment. These tools are the photographer's means of communicating his personal vision of a subject. Carmichael uses a 100mm macro to move his eye inside the passion flower, where the bright red color and shape of the petals provide a dramatic setting for an elaborately detailed pistil and stamen. To sharpen the color and the details, he placed dark paper behind the blossom. Carmichael's cactus (opposite, top), photographed in subdued natural light from above, is transformed to a subtle pattern of textures by the angle of the shot.

Robert Carr finds the first few inches of space above the earth a good place to look for plant subjects for macro work. His ground-level view of 6-inch horsetails (left) is composed of simple vertical variations which give depth to the shot as they fade softly into the background. Light from a reflector highlights the slender stalks and reinforces that verticality. Below, shallow depth-of-field and strong directional lighting help photographer Leland Payton single out a sunflower from its gold-speckled, green surroundings.

cloth can be kept moving, it will provide a perfectly plain background.

A piece of coated nylon is good to use as a ground cloth in wet areas. I carry a small atomizer, too, to add "dew" when there isn't any. And a polarizing filter enables you to control reflections from shiny leaves or water.

One of the handiest things any flower photographer can carry is a small square of aluminum foil. Foil reflects light into dark places and illuminates the shaded parts of flowers and plants.

Shooting plants is an excellent way to utilize a foggy or cloudy day; often the results are better than the bright-sun pictures. When you find a good specimen, take time to look at it from all angles to see what will make the best composition. Decide what to emphasize and minimize, by lighting, angle of view, filters, or selective focus.

It's fun and it sharpen's one's eye to make a good-natured contest out of flower photography. When someone finds a good specimen, each member of the family takes one picture without the others watching. Then the pictures are compared after they come back. It's common for them all to be quite different! One backlighted, one with dew, one with flash, others without. You can learn surprising things by seeing how imaginatively other people shoot the same subject.

Whether shooting flowers with members of his family or sneaking up on wildlife by himself, a nature photographer is confronted with the exciting challenges of seeing what surrounds him and learning about it and how to capture his personal vision of it on film. The sensitive, trained eye of the photographer opens wide new vistas of experience, knowledge, and understanding. Take it all in, in fantastic Wildlife Country!

Although the camera frames only a portion of a landscape that to the eye seems boundless, one with a wide-angle lens embraces more of the panorama than any other. In Keith Gunnar's scenic of Washington's Cle Elum Valley, the great depth of field of his 35mm lens exaggerates the distance to the mountains that beckon visitors to explore.

Bibliography

Backpacking and Camping: Where to Go

Sterling, E.M. *Western Trips and Trails.* Harrisburg, Pa.: Stackpole Books, 1974. 351 pp.; $4.95; paperback.

For nine western states, Sterling selects what he thinks are some of the best vacation spots for hiking and camping in the mountains and on the beaches. Brief descriptions of the flora, fauna, and geography of each site provide an idea of what it is like to be there. Names of access routes tell how to get to each place; enumeration of the activities available (scenic drives, hiking, canoeing, and camping) helps in deciding what to do once there; and information on permits and reservations required before arriving helps with preplanning. There are also addresses of sources of more detailed information. Maps and black-and-white photos.

Sutton, Ann and Myron. *Wilderness Areas of North America.* New York: Funk and Wagnalls, 1974. 406 pp.; $10.00; hardbound.

Immensely useful, this book lists over 500 national and state parks and refuges, most of them over 5,000 acres. It describes "geology, flora and fauna, size, location, approach routes, what to see and do, where roads and/or trails reach, packers and outfitters available, campsites in the vicinity, accommodations nearby, who administers the area, unusual regulations, special features that should not be missed, and where to write for information." All this is done concisely.

Thomas, Bill. *Eastern Trips and Trails.* Harrisburg, Pa.: Stackpole Books, 1975. 253 pp.; $4.95; paperback.
.........., *Mid-America Trips and Trails.* Harrisburg, Pa.: Stackpole Books, 1975. 238 pp.; $4.95; paperback.

Each of these guides lists over 50 different hiking and camping areas. Instead of giving details about each trail, Thomas presents basic facts and descriptions to give the reader a feel for each area and to help him choose a vacation spot. In addition to providing a brief description of each area (what animals, plants, trees are there; how large it is; major rivers; flyways, etc.), he tells how to get there and where to drive, hike, canoe, or camp. Guidance for backpackers includes information on permits and reservations. Finally, Thomas advises where to write to obtain more detailed information on each area. Both books are illustrated with maps and black-and-white photos.

Backpacking: Equipment, Food, Techniques

Cunningham, Gerry, and Hansson, Margaret. *Light Weight Camping Equipment and How to Make It.* New York: Charles Scribner's Sons, 1976. 150 pp.; $5.95; paperback.

Gerry Cunningham, the founder and designer of the well-known GERRY line of backpacking equipment, is an authority on this subject. He and Ms. Hansson describe in detail different fabrics and insulation and methods of pattern-making and sewing. Includes detailed instructions and diagrams for specific projects ranging from a belt pocket to a sleeping bag. The text also teaches how to evaluate the quality of commercial products. Excellent.

Fletcher, Colin. *The New Complete Walker: The Joys and Techniques of Hiking and Backpacking.* 2nd rev. ed. New York: Alfred A. Knopf, 1974. 485 pp.; $10.00; hardbound.

This classic describes in detail techniques of hiking and types of hiking equipment, for beginner through expert outdoorsman. Fletcher has carefully updated and revised the first edition, but his thoroughness is not tedious. He writes that "equipment and techniques are mere means to an end," and he means it. The descriptions and explanations are often accompanied by anecdotes from Fletcher's experience hiking in the Grand Canyon and in California deserts and are always in line with his basic criterion of outdoor excellence: "Keep things simple."

Frostline Kits. *The Personal Touch II.* Frostline Circle, Denver, Colo., n.d. 59 pp.; $2.95; pamphlet.

This pamphlet, full of photographs of customized kits, gives simple patterns and instructions on how to customize clothing, sleeping bag, and tent kits. The ideas are applicable to other kit manufacturers' products as well as Frostline's. Suggestions for both decorative and functional alterations include tips on how to add embroidery, appliques, yokes, contrasting accents, pockets, and detachable sleeves.

Kemsley, William, Jr. et. al. *Backpacking Equipment: A Consumers' Guide.* New York: Macmillan Publishing Co., Collier Books, 1975. 160 pp.; $4.95; paperback.

This comprehensive guide is full of useful evaluations of packs, sleeping bags, tents, boots, and freeze-dried foods by brand name. Articulate, even-handed comparisons are coupled with clear explanations of the theories behind the designs. Tables, graphs, line art, black-and-white photographs.

Manning, Harvey. *Backpacking, One Step at a Time.* New York: Random House, Vintage Books, 1973. 353 pp.; $2.95; paperback.

Besides giving complete, well-thought-out advice on how to buy essential equipment, veteran backpacker and mountain climber Manning tells how to walk comfortably, cross fast-running streams, and climb steep, rocky hills safely. His excellent chapter "Suffer the Little Children" tells you how to include your children and still enjoy your trip by keeping the activity "not only within the *physical* limits but the *fun* limits." Delightful cartoon illustrations; black-and-white photos.

Roberts, Harry N. *Movin' Out: Equipment and Techniques for Eastern Hikers.* Lexington, Mass.: Stone Wall Press, 1975. 139 pp.; $3.95; paperback.

This book presents facts and an outfitter's entertaining opinions about how to buy the right equipment, how to carry it, how to find your way with map and compass, how to give first aid for common trail ailments. There is even some good advice on how to get your mate and children happily hiking the trails with you. Nitty-gritty information on what goes into quality gear, given by an expert—Roberts is a design consultant to outdoor equipment manufacturers. Illustrated with line art.

Silverman, Goldie. *Backpacking with Babies and Small Children.* Lynwood, Wash.: Signpost Publications, 1975. 144 pp.; $4.95; paperback.

The author and her husband write from personal experience, having gone on hiking trips with three children, ages 15 months, 6 and 8 years. Her advice? Start with day hikes, then go on longer journeys. Practical information on the differences between traveling with infants and small children; tips on infant carriers and packs for children; and advice on how to spoon feed without a high chair, how to go about "toileting" (but *don't* follow her advice to bury disposable diapers!), and how to get children to help with campsite chores—and enjoy it. She also describes simple games and diversions using camping gear.

Stout, James H. and Ann M. *Backpacking with Small Children.* New York: Funk and Wagnalls, 1975. 223 pp.; $6.95; hardbound.

The authors consider their book a "supplement to be read and used by parents already experienced in backcountry travel," but it is useful for beginners, too. There are chapters on how old children should be before taking them on the trail, how to buy and make children's clothing and equipment, and how to prepare for a trip that is fun for the kids as well as for the parents. It is especially good on how to motivate children (for example, by selecting goals in which they will be interested) and on how to meet children's special physical and psychological needs. Photographs, tables, useful bibliography.

Sumner, Robert. *Make Your Own Camping Equipment.* New York: Drake Publishing Co., 1976. 168 pp.; $6.95; paperback.

Profusely illustrated, this book has chapters on materials, construction techniques, and making your own patterns. Patterns and design criteria are given for both simple and advanced projects. Also covers maintenance and repair of equipment.

Canoes, Rafts, and River Tours

Arighi, Scott and Margaret. *Wildwater Touring.* New York: Macmillan Publishing Co., 1974. 334 pp.; $8.95; hardbound.

This book is "a guide to extended tripping by canoe, kayak, drift boat, or raft," and it "attempts to provide enough information for the would-be wildwater tourist to make a tour safely without hiring an outfitter or guide." There is much on how and where to tour, but not on how to handle a boat. It has sections on boat accessories and repair, camping gear and personal equipment, photography, fishing, and safety. The Arighis describe nine self-guided tours of rivers in Idaho and Oregon, giving detailed maps and descriptions of the rivers, difficulty ratings, best seasons to go, and advice on which types of boats to use.

Evans, G. Heberton, III. *Canoeing Wilderness Waters.* Cranbury, New Jersey: A. S. Barnes & Co., 1975. 211 pp.; $17.50; hardbound.

Although this book caters to "wilderness canoeing [which] differs from paddling around the summer cottage," it offers advice and instruction applicable to all types of canoeing and canoers. Tells and shows with black-and-white photographs and diagrams how to perform many different strokes; how to travel upstream and downstream and in windy weather; how to portage; and how to repair aluminum, fiberglass, and canvas canoes. Prospective buyers will appreciate the tables giving dimensions of common types and brands of canoes.

Jenkinson, Michael. *Wild Rivers of North America.* New York: E. P. Dutton, 1973. 413 pp.; $12.95; hardbound.

This is a "where to," not a "how to," book. Jenkinson covers 115 rivers, 8 in rich detail about their history and lore. Fascinating tales of early adventurers and modern river runners are combined with a great deal of information on where to get maps, sources of river-running information by state and province, the names and addresses of professional outfitters and of whitewater organizations. There is a selected bibliography of books on river running. Illustrated with maps and black-and-white photos.

McGinnis, William. *Whitewater Rafting.* New York: Quadrangle, The New York Times Book Co., 1975. 361 pp.; $12.50; hardbound.

McGinnis, a professional outfitter and river guide, offers much information about rafts (what they are, how to care for and equip them) and how to use them (oar techniques, scouting rapids, planning a course, safety, notes for beginners). He has chapters on coping with emergencies, giving first aid, and camping and cooking along rivers. Roughly half the book is a guidebook to eastern, midwestern, northwestern, Californian, and southwestern rivers. He describes 28 rivers in detail, lists maps and guidebooks, and tells about special regulations. Also included are lists of white-water schools and rafting outfitters. Illustrated with black-and-white photos and line drawings.

Riviere, William A. *Pole, Paddle, and Portage.* New York: Van Nostrand Rheinhold Co., 1969. 259 pp.; $6.95; hardbound.

Besides telling how to select canoes and oars, paddle, and negotiate whitewater, Riviere tells how to pole a canoe, how to hunt and fish from a canoe, and how to pick the types of tents and sleeping bags best suited for canoe trips. One chapter is devoted to canoeing specific rivers and how to get up-to-date information on each one. Rivers are listed by states.

Cooking on the Trail

Barker, Harriett. *The One-Burner Gourmet.* Chicago: Greatlakes Living Press, 1975. 280 pp.; $4.95; paperback.

A trained home economist and veteran wilderness traveler provides over 700 inviting recipes appropriate for a wide range of trips. Most of the one-burner recipes take about 30 minutes to prepare. Foil cookery and Dutch oven recipes run a little longer. Special chapters deal with cooking nature's wild harvest, choosing campstoves, and drying fruits and vegetables. "Make-aheads" for the first day(s) out are accompanied by trail-wise suggestions for packing the grub box.

Bunnelle, Hasse, and Sarvis, Shirley. *Cooking for Camp and Trail.* San Francisco & New York: Sierra Club, 1972. 198 pp.; $3.95; paperback.

.............., and Thomas, Winnie. *Food for Knapsackers.* San Francisco & New York: Sierra Club, 1971. 144 pp.; $3.95; paperback.

Pocket-sized Totebooks for campers who enjoy gourmet meals outdoors. Tasty, trail-tested foods calling for such ingredients as jalapeno peppers, freeze-dried prawns, and lamb, and for such condiments as tumeric, parsley flakes, rosemary, and marjoram. So plan ahead! Some recipes are suited for canoe- and car-camping groups while others are for backpacking couples. Their hints on improving the taste of freeze-dried food and advice on nutrition are helpful.

Cross, Margaret, and Fiske, Jean. *Backpack Cookbook.* Berkeley, Cal.: Ten Speed Press, 1973. 143 pp.; $3.00; paperback.

This is a top-notch book for camp cooks. It sends the backpacker down the trail well-prepared and carefully organized to cook meals that utilize its fine collection of trail recipes. A bonus is the authors' pattern for making a food bag that will hold all the ingredients for one meal or a day's meals.

Food Editors of Farm Journal Magazine. *How to Dry Fruits and Vegetables at Home.* Garden City, N.Y.: Doubleday & Co., 1975. 122 pp.; $2.95; paperback.

For the backpacker or anyone else who wants to know how to dry fruits and vegetables in the sun, in the oven, or in a dehydrator. This practical guide also outlines how to make a dehydrator and provides 50 very good recipes utilizing the dried foods. (Does not include ways of drying meat.)

MacManiman, Gen. *Dry It—You'll Like It.* Fall City, Wash.: Living Foods Dehydrators, n.d. 74 pp.; $3.95; paperback.

This attractive paperback book, published (and sold) by a dehydrator manufacturer, provides every incentive to try drying foods. Its ideas will be useful to those who do their drying in an oven as well as in a dehydrator. It tells how to dry meat, fruit, and vegetables and provides good trail recipes for using the foods. MacManiman stresses organic gardening and health foods and tells how to build a dehydrator from a kit or from parts.

Mendenhall, Ruth Dyer. *Backpack Cookery.* Glendale, Cal.: La Siesta Press, 1974. 50 pp.; $1.50; paperback.

A sound guide to planning, purchasing, packing, and preparing backpack foods. Includes many recipes, though the focus is on pre-trip planning. Other useful features are a table of various foods' energy values and advice on adapting to high-altitude cooking. A good book for beginners.

Reiger, George and Barbara. *The Zane Grey Cookbook.* Englewood Cliffs, N.J.: Prentice-Hall, 1976. 239 pp.; $9.95; hardbound.

Writer-outdoorsman Zane Grey's taste for fresh fish, fowl, and game is the basis for this new outdoor cookbook. Indoor cooks and car campers, hunters, and horsepackers able to carry fresh foods and heavy equipment will find tasty suggestions in chapters on soups, vegetables, large and small game, fish, and desserts. Even includes a few South Sea favorites, since Grey

fished in those waters. Advice on storing and carrying equipment and gear as well as anecdotes on Grey's outdoor experiences.

Cross-Country Skiing, Snowshoeing, and Winter Trails

Brunner, Hans, and Kälin, Alvis. *Cross-Country Skiing.* Translated by Wolfgang E. Ruck. New York: McGraw-Hill Ryerson Limited, 1973. 79 pp.; $4.95; hardbound.

This short book is based on its authors' experiences in cross-country ski races and in teaching cross-country skiing in Switzerland. Relying heavily on easy-to-understand illustrations, the authors emphasize technique, including how to use terrain to advantage. Useful for beginners and experts.

Colwell, Robert. *Robert Colwell's Guide to Snow Trails.* Harrisburg, Pa.: Stackpole Books, 1973. 185 pp.; $3.95; paperback.

Whether you live in the East, the Midwest, or the West, you can find out from this book where to go for cross-country skiing and snowshoeing fun. The book lists ski-touring centers and resorts, many offering instruction and marked trails, as well as places where experienced tourers can cut their own paths. A "City-Trail Index" lists over 100 cities and the trail areas within a 125-mile radius of each one. Another index lists areas by state and name of facility, national park, etc. For each site, Colwell gives the dates of the season, location, access routes, transportation services, accommodations, medical assistance available, sports offered, and local reference from which to get still more information.

Liebers, Arthur. *The Complete Book of Cross-Country Skiing and Ski Touring.* New York: Coward, McCann & Geoghegan, 1974. 285 pp.; $8.95; hardbound.

Besides explaining how to cross-country ski, Liebers outlines the sport's history, gives tips on selecting equipment—including winter clothes and tents as well as skis, boots, and bindings. There is advice on safety and survival, information on cross-country competition, and a guide to ski-touring areas in the U.S. and Canada.

Osgood, William, and Hurley, Leslie. *The Snowshoe Book.* 2nd ed. rev. & enlarged. Brattleboro, Vt: The Stephen Greene Press, 1975. 163 pp.; $4.50; paperback.

Almost any question you can ask about snowshoes and snowshoeing is answered in this truly complete guide to how, why, and when to snowshoe. It explains clearly, in text and illustrations, the advantages and disadvantages of the different types of snowshoes. There is advice on dressing for the winter outdoors and on selecting equipment, including a list of snowshoe manufacturers. Even a chapter on games played on snowshoes!

Prater, Gene. *Snowshoeing.* Seattle, Wash: The Mountaineers, 1975. 109 pp.; $3.95; paperback.

Expert snowshoer Gene Prater offers advice based on over 20 years of snowshoeing experience. Divided into two sections, one on equipment, one on technique, this book tells you all you need to know about what to buy in the way of snowshoes, bindings, and traction devices; how to walk with snowshoes; what to do in emergencies and how to prevent them, what to wear and take along for snow camping. Useful for the beginner as well as the person who has forayed out before. Black-and-white photographs and line art.

Edible Wild Plants

Fernald, M. L., and Kinsey, A. C. *Edible Wild Plants of Eastern North America.* 1943. Revised by R. C. Rollins. New York: Harper and Row, 1958. 452 pp.; $12.50; hardbound.

Beginning with the classification of wild plants according to their uses as foods, this authoritative, easy-to-use book discusses flowering plants, ferns, mushrooms, seaweeds, and lichens. Besides precise information on identification, habitat, range, and seasons when plants are available, there are recipes useful both in survival situations and at home. Tells how the Indians and settlers used plants as food, with fascinating excerpts from historic journals. There's also a chapter on poisonous plants that are often confused with edible plants. Illustrated with drawings and a few black-and-white photographs.

Hall, Alan. *The Wild Food Trailguide.* New, expanded edition. New York: Holt, Rinehart and Winston, 1976. 230 pp.; $8.95; hardbound.

Sized to fit in a backpack, this book gives the common names, size, habitat, seasons when each edible part of each plant is safe to eat, the identifying characteristics, and tips on the collection and use of 85 of the most common edible wild plants in the United States. One section lists plants by their uses (salads, trail nibbles, potherbs, etc.), and there is a chapter on poisonous plants that look like edible ones. Illustrated with line drawings, maps.

Kirk, Donald R. *Wild Edible Plants of the Western United States.* 2nd ed. Healdsburg, Cal: Naturegraph Publishers, 1975. 324 pp.; $5.95; paperback.

This book divides the Western U.S. into three regions—Northwest, Southwest, and Rocky Mountain States—and lists the edible plants found in each region. Indexed by common and scientific names, by uses other than food, and by use as food, this book helps you look up quickly which plants are suitable for salads or potherbs or main courses. For each listing there is a description of the plant's habitat and distribution, a description of the plant, a line drawing of the plant, and a concise explanation of its preparation and uses as a food. It does *not* describe any poisonous plants. Illustrated with line drawings and a few color photos.

First Aid

American National Red Cross. *Advanced First Aid and Emergency Care.* New York: Doubleday and Co., 1973. 318 pp.; $2.50; paperback.

This is the classic text on first aid. It's an excellent idea to study it and to take classes to master the skills it teaches *before* going on a camping trip. A textbook designed for use by policemen, firemen, ambulance attendants, and others responsible for giving first aid, it is clearly organized for quick, easy reference. Some techniques, such as evacuation carries, require several people and may not be of much use to backpackers. Especially useful to the outdoorsman are the sections on wounds (cuts, abrasions, etc.), injuries (to eyes, hands, feet, etc.), and poisoning (from plants, insects, snakes). Helpful, easy-to-understand illustrations.

Nourse, Alan E. *The Outdoorsman's Medical Guide.* New York: Harper and Row Publishers, 1974. 135 pp.; $3.95; paperback.

Nourse begins with an explanation of the general procedure for handling any medical emergency (take time to determine the extent, the nature, and the severity of the emergency, then

control hemorrhage, restore breathing, re-establish circulation, and combat shock). He explains all that a camper will probably need to know about injuries and about illness caused by heat, cold, bites, and stings. There is advice on preventing as well as caring for sunburn, dehydration, heatstroke, frostbite, hypothermia, and more common ailments like blisters and muscle cramps. There is a concluding chapter on first aid kits. Illustrated with line drawings.

Map and Compass

Kjellstrom, Bjorn. *Be Expert with Map and Compass.* 1955. New enlarged ed. New York: Charles Scribner's Sons, 1976. 214 pp.; $6.95; hardbound.

The book on map and compass probably most frequently found in outdoor bibliographies. A leader in its field for 22 years, it combines clearly written text with many, many illustrations to explain the skills of using map and compass. An actual map and practicing compass come with the book to enable the reader to master the principles by using them as he reads. The author concludes with a description of competitive orienteering, an international sport which he introduced to the United States.

Mooers, Robert L., Jr. *Finding Your Way in the Outdoors.* New York: E. P. Dutton, 1972. 275 pp.; $6.95; hardbound.

This book was "written for the beginning navigator who wants to understand his own particular type of compass." A chapter is devoted to each of the three basic types of compass—the Silva, the lensatic, and the cruiser. Step-by-step instructions for their use are clearly illustrated. Thorough coverage of all aspects of wilderness navigation includes a chapter on reading weather signs, a guide on what to look for in buying a compass, and a useful glossary.

Owendoff, Robert S. *Better Ways of Pathfinding.* Harrisburg, Pa.: Stackpole Books, 1964. 96 pp.; hardbound. Not in print; check your library.

A serious book for the committed wilderness traveler who wants to sharpen his survival skills. Owendoff provides an excellent text on map and compass reading, but he stresses finding one's way without a compass. He invented the "shadow-tip" method of route-finding which was adopted in

1962 by the U.S. Army and Air Force, National Park Service, U.S. Forest Service, and other agencies professionally involved in outdoor work.

Rutstrum, Calvin. *The Wilderness Route Finder.* New York: Macmillan Co., 1967. 214 pp.; $4.95; hardbound.

Emphasizing use of the cruiser-type compass, Rutstrum gives "direct, step-by-step, nontechnical explanations of procedure. . . ." He includes a fascinating discussion on why people get lost and debunks such hoary misconceptions as that people have an innate sense of direction and that moss grows heaviest on the north side of a tree. The last chapter, about sextants and other expensive equipment, goes beyond the needs of the ordinary backpacker.

Observing and Photographing Wildlife

Adams, Ansel. *Camera and Lens: The Creative Approach.* Boston: New York Graphic Society, 1976. 304 pp.; $14.95; hardbound.

This new version of the first volume of Adams' Basic Photo Series teaches a technique designed to "simplify and clarify the statement of the photographer's concept" of his subject. Articulate, concise discussions of equipment (cameras, lenses, filters, films) increase the reader's understanding of the capabilities of these tools as part of the creative process. Illustrated with charts, diagrams, and black-and-white photographs.

Angel, Heather. *Nature Photography: Its Art and Techniques.* London: Fountain Press, 1973. 222 pp.; $16.50; hardbound.

An extremely practical approach to basic techniques for shooting the major groups of plants and animals. Each chapter deals with a single nature subject and explores elementary to advanced techniques for capturing it on film. Scientific applications and a bibliography conclude the chapters. At a conceptual level, the book also serves as a bridge between scientific and artistic orientations to nature photography. It is illustrated with numerous useful charts and black-and-white and color photographs.

Bauer, Erwin A. *Hunting with a Camera: A World Guide to Wildlife Photography.* New York: Winchester Press, 1974. 324 pp.; $12.95; hardbound.

Based on his own travels as a wildlife photographer, Bauer's guide to good photo opportunities in the field is informative reading for photographers at every level of expertise. Place descriptions consist of tips on where, when, and how to go, and what to expect to shoot in North America and abroad. Chapters on equipment and techniques precede the surveys of places to visit. Illustrated with the author's black-and-white and color photographs.

Blaker, Alfred A. *Field Photography: Beginning & Advanced Techniques.* San Francisco: W. H. Freeman and Co., 1976. 451 pp.; $19.95; hardbound.

This is a basic text for both scientists and laymen interested in biological field photography. It assumes no prior familiarity with the subject matter, so the beginner will find concise information on basic photographic principles. The more knowledgeable photographer will be interested in the discussion of such field techniques as building blinds and stalking animals that are readily applicable to a variety of subjects. The book also includes chapters on darkroom procedures, aesthetic and ecological considerations, and climatic problems. Illustrated with excellent diagrams and photos.

Ettlinger, D. M. Turner, ed. *Natural History Photography.* New York: Academic Press, 1974. 395 pp.; $26.75; hardbound.

This is a book for the naturalist with a camera. It focuses primarily on accurate recording techniques that do not jeopardize the welfare of the subject. The authors also examine subjects from an artistic standpoint, showing how to add interest to scientific studies. The book consists of chapters written by 18 specialists and is organized by subject matter. A basic reference for amateur and advanced wildlife photographers.

Kinne, Russ. *The Complete Book of Nature Photography.* Garden City, N.Y.: Amphoto, 1971. 192 pp.; $10.95; hardbound.

A general text covering the field of wildlife photography, the book is informative reading for novice as well as experienced photographer. Kinne's examination of equipment and its applicability to a variety of shooting situations will help the consumer assess a complex market as well as his own needs. Chapters deal with single sub-

jects (e.g., mammals, birds), describing equipment and techniques needed to get close, explaining aesthetic considerations, and telling about the author's personal experiences. Illustrated with instructive black-and-white photos and some color.

Nuridsany, Claude, and Perennou, Marie. *Photographing Nature: From the Magnifying Glass to the Microscope.* New York: Oxford Univ. Press, 1976. 157 pp.; $17.95; hardbound.

Exquisite color photographs and informative text take the reader into the world of close-up photography, with information on macro lenses, extension rings, bellows, reversing ring, telephoto lenses, and shooting through microscopes. Besides providing practical advice for both amateurs and experts, the authors give enlightening accounts of their plant and animal subjects. Appendices of practical information include a simple naturalist's calendar telling what to look for in meadow, pond, and forest in the four seasons; charts comparing photographic equipment; formulas to correct for distortion; and a bibliography.

Time-Life Books. *Photographing Nature.* New York: Time-Life Books, 1971. 234 pp.; $9.95; hardbound.

"The natural world in its infinite variety" is the subject of this photography book for the nonprofessional. Introductory chapters highlighting the history and scope of the field are followed by detailed treatment of several specialized pursuits: underwater, safari, zoo, close-up, and landscape photography. The tools for shooting each type of nature photo are carefully examined in text, diagram, chart, and black-and-white photo. Color photographs illustrate approaches to various subjects and shooting situations.

Warham, John. *The Technique of Bird Photography.* 3rd ed. Garden City, N.Y.: Amphoto, 1974. 218 pp.; $12.95; hardbound.

With knowledge gained from nearly 40 years as a zoologist, Warham describes step-by-step methods of getting close to birds in every imaginable shooting situation. There are chapters on equipment and photographic technique as well as on shooting in extremes of temperature, photography for the ornithologist, and birds in Britain. Drawings and black-and-white photos illustrate techniques.

Survival

Angier, Bradford. *Survival with Style.* New York: Random House, 1974. 322 pp.; $2.45; paperback.

Angier has written many standard books on how to get along in the outdoors. In this one, he tells how to survive in all seasons and in climates as different as California deserts and Alaskan snow fields. His advice, based on years of experience living and camping in U.S. and Canadian wilderness, ranges from how to build a log cabin to how to sleep warmly in cold weather without a sleeping bag.

Fear, Eugene H. *Surviving the Unexpected Wilderness Emergency.* Rev. ed. Tacoma, Wash: Survival Education Association, 1976. 196 pp.; $3.95; paperback.

Gene Fear is well-known among mountaineers and backpackers for his work within the Mountain Rescue Association. In this book, he succinctly and thoroughly covers the basics of staying alive in an emergency. More than most books in this genre, this one stresses the attitudes that spell the difference between one person's living and another's not living through similar difficulties. For example, the author describes ten common fears and tells how to recognize and control them in others and in yourself. He does *not* give a guide to catching animals or identifying wild edible plants. Because human beings can live for two weeks or more without food, he thinks it is better to concentrate on staying dry and warm and keeping up morale. Illustrated with line drawings and cartoons.

Merrill, W. K. *The Survival Handbook.* New York: Winchester Press, 1972. 312 pp.; $1.95; paperback.

This is truly a *handbook* that fits neatly into a hiker's pack. Merrill believes that "survival situations can be nothing more than adventures, if you have the proper know-how." His book provides the know-how for surviving in deserts, cold weather, water, and the mountains. Merrill stresses the importance of not getting lost in the first place and knowing how to orient yourself if you do become lost. The chapters on signaling, shelters, fires and cooking, edible wild animals and plants, woodlore (knots, rafts, lashes), and first aid are replete with basic information the average camper can easily comprehend.

Appendix

Equipment Catalogs

Ready Made Clothing and Gear

Adventure 16
656 Front Street
El Cajon, California 92020

Alpine Designs
6185 East Arapahoe
P.O. Box 3561
Boulder, Colorado 80303

Cabela's, Inc.
812 13th Avenue
Sidney, Nebraska 69162

Camp 7
802 South Sherman
Longmont, Colorado 80501

Camp Trails Company
P.O. Box 23155
Phoenix, Arizona 85063

Cannondale
35 Pulaske Street
Stamford, Connecticut 06902

Class 5
2010 Seventh Avenue
Berkeley, California 94710

Cozy Quip
Curtis Industries, Inc.
P.O. Box 1631
Santa Fe, New Mexico 87501

Eastern Mountain
Sports, Inc.
1041 Commonwealth Avenue
Boston, Massachusetts 02215

Eddie Bauer
P.O. Box 3700
Third and Virginia
Seattle, Washington 98124

Gerry Division of Outdoor Sports
  Industries, Inc.
5450 North Valley Highway
Denver, Colorado 80216

Great World, Inc.
250 Farms Village Road
West Simsbury, Connecticut 06092

Herters, Inc.
Waseca, Minnesota 56093

Hancock Village Outfitters, Inc.
Hancock, New Hampshire 03458

Holubar Mountaineering
Box 7
Boulder, Colorado 80302

JanSport
Paine Field Industrial Park
Everett, Washington 98204

Kelty Mountaineering-Backpacking
1801 Victory Boulevard
Glendale, California 91201

Kreeger and Sons
30 West 46th Street
New York, New York 10036

L. L. Bean, Inc.
Freeport, Maine 04033

Moor and Mountain
63 Park Street
Andover, Massachusetts 01810

Mountain Equipment, Inc.
3208 East Hamilton
Fresno, California 93702

Mountain Sports
821 Pearl Street
Boulder, Colorado 80302

The North Face
P.O. Box 2399
Station A
Berkeley, California 94702

Recreational Equipment, Inc.
1525 11th Avenue
Seattle, Washington 98122

Sierra Designs
4th and Addison Streets
Berkeley, California 94710

Snow Lion
P.O. Box 9056
Berkeley, California 94701

Trail Tech
Division of Gibralter
Industries, Inc.
254 86th Street
Brooklyn, New York 11232

Wilderness Experience
20120 Plummer
Chatsworth, California 91311

Make-Your-Own Kits

Altra, Inc.
5441 Western Avenue
Boulder, Colorado 80301

Calico
P.O. Box 1222
1275 Sherman Drive
Longmont, Colorado 80501

Country Ways, Inc.
3500 Highway 101 South
Minnetonka, Minnesota 55343

Eastern Mountain Sports, Inc.
1041 Commonwealth Avenue
Boston, Massachusetts 02215

Frostline Kits
Dept. C, 452 Burbank
Broomfield, Colorado 80020

Holubar Mountaineering
Box 7
Boulder, Colorado 80306

Mountain Adventure Kits
P.O. Box 571
Whittier, California 90608

Plain Brown Wrapper, Inc.
1150 West Virginia
Denver, Colorado 80223

Sun Down
Box 1023
Burnsville, Minnesota 55337

Map Sources

States East of the Mississippi River (including Minnesota):
Branch of Distribution, Eastern Region, U.S. Geological Survey, 1200 South Eads Street, Arlington, Virginia 22202.

States West of the Mississippi:
Branch of Distribution, Central Region, U.S. Geological Survey, P.O. Box 25286, Federal Center, Denver, Colorado 80225.
  Ask for: Free state index maps showing topos available and listing stores in which they can be bought over the counter; the pamphlets "Topographic Maps," "Topographic Maps—Silent Guides for Outdoorsmen."

U.S. Map Info: National Cartographic Information Center, USGS, 507 National Center, Reston, Virginia 22092.
  Provides: Information about the status of USGS mapping in any state and availability of maps of other federal and state agencies.

Canada: Canada Map Office, Dept. of Energy, Mines, and Resources, 615 Booth Street, Ottawa, Ontario K1A 0E9, Canada.
  Ask for: Free index charts, map symbol guide.

Commercial Map Outfitter:
U.S.-Canadian Map Service Bureau, Ltd.: Midwest Distribution Center, Box 249, 1066 America Drive, Neenah, Wisconsin 54956.
  Provides: U.S. and Canadian land maps and water charts. Most topos cost about $2.00.
  Ask for: "Eastern North America" or "Western North America" catalog. Each catalog currently costs $4.95 plus 90 cents postage.

Index

Illustrations appear in **Boldface** type

Picture Credits

Page 1: Boots and pack, Lowell Georgia. 2-3: Camping in the Blue Ridge Mountains, David A. Harvey—Woodfin Camp.

RETURN TO THE WILD
Pages 6-7: City family camping, Brown Brothers. 8-9: Flipping flapjacks, Library of Congress. Tent city, National Archives. 9: Feeding deer, National Park Service. Woman pointing to Park decals, National Park Service. 10: Backpacker, National Park Service. Canoeists, Brown Brothers. 10-11: Woman photographing fisherman, Library of Congress. 11: Trail riders, Library of Congress. 12-13: Hikers at Paradise Glacier on Mt. Rainier, National Park Service. 13: Snowshoers, National Archives.

MAKE IT A FAMILY ADVENTURE
Page 14: Grand Canyon, Kenn Petsch. 15: Surveying Grand Canyon, Kenn Petsch. 16: Hikers on switchback, Kenn Petsch. 17: Andrew Kemsley, Kenn Petsch. Map, William Kemsley. Family on Trail, Kenn Petsch. 18: Hiking in Canyon, Kenn Petsch. 19: Kenn Petsch, Thomas W. Davison. Bridge, Kenn Petsch. 20: Katie at creek, Thomas W. Davison. Backpackers and burros, Thomas W. Davison. Whiptail lizard, Kenn Petsch. 21: Desert bighorn, Thase Daniel. 22: Campsite, Thomas W. Davison. 23: Meal bags, William Kemsley. Lunch, Kenn Petsch. Feeding Maggie, Kenn Petsch. 24: Agave cactus, Don Briggs. Anasazi ruins, Thomas W. Davison. 25: Deer Creek Gorge, David Muench.

EQUIPMENT—YOUR KEY TO COMFORT ON THE TRAIL
Pages 26-27: Campsite, Erwin A. Bauer. 28: Tying boots, Erwin A. Bauer. 31: Waxing skis, Keith Gunnar. 35: Climbing mountain, Peggy Bauer. 36: Airing sleeping bag, Mel Baughman, NWF. 38: Blue and yellow tent, Erwin A. Bauer. Red tent, Mel Baughman, NWF. Red and blue tent, Erwin A. Bauer. Blue and green tent, Erwin A. Bauer. 40: Cooking, Keith Gunnar.

PADDLE THROUGH WILDERNESS WATERS
Page 42: Loon, Kip Taylor. 43: Canoeist, Clyde H. Smith. 44: Bus, Clyde H. Smith. 44-45: Getting into canoes, Clyde H. Smith. Three canoes, Clyde H. Smith. 45: Canoeist, Clyde H. Smith. Girls packing canoe, Clyde H. Smith. 46: Adirondacks' Chain Lakes, Clyde H. Smith. Eric Hixson helping carry canoe, Clyde H. Smith. 47: Canoeist at culvert entrance, Clyde H. Smith. Portaging, Clyde H. Smith. Carrying packs and paddles, Clyde H. Smith. 48: Deer, Clyde H. Smith. Canada goose, Clyde H. Smith.

48-49: Canada geese, Clyde H. Smith. 49: Osprey, Laura Riley. 50: Foggy morning, Clyde H. Smith. 51: Fishing, Clyde H. Smith. Climbing mountain, Clyde H. Smith. 52: Two canoes, Clyde H. Smith. 52-53: Swimming in pothole, Clyde H. Smith. 53: Pot-watching group, Clyde H. Smith. Diving for pebbles, Clyde H. Smith.

EAT WELL—IT'S HALF THE FUN
Pages 54-55: Serving trailriders' breakfast, Mel Baughman, NWF. 57: Mess kit, Mel Baughman, NWF. Assembling mess kit, Mel Baughman, NWF. Backpack foods, William Kemsley. Repackaging dry ingredients, Bretton Littlehales. Poly bottle filled with eggs, Robert S. Harris, M. Photog. 58: Peeling a fruit leather, Mel Baughman, NWF. Removing fruit slices from a dehydrator, Mel Baughman, NWF. Slicing meat, Mel Baughman, NWF. Putting meat in marinade, Mel Baughman, NWF. Blotting meat, Mel Baughman, NWF. Putting meat on oven rack, Mel Baughman, NWF. Jerky, Bretton Littlehales. 59: Trail snacking, Bretton Littlehales. 60: Camp breakfast cooking, Clyde H. Smith. Sequence, making bannock biscuits, Mel Baughman, NWF. 62: Cooking over a mini-stove, Ed Park. Washing skillet, Mel Baughman, NWF. Melting snow, Charlotte Bull. "Coffee please," Lowell Georgia/Photo Researchers, Inc. 63: Cooking over a campfire, Clyde H. Smith. Lighting campfire, Mel Baughman, NWF. Dousing campfire, Keith Gunnar.

IN SEARCH OF WINTER WILDLIFE
Page 70: Ski touring, Kent and Donna Dannen. 71: Skier after fall, Kent and Donna Dannen. 72: Bison, Harry Engels. 73: Bison herd, Kent and Donna Dannen. Bison, Erwin A. Bauer. 74: Castle Geyser, Kent and Donna Dannen. 75: Snowshoers resting, Kent and Donna Dannen. 76-77: Sketching, Kent and Donna Dannen. Elk, Kent and Donna Dannen. Snow-draped branches, Kent and Donna Dannen. 78-79: Two ptarmigan, Kent and Donna Dannen. 79: Ptarmigan roosting, Kent and Donna Dannen. Photographing ptarmigan, Kent and Donna Dannen. 80: Dog and skiers, Kent and Donna Dannen. Snow cave, Kent and Donna Dannen. 80-81: Ski touring, Kent and Donna Dannen. 81: Lunch break, Kent and Donna Dannen.

LET MAP AND COMPASS LEAD THE WAY
Pages 82-83: Hiker studying map, Shostal Associates. 84: Relief and topographic maps, United States Geological Survey. Topographic map symbols, United States Geological Survey. 85: Segment of Lake